The Hunt for the Czar

ALSO BY GUY RICHARDS

TWO ROUBLES TO TIMES SQUARE (a novel)
IMPERIAL AGENT

THE HUNT FOR THE
CZAR

GUY RICHARDS

PETER DAVIES : LONDON

PHOTO CREDITS

PLATE 29: From *Le Matin*, Paris, August 24, 1927
PLATE 32: Ted Russell, LIFE Magazine, © 1963, TIME Inc.
PLATE 35: Robert Speller, Jr.
PLATE 38: Susan Barclay

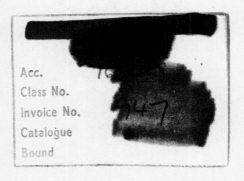

Printed in Great Britain by
FLETCHER AND SON LTD, NORWICH

To
Mary, Toni, Pam, and Bab,
with love

Author's Note

This book is a detective story as much as it is anything else. It is a narrative of obstacles, frustrations, and breakthroughs. The names of those who scored the advances are duly noted in the text, along with the locales and circumstances. In a sense, then, its pages comprise a comprehensive list of my indebtedness to others, and precisely who they are. The reader will discover why I don't have to emphasize a dozen times over that there never would have been a book without the help of two hundred or more other persons. Nevertheless, I'm going to emphasize it anyway.

Some of the breakthroughs were in archives, libraries, and the private papers of individuals. These sources are only as good as the skill with which their custodians can help you find the right areas to search. On behalf of my colleagues and myself, I would like to express our particular gratitude on that score to Mrs. William C. Tesche, Mrs. Mark R. McGarry, and Florida State Circuit Court Judge Mark R. McGarry, Jr., respectively the daughter, daughter-in-law, and grandson of William Rutledge McGarry, for their help in assembling and exploring the more than thirty containers of McGarry papers; to Mr. and Mrs. James Marston Fox for their assistance in rounding up the letters and documents kept by Charles James Fox, Mr. Fox's father; to Mrs. Gerald Hagar for her permission to examine the private papers of her father, David Prescott

Barrows, former President of the University of California at Berkeley; to Mrs. Sylva Butler and her son, Bruce J., for lending us the journals and letters of Captain Lawrence D. Butler; and to Mr. John Frederick Schlafly for arranging with the descendants of our World War I Ambassador to Russia, David R. Francis, for us to study the Ambassador's personal papers in the archives of the Missouri Historical Society in St. Louis.

We owe thanks also to the staffs of the New York Public Library and its Annex, where old newspapers are preserved on microfilm; the New York Society Library; the New-York Historical Society; the New York Genealogical and Biographical Society; the Towne Laboratories of New York for their exceptional help in processing old and new photographs; the Library of Congress in Washington; the University of Chicago Library, Harper Collection; the Yale University Library; the University of Minnesota Library; The Sutro Library of San Francisco; the Bancroft Library of the University of California at Berkeley; the Mendocino, California, Public Library; the State Library of California at Sacramento; the Redwood City, California, Public Library; James T. White & Co. of Clifton, New Jersey, publishers of the National Encyclopedia of American Biography; the library of the American Bar Association in Chicago; and the Library of the British Museum in London.

We are also indebted to a certain Mr. "Fox" for a helpful literary device. He is one of the two diarists in a bizarre book described in Chapter I. He refers to the Grand Duchess Marie, one of the Czar's four daughters, as "Maria." This version of her name was used by many in Saint Petersburg and Tsarskoe Selo to distinguish her from a more prominent Marie, her grandmother, the Dowager Empress. Because of the frequent juxtaposition of the two personages on the following pages, we, too, to avoid confusion, use "Marie" for the Czar's mother and "Maria" for his daughter. We feel justified in so doing because the younger of the two often called herself Maria, depending on her mood.

Contents

CONTENTS

PART TWO: FOR THE RECORD

List of Illustrations

Preface

I doubt that anyone ever backed into a subject more reluctantly than I backed into the subject of what happened to the Romanovs in 1918. I brought to the task a unique array of disqualifications. My ignorance of the known facts was vast. My lack of interest was almost unlimited. Of all the royal dynasties I had read about, the Romanovs appealed the least. Long before they were done in, it seemed to me, they had shown a perverse delight in avoiding the courses and measures that might have saved their country from the outrage of an exploited and impoverished population.

I was as convinced as most people that the seven members of the family of Czar Nicholas II ended their earthly existence in a fusillade of Bolshevik bullets at Ekaterinburg, Siberia, on the night of July 16–17, 1918. It was a sorrowful event. But then, it seemed, it might have been the least of the sorrows. The seven Romanovs tallied only a minute fraction of the total number of victims of the butchery that took the lives of thousands from the Baltic to the Pacific during the nightmare that started with the Revolution and kept on for years under Stalin.

There was an influx of Russian refugees into America at the end of World War I, and I remember them vaguely. After their sudden uprootings and often melodramatic escapes, the newcomers made brave new beginnings in the Western Hemisphere as miners, musicians, janitors, taxicab drivers, clerks, storekeepers, farmers, and farmhands. Some scored notable successes. These included people like the Sikorskys, the De Severskys, the Obolenskys, the Cassinis, etc.

Even the old Grand Duchess Olga, the Czar's younger sister, put in a brisk day's work on her Canadian farm, tending to her flowers and her welfare projects.

The Russians' all-round gusto, their capacity for hard work, their eloquent moods of sadness, the intensity of their play, and even the grandiosity of their humor with its penchant for gross exaggeration—all these qualities made it easy for them to blend into the American scene. In fact, it was virtually ready-made for them. Their advent here looked like a mutually happy development.

If there was anything about them to cause wonder, it was how and why they and the other Russians back in the old country had been willing to let their empire languish so long under an absolutely autocratic ruler.

It was known that some of the Russian nobility, particularly those who traded on their titles, hoped that some near miracle would resurrect a member of the Imperial Family—if not all seven—and give them an image to rally around. Others were far too busy becoming a part of the American mainstream to indulge in such dreams.

In Russia, there was still another group left who found that it didn't pay to let your secret feelings be known to the White Army, even if you hoped against hope for the return of Nicholas. Many of the Whites, in the early months, were both anti-Bolshevik and anti-Monarchist. So the secret Monarchists joined the White ranks and kept silent. Of the few members of titled families who threw in with the Reds, some were idealists, some were pragmatists, and some were just desperately hungry.

Over the years, the whole issue of European nobility on our shores might have faded away like a defeated presidential candidate's campaign slogans were it not for a peculiar schizophrenia in the American make-up.

On the one hand, we damn all emperors and kings and swear that none will ever again be allowed to determine the course of events in the land of Lexington and Concord. We take pleasure in decrying the "false values" of those celebrated studbooks, the Almanach de Gotha and Burke's Peerage. We frequently repeat clichés such as "Our only aristocracy is the aristocracy of achievement." But on the other hand, we often fail to live up to these noble democratic sentiments.

Many of our hostesses and party-throwing dowagers fawn over any title from baron up. Mothers with an eye out for a son-in-law are often guilty of trying to nudge their daughters in the direction of a foreign title, and the guiltiest mothers frequently are the richest. Dinners, cocktail parties, and fund-raising balls are pitched around titled personages the way circus tents are tied to ridgepoles. Since there are not enough to fill the demand, we keep busy trying to create our own kings, queens, and princesses, whether it's out of promising material like Jacqueline Kennedy Onassis or out of a less-glamorous, Oregon beauty who has nervously outsmiled all competition to win the title of Apple Queen.

In all my years in the newspaper business, neither the Romanovs nor the society page had fixed my interest. Therefore, when, five years ago, a Romanov tinge began to show up in one of the most fascinating and complicated stories of my career—the Michal Goleniewski espionage case, I felt very inadequate, not to mention dismayed.

A few months later, in 1965, the Romanov tinge deepened. It soon became apparent that the riddle of what happened to the Russian Imperial Family in 1918 was at the very heart of the Goleniewski case. That was because Lieutenant Colonel Michal Goleniewski (Goleniewski is pronounced in the Polish style, "Go-le-*nyef*-ski"), a defector from Polish Military Intelligence, and a member of the "Heckenschuetze" anti-Communist spy ring, which has sent us enough information through the Iron Curtain to expose dozens of KGB operatives in the West, claimed to be Alexei Nicholaevich Romanov, the supposedly long-dead son and heir of Czar Nicholas II.

When I heard this I groaned. Why should a man with such a notable record, I wondered, cloud the atmosphere with a claim like that? All sorts of theories were advanced. Some intelligence pros contended, "The poor chap has flipped his lid—you know what pressure some of these defectors are under." Others argued that it was a calculated gambit to convince the Russians that he had, indeed, lost his mind, and therefore wasn't worth the trouble to stalk and murder here.

But Goleniewski stuck to his story. With unwavering zeal and infinite narrative detail, he described how the seven Romanovs were spirited out of Ekaterinburg in three groups, hidden in the backs of trucks, and how they lived for years under cover names in Poland and Germany.

I worked on the Goleniewski case for two years and wrote a book on it (*Imperial Agent,* New York: Devin-Adair, 1966). I discovered that, whether or not Goleniewski was who he claimed to be, the "Heckenschuetze" network—one of the most important allies ever gained and lost by the United States and composed of many anti-Communist Russians—undoubtedly thought he was.

Was it likely that the "Heckenschuetzes" were wrong about him? Was it likely that they, who had told us other things, which turned out to be true, about Stig Wennerström, George Blake, Gordon Lonsdale, Israel Beer, John Vassall, etc., were wrong about Goleniewski?

At any rate, Congress seemed to be preparing to unravel the mystery, in late 1964, as to both his parentage and his political affiliations. Goleniewski was subpoenaed to appear before secret sessions of the Senate Internal Security Subcommittee. I looked forward to finding the answers from those who had the authority to question witnesses under oath and cross-examine them.

It was a false hope. The careful interrogation never took place. After a couple of postponements, the Senate subcommittee finally decided not to put Goleniewski in the witness chair. The pressures that brought this turnabout in the Senate must be left to conjecture unless the most powerful member of the subcommittee, its vice-chairman, Senator Thomas J. Dodd, decides to change his mind and talk about them. For a while, the Goleniewski case drifted into the shadows.

Then, starting in 1968, the story began to stir again. A report by sixteen members of the staff of the *Sunday Times* in London described how Goleniewski had clinched the exposure of Harold "Kim" Philby, the Cambridge-bred Soviet agent high in the councils of Britain's MI-6, who for more than a decade had passed along to Moscow the secret plans of his agency and those of our own CIA. Goleniewski's achievement, in Philby's instance, was racked up in 1963. That was two years after Goleniewski's defection.

In 1969, a rather mysterious volume came to light on this side of the Atlantic. Stripped of many names and vital dates, and often couched in ambiguous language, it consists of reports— if genuine—of two secret agents who said they had helped to smuggle the Romanovs out of Ekaterinburg. The reports are in the form of diaries. I learned that the Justice Department had been informed by Colonel Goleniewski that the operations recounted in the diaries of one of the agents, "Fox," were substantially correct.

The emergence of the name of "Fox" was especially exciting. For several years I had known about two covert letters to "My dear Fox," presumably written in post-World War I days. One was signed "Wilhelm" in what looked like the handwriting of the German Kaiser. The other was signed "Nicolas" in a hand resembling that of the Russian Emperor. The latter was dated "Six Jan'y '19," nearly six months after the Czar was supposed to have been murdered. It thanked Fox for all he had done "towards consummating my escape." It expressed confidence that Fox would help "to maintain my State Secret." I had never seen the originals. I had never been able to determine who Fox was.

But the hint that Fox's diary might now be available recalled another piece of information I had received a few years previously that Nicholas himself was very much alive, but incognito, and that he had visited California some time in 1919 or 1920 to confer with friends and supporters. Could one have been Fox?

If these bits of evidence were valid, another, but much more extensive, probe of the whole Romanov conundrum was called for. It would have to delve into the "diaries," of course, but it would have to go far beyond them to follow the traces and trails of seven persons reported dead more than a half century ago and of several others who presumably helped the Romanovs escape and hide.

This probably would have consumed a year or two or three were it not for a happy discovery. I found that a number of others around the country were well along in their own inquiries into the Goleniewski case, or the Romanov case, or some part of one or the other. We decided to pool our findings—to my great advantage. (The team we formed soon came to be known, somewhat irreverently, as the Three Gs, or the Goleniewski Go-Gos).

To me, the discovery of the existence of the others was one of the most astonishing developments of all. In age, experience, jobs, professions, and political alignments, they vary as widely as any random selection of passers-by on a crowded sidewalk. They are scattered from coast to coast. Some are amateur sleuths, some professionals; some are those whose investigative acumen in fields like the law and heraldry was stimulated by the challenge posed by Michal Goleniewski. (See Chapter III.) A few bear out the theory that there is a certain breed of individualist, the kind of man who will roll up his sleeves and start poking into a subject the minute he gets the idea that his government has found it too fraught with political boomerangs. This breed—and what characters some of them are!—really comprises America's "Fourth Branch."

I learned quickly that some of the others had come up with leads in documents, books, letters, and memos written by Finns, Poles, Frenchmen, Russians, and Germans. Translations were made of all that was pertinent. The work of a man in a San Francisco library was made easier by a discovery in Chevy Chase, Maryland. The translation of a book published years ago in Paris guided the questioning of a former resident of Tsarskoe Selo, the "Czar's Village," near Leningrad, which the Soviets have renamed Pushkin. Little by little the gains added up. Distribution to all, however, of the news of an advance on any one front became a heavy communications problem. It must have added a tidy sum to airmail revenues. Airlines, railroads, and bus lines also got a lift. Some of us did a lot of traveling. As for long-distance calls, I think the new-business department of the phone company owes us a dinner.

The book on the following pages is the result of all this burrowing, scanning, reading, phoning, letter writing, and accosting of persons all over the country and in several foreign countries. It is not the only by-product of the investigation. We made a few discoveries that may be worth volumes in themselves.

But by far and away the most valuable findings from the quest, and quite a surprise to the searchers, were the wealth of material found in the memories of men and women and in cubbyholes, drawers, shelves, private papers, and old notes that bear on these questions:

What really happened to the Romanovs?

Does any of the Czar's fortune still exist?

If so, are the Soviets trying to latch onto it by secretly backing a spurious "Czarevich" who poses as an ex-double agent and who claims that the Romanovs weren't killed?

Is there a hidden contest under way for the Romanov inheritance? Is the Russian Orthodox Church Outside Russia (and/or in Mother Russia) aligned with one of the Romanov factions in a plan to share the money that would be their due because Nicholas was head of the Church?

G.R.

New York, 1970

The American struggles against the natural obstacles which oppose him; the adversaries of the Russian are men; the former combats the wilderness and savage life; the latter, civilization with all its weapons and its arts; the conquests of the one are therefore gained by the ploughshare, those of the other by the sword. The Anglo-American relies upon personal interest to accomplish his ends, and gives free scope to the unguided exertions and common sense of the citizens; the Russian centers all the authority of society in a single arm; the principal instrument of the former is freedom; of the latter, servitude. Their starting point is different and their courses are not the same; yet each of them seems to be marked out by the will of Heaven to sway the destinies of half the world.

Comte Alexis de Tocqueville

Part One

THE HUNT

I

"Rescuing the Czar" and the Phenomenal Mr. Fox

If some books remain mysterious for one reason or another, then *Rescuing the Czar* must be entered for the grand championship. It is a mystery for thirty or forty reasons.

Its several authors are unaccounted for. Its principal characters are unidentified. Its purpose is unknown. Its narrative contradicts accepted history in almost all details. The U. S. Army officer who is supposed to have obtained the manuscript by accident remains, in the text of the book, anonymous. The man who paid for the printing insisted that the publisher keep it a secret. His name appears nowhere, from cover to cover.

All copies were delivered to its secret sponsor, who paid twelve thousand dollars for the production of two thousand copies nearly a half century ago in San Francisco. The plates were destroyed. The printer was not allowed to keep a single copy. Neither was the bookbinder.

Still alive, in his seventies, the printer says he "never heard" of what happened to the book afterwards, never saw a line about it anywhere, never received any inquiries about it until I wrote to him November 11, 1968. It seems inconceivable that any literary work

3

with such a shadowy background should be taken seriously by anyone. But this one is.

Among other things, it tends to confirm all claims that the last Imperial Family of Russia wasn't wiped out by the Bolsheviks.

It appears that the book was never put on sale. Not a line of biographical material appears in it about anyone connected with its publication. That includes "the arranger and translator," James P. Smythe, A.M., Ph.D., and the author of the foreword, who, on subsequent investigation, stands revealed as a distinguished physician, lawyer, and man of letters, Dr. William E. Aughinbaugh, who died twenty-eight years after his literary contribution. He was on the faculty of New York University. He was hardly a figure to associate himself with a fraud.

Few persons ever heard of the book. No news releases were issued before publication to the trade, press, or book-review editors at the time of publication or afterward. Its title appears in none of the bibliographies of Nicholas II or the Romanovs that I have been able to find.

Only a handful of copies are known to exist. The few libraries that own it seem to have acquired it from six to eight years after its publication date, as though someone waited to sneak it in when no one was looking. The New York Public Library, for instance, got its two copies in April 1926.

Among the places where copies have been placed are the Library of Congress, in Washington; the library of Chicago University, Harper Collection (restricted to researchers, by appointment); the British Museum in London, and the public libraries of New York and Los Angeles (in each case in only the central collection). None of the personnel of these institutions said they had read it or heard of it before we made inquiries in the final weeks of 1968 and early 1969.

The light olive volume with the faded white nameplate and 269 pages purports to be the diaries of two secret agents who helped to liberate Nicholas II, the Empress Alexandra, and their five children from the Bolsheviks at Ekaterinburg in the summer of 1918. If, as history says, they were all assassinated, no bodies or skulls were found. Only one human finger and such family items as gems, corset stays, and buttons were uncovered from the abandoned mine shaft near Ekaterinburg where, according to some accounts, the remains were dumped, after the bodies were partially incinerated near the top of the mine pit.

But, according to *Rescuing the Czar,* even the questionable evidence recounted above is pure fabrication. The book describes how the Romanovs were spirited out of Ekaterinburg in the backs of trucks, hidden under folds of tents and canvas. It further describes their escape route through Turkestan and Tibet; how they were disguised at times as Buddhist pilgrims; how the sick boy, Alexei, suffered on the journey; how they were safely delivered aboard a gunboat of unspecified but "foreign" nationality at Chungking, on the upper Yangtze.

The first agent is a man named "Fox" who it is implied is probably an American. He speaks several languages. He's clearly a professional in secret operations, a man of dash and derring-do, with an eye for a blond baroness in Berlin and another for a Mediterranean beauty in the Balkans. He is flabbergasted when a courier from intelligence headquarters in London flags him off a sidewalk and tells him to hurry back to the office along a specified route.

As the introduction puts it:

"I had walked from Euston Station to Madame Tussaud's, when the messenger jumped from his motorcycle and rushed up to me.

" 'Go to Birdcage and walk slowly back to Queen Victoria Memorial. As you pass Buckingham, observe the heavily veiled lady wearing white lace wristlets who will follow on behind. If she utters the *correct phrase,* go with her at once to Admiralty

Arch and follow the Life Guard to the War Office. Meet number
. . . there; receive a small, orange-colored packet, and cross the
Channel at once.'"

The book has such a jigsaw construction that one must turn
dozens of pages, read several flashbacks, and weave together out-
of-context sentences, before learning Fox's reactions when he gets
to the War Office.

There his aplomb is further shaken. His first mission, says his
chief, is to get into civilian clothes that won't attract too much
attention in Belgium and Holland. He is then to cross into Germany,
with his destination Berlin. Fox is incredulous. World War I is
still raging, and Germany is enemy territory. The diary's excerpts
are not dated, but the time is apparently the spring of 1918. Fox
is still more incredulous when he hears that his second mission is
to go to an office in the Wilhelmstrasse, Berlin, and see a certain
German colonel for a briefing on a mission of humanity he is to
undertake.

Humanity? On behalf of the Germans?

The rest of Fox's reactions and experiences in London are edited
out of the book for "prudent" reasons, but the reader by now
knows that such a sagacious operative would never have risked his
neck venturing into hostile territory unless he knew that his credentials were issued from Kaiser Wilhelm II, as well as King George;
that the object of the mission of humanity was the Imperial Family
of Russia; that the newspaper headlines were a good and sufficient
source to inform anyone that the Romanovs were in trouble; that
the three royal families were all related; that the mercy errand was
a family affair, which superseded all other considerations.

The book prepares us to accept the concept of a royal protective
association ready to move into action in order to help the imperial
prisoners of the Bolsheviks. The cue comes early in the book, in a
preamble by Mr. James P. Smythe, the "arranger" and "translator."

". . . there were a few men in Europe and America, as well as in India and Tibet, who were slowly converging in the direction of the victims with a phrase upon their lips, which no one but Royalty and themselves were privileged to use. It was that ancient secret code transmitted by Lycurgus, as well as by Solomon and Justinian; and it was again employed by the partisans of Louis XVIII to save the House of Bourbon. It is that mystic code which binds Royalty together and is given only to those whom Royalty may trust. That ancient code meant freedom if it reached the prisoners in time! It rested with these silent men to pass the scrutiny of a million eyes to liberate the victims from the fury of the mob."

By the lordly, romantic tones of these sentences, and the genu-flecting usage of a capital "R" for royalty, Mr. Smythe takes a slightly more fawning posture toward the Romanovs than the aver-age reader would allow himself. Fox, on the other hand, is much more a man of the people. He is not awed with Nicholas or his family, at least not until he meets them.

In Germany, Fox's credentials were golden. He had no trouble gaining audiences with several ranking Army officers. He got his final orders from the Kaiser himself:

"I was taken downstairs, along a wide corridor to a solid-oak door guarded by two sentries and an attendant in the Royal livery. The door was opened by an officer of the Erste Garde; I entered a large room, advanced to the center, and faced the divided portieres of an adjoining chamber! There sat the man whose nod shook the earth! . . . Behind a heavy, old-fashioned desk, in a dim light, apparently absorbed in writing, sat a deeply tanned, lean-faced, blue-gray-eyed counterpart of Frederick the Great—the very embodiment of Majesty! . . . I stood there fully five minutes before I heard the sharp, high-pitched voice pierce through the portiere saying: 'Adell, I will see the C———'"

From the Kaiser, Fox got written instructions "in black and white. . . . And I could not ask a solitary question!"

Soon he's on his way to Russia by way of the Balkans. His

diary becomes a blend of descriptive window dressing and primitive heroics. He is given a firing-squad test of his courage, in which other standees are shot and he isn't. The scene is in one of the little kingdoms through which he winds his way to South Central Russia. In these sticky situations, the literary style becomes a blend of Zane Grey and E. Phillips Oppenheim, with additional dollops of pure corn.

These excerpts are sandwiched between flights of perceptive and incisive writing. There is a dramatic account of the Romanovs' passage from Ipatiev House, Ekaterinburg, in a tunnel leading to "the medical office of a foreign consulate a thousand feet away." The office harbors a "Union Jack" and a steel engraving "of King George of England." It was an old, abandoned cistern tunnel they came through, pocked by earthslides and cave-ins. They made the transit, and after many scares and frustrations they squeezed through a trap door into the medical office.

(It is true that the British, as well as the French and the Americans, had consulates in Ekaterinburg in 1918. Already it was a railroad and mining metropolis and a center of platinum production. The British Consulate was near Ipatiev House.)

There are profound soliloquies about Russia and the war from "my prisoner" (the Czar). There are charming tributes to the personality of the Grand Duchess Maria,[1] then nineteen, and to Alexei, then fourteen. The rest of Fox's diary is the tale of an ordeal over roads, through mountain passes, etc. But there are several more trenchant dialogues with "my prisoner" and more glowing anecdotes about Maria, whose attitude impresses him for its sustained triumph over adversities.

There are also many piquant clues. For example, the Romanovs seem to be as curious about Fox's identity as the reader of his diary becomes.

---

[1] The Grand Duchess Marie was called "Maria" by some Russians, Germans, Americans, and Englishmen—as Fox does here—in order to distinguish her from her more-famous grandmother, the Dowager Empress Marie.

"Maria asked me today," he writes, "if I were any relation to Charles James Fox, whose oratory she claims to greatly admire. [The most famous Charles James Fox was an eloquent British statesman of the U. S. Revolutionary period.]

"When I informed her that I had never met this gentleman her eyes grew very big.

" 'What are you?' she inquired. 'Are you an Englishman or a Russian? You cannot be a German—or are you an American? Oh, I hope you are an American!' . . . When I informed her that my ancestors fought beside Kosciusko and Pulaski and that their names might be found on the muster rolls of the First Line Regiment of New York Colony and State, along with the names of Goose Van Schaick and Jeremiah Van Rensselaer, she burst her sides with laughter . . . 'What a happy family you must have been!' she rippled. 'When a Fox and a Goose may dwell in peace and amity together there is nothing that is not possible for their race!'

"This quick-witted girl, certainly, belongs in the United States— the plains of Eastern Turkestan are no place for her!"

It so happens that there were a Goose Van Schaick and a Jeremiah Van Rensselaer in the First New York Line Regiment. There was also a Philip Fox. He was a private.

Fox, the professional agent, leaves the Romanovs on the gunboat in Chungking. The other diarist never gets that far.

He's a Russian aristocrat. From the entries in his Cyranoesque gazette, it becomes apparent that he has never heard of Fox and is working independently of him. His name, apparently, is "Alexei," but he certainly isn't the Czarevich. It's a wonder, from his attitude, that anyone ever got him to work at all.

He doesn't think much of the Imperial Family. He thinks even less of Nicholas, who, he laments, couldn't even run his family or handle his wife, to say nothing of ruling the world's largest nation. He sneers at Nicholas' inability to keep pixilated monks (like Rasputin, presumably) out of the pantry and the palace. He turns

9

down a couple of quiet bids to help a network planning to spring the Romanovs from captivity. It is only after he has been beaten and mugged a few times by rampaging Bolsheviks in Saint Petersburg, and later in Moscow, that he lends a more open ear to further blandishments from the pro-Romanov cell. Then he expresses disgust for himself. His growing willingness to help, he realizes, is not due to a flicker of loyalty or patriotism or devotion to the Emperor, but strictly for creature comforts, for more money, food, and protection from roughing-ups by the pillaging Bolshevik hoods. They find his aristocratic features a sure sign that he's one of the Imperial family's allies.

Alexei's plight is that of the unaffiliated and unmotivated snob caught in the turmoil of an exploding world. He despises almost everyone, but himself the most.

Alexei adds nothing to the details of the freeing and escape of the Romanovs described by the first diarist, Fox. This second diarist—Alexei—seems to have been killed before the prisoners left Ipatiev House. All his remaining pages add to the story is that there are many plotters, from all ranks of society, who are trying to free the Romanovs. He doesn't mention Fox by name. It is the reader who must note the black-and-white differences between the tones and attitudes of the two agents.

The book doesn't try to propagandize anything except the "fact" that there was not any mass murder of the Czar, the Czarina, and their children.

At its most dubious, then, this superanonymous book may be a spook or an ingenious hoax. At its least dubious, however, it may be a gem, a Rosetta stone of the Revolution, a carefully prepared decoding device emplaced in a time capsule, ready to unscramble all the hieroglyphics the moment the right signal is given.

Two factors tend to bear out the Rosetta theory. One is that the book was quietly placed in the repositories most respected by scholars and historians—libraries and universities. There was no fanfare over its debut. Personal publicity, exploitation, the itch for a fast buck from a fleeting sensation—all signs of these are distinctly missing.

The other comes from the comment of the "publisher," Henry Haskin, founder and head of the California Printing Company, who, at seventy-four, is hearty and physically fit, and "very interested in the whole story of this book." I interviewed him while he was vacationing at Palm Springs, California.

Rescuing the Czar was published in 1920. Mr. Haskin said he had arrived in San Francisco in 1916 as a rather impoverished Russian immigrant. He had been trained as a printer in Romny, in the Ukrainian province of Poltava, and he had brought a font of Russian type with him. But he had worked for months at odd jobs before he was able, with three partners, to set up a small printing establishment. He said:

"The manuscript was given to me by a Mr. Romanovsky, the White Russian consul in San Francisco. It must have been sometime around the end of 1919. [The Reds had not yet taken over. It would be more than thirteen years before their government received diplomatic recognition by the U.S.]

"Mr. Romanovsky told me: 'This is the real story of what happened in our country. I want it kept a secret right now. Please talk to no one about it. See that none of the printers talk about it.' "

George S. Romanovsky was a Russian consul general in San Francisco from 1918 to 1920. He must have been a busy man. Russian *émigrés* by the hundreds were landing in our West Coast ports.

Mr. Haskin was asked if he met a "Mr. Fox" at the time, and he answered:

"Yes, I seem to remember getting business from a Mr. Fox. It was just after I had finished with the book. I got the impression I received the business through the kindness of Mr. Romanovsky.

The orders were for printing forms. I think they were Justice Department forms, maybe applications or affidavits or something like that.

"Fox had an office in the Post Office Building. He asked me to come over several times, but I always got my directions from a young assistant in Fox's office. He was a young man, very polite. Fox had a bushy moustache, as I remember. Maybe a goatee, too. He was tall, dark, very distinguished-looking. His hair was pompadour style. A very nice man. After a few months he left town. I never saw him again.

"Romanovsky was in San Francisco more than a year after that. I remember I was once invited to a party he was attending, but I didn't go. He left San Francisco in a year or so. I never saw him again, either."

II

New Leads pro and con Assassination and Two Emperors' Purported Letters to Fox

From all the information we could find in the book, and about it, a number of inferences could be arrayed on both sides of the assassination versus no-assassination debate.

PRO ASSASSINATION

Romanovsky, a White Russian, wanted to arouse false hopes that the Czar was still alive in order to give his adherents a figure to rally around, and

To freeze Czarist funds in this country against a Bolshevik seizure, or

To lay the groundwork for imperial pretenders.

AGAINST ASSASSINATION

Romanovsky knew or believed there had been no killings, or

He knew that Nicholas II, though spared along with his family, was for reasons of honor or security required to stay submerged and could not at that time disclose his survival, or

The Czar's survival was a state secret to be locked in the archives of several nations and that, therefore, this anonymous diary gimmick was the only way to tell the story without invoking the fury, if not the prosecution, of one or more sovereign states.

This thought had been broached before in an investigation of the Goleniewski case. There were rumbles that the Vatican had lent a hand to the Romanovs. If so, it could have been one of the most notable unpublicized ecumenical acts by the Holy See on behalf of the Russian Orthodox Church.

An additional interesting surmise, good for either side: was Fox, perhaps, an American agent? Is that why his office, before he left San Francisco, was in the Post Office Building?

But there is a problem that reduces the satisfactoriness of the claims from both sides. Why no announcements, no drumbeating, no publicity about the book? And, furthermore, what was it at this time, a half century after the alleged assassination, that suddenly stirred things to life and stirred up an arduous search for the book and its publisher, sponsors, and authors?

The answer is one three-letter word that is now quite familiar—"Fox." In the winter of 1968, "Fox" entered the story for the third time, and it was this third "Fox" who made it apparent that, with almost imperceptible motion, the "Fox" of the book, who had been biding his time in libraries for all these years was on a collision course with two others.

One Fox appeared in the Goleniewski case. Shortly after he arrived in the United States in 1961, Lieutenant Colonel Goleniewski, the defector from Polish Army Intelligence, told the CIA that an agent called Fox had been instrumental in spiriting the Imperial Family out of Ekaterinburg in 1918. He told me that same thing during the course of a number of interviews in 1965. *That was Fox Number 1.*

Whether or not the Romanovs had been massacred, and whether or not Goleniewski was in any way connected with them, one thing was clear: whoever was at work on the escape story was relying heavily on the role, real or conjured, of a "Fox."

Fox Number 2 blew in from an entirely different quarter. While I was working on the Goleniewski case I received information about two letters addressed to "My Dear Fox." One, presumably, was from Germany's Kaiser Wilhelm II, undated, written in longhand verified as his own. The text was made available to me, along with a blueprint of the reported original, by a friend of a friend of the late Boris Brasol, who was a former prosecuting attorney of Nicholas II's government. Brasol had come to the United States in World War I as Russian representative on the interallied Conference. He stayed here and died in New York on March 19, 1963, at the age of seventy-seven. Here's the text of the Wilhelm letter. A photograph of the letter is reproduced in the photographic section following text page 98.

My Dear Fox—

I am profoundly pleased to learn that G_____ has so good an opinion of my efforts in that matter. It strikes me—with such eminent support you cannot fail to fulfill your arduous task with the very best results . . . *Pense à bien—*

Wilhelm.

(The "G_____" in this letter could have been King George V.)

The other letter, signed "Nicolas," is dated "Six Jan'y '19"— six months after the reported Romanov murders. It also came from a blueprint shown by Brasol to his friends. It was in the longhand of Nicholas II. A photograph of the letter is reproduced in the photographic section following text page 98.

My Dear Fox:

I need not tell you how I feel indebted for all that you have done towards consummating my escape.

I feel that you will do all you can to maintain my State Secret. Believe me sincerely,

Nicolas.

The first letter (if it isn't a fake) apparently was written before Fox's mission was carried out, the second *afterward*.

That they're both in English is not surprising, for the two crowned heads often corresponded in that language. Nicholas disliked German. Wilhelm floundered in Russian. Furthermore, in this instance, English seems to have been the appropriate language for Fox.

But what is surprising is that to this day Brasol's friends disagree about his attitude toward the letters. Some say he considered them proof that the Romanovs were freed by a joint German-British adventure. Others say Brasol considered them frauds, but highly important as evidence of the pains some circles were taking to make the world believe the murders never took place.

Norman Dodd, a Yale graduate and retired New York banker who has become a buff of the Russian Revolution, and to whom Brasol bequeathed many of his books and papers, told me,

"There's no doubt Boris Brasol considered these 'Fox' letters highly important. If I remember correctly, though, I think he believed they were forgeries. . . .

"You must remember he was in the States at the time of the big blowup at home. He was quite convinced that it wasn't a revolution in the true sense of the word but, rather, the theft of a country by a small minority of foreign conspirators.

"As far as the letters are concerned, I think he believed that if one could trace where they came from, one could trace those who conspired against Czarist Russia and the Romanovs. . . ."

But the Brasol letters supplied more evidence that "Fox"—real or imaginary—was cast in a big role in the clandestine story.

Fox Number 3 tiptoed very quietly into my life by mail in

November 1968. He was so unobtrusive, in fact, that at first I barely noticed him. The Justice Department, a letter informed me, had just been notified by Colonel Goleniewski that a book called *Rescuing the Czar* was based "on true facts" about the Romanovs' escape in 1918; that the part played by a man called Fox, as described in the book, was accurate.

I must have been distracted that day. I had never heard of the book. Colonel Goleniewski had never mentioned it to me in the months I was in contact with him. He surely would have cited it then, I thought, if he had known about it. He had been more than eager to show me data of all sorts that supported his claim.

But I dawdled about searching for a copy of *Rescuing*. I had to be jogged by the man who gave me the tip about it—an indefatigable digger and researcher, M. Robert Samborski, a Chicago lawyer. But where should I start checking? Since early 1966 Goleniewski had cut off his relationships with virtually every American who was interested in his case and working with him on it.

By November 1968, I didn't have to be told that the main components of the enigma were heating up and that an explosion could come at any moment. Whoever and whatever was really behind all the tales, letters, and diary entries bearing the name of Fox, were edging toward a showdown.

Soon, very soon, it seemed, evidence would emerge that was going to prove the Ekaterinburg massacre a myth, or, quite contrarily, that the "myth" peddlers were the real liars—perhaps criminals twice over; men who contrived the mass murder, and then, harried by the stigma of historical guilt, plotted to have the deed expunged.

And what a conflict of versions beclouded the status of Fox! Either he was one of the great unsung heroes of World War I, or he was a man who never was, one of the most dynamic and resourceful ciphers who never bothered to draw the breath of life! I knew it was imperative for me to find a copy of the book, read it, and garner as many new clues as possible about its origins and Fox.

After a few false starts I found a copy in the New York Public Library. I read it carefully. I filled a scratch-pad with notes.

I was surprised to discover that the book had a familiar effect on me—one that I could only describe as "the Romanov effect." I sensed in its pages a very ornate, very calculated mixture of fact and fiction. The job was to separate them. The Goleniewski case has posed the same challenge. That had plunged me into my first encounters with the Romanov relatives, who are scattered all over the United States and Europe. It is not an experience that is likely to slip one's mind. It means a painful exposure to that quicksilverish combination of candor and cajolery, of frankness and deliberate put-on, with which members of Russia's centuries-old sovereign family have always treated Westerners. Riddles, ambiguity, revelations that are only partly true—all seem to be as dear to the hearts of the Romanovs as poison to the Borgias, and the effects on the rest of us are not entirely dissimilar.

Among the hundreds of other wonders the Romanov family intrigues have produced since World War I, are at least two self-proclaimed Anastasias, each claiming she escaped the assassination that killed the other six members of the Imperial Family; several Alexeis each claiming that he, too, eluded the Bolshevik executioners; one Alexei who contends that all seven members of the Czar's family survived Ekaterinburg; and clusters of more or less mutually hostile coteries of Romanov relatives, strewn from Madrid to California, all rather oddly refraining from entering a claim to the Czar's estate (as if they were deterred by the knowledge that Nicholas' children are alive). There is also the final rejection by a German court in Hamburg, after years of litigation, of the claims of Anna Anderson that she is the Grand Duchess Anastasia and entitled thereby to a share of Nicholas II's estate; a supercharged confrontation scene in New York, on December 31, 1963, between a "long lost" brother, Alexei (Goleniewski) and a "long lost" sister, Anastasia (Mrs. Eugenia Smith) in which they "acknowledged" each other's identity after an emotional colloquy and embraced— only to become estranged after a few subsequent meetings;[1] and, finally, one Alexei alias Lieutenant Colonel Michal Goleniewski.

It is Goleniewski's association with the "Heckenschuetze" group —a group that seems to survive all KGB purges—that lifts his importance, Romanov or not, head and shoulders above all the others. He is apparently the only one of the claimants who risked his life many times over in the course of rendering great service to the West. He seems to have passed the test of time required to determine whether he came as a KGB stand-in or as a double agent. In 1963, two years after his arrival in America, he was given credit for supplying the leads that ended Philby's spying career. (The *Sunday Times'* findings were published in 1968 in *Philby: The Spy Who Betrayed a Generation.* London: André Deutsch).

From the very start of our investigation, then, the Goleniewski case gave promise of a link to four objectives: the truth about Fox, Ekaterinburg, the fight over the Romanov fortune, and the aims and purposes of the "Heckenschuetzes." Let's take a look at the case and its principal figure, Lieutenant Colonel Michal Goleniewski, formerly of Polish Army Intelligence, who says he really is Alexei N. Romanov, son of Czar Nicholas II.

---

[1] A full description of this meeting appears in Chapter XII.

III

The Defector with a Credit Card
Signed "Heckenschuetze"

For thirty-three months, starting in 1958, from somewhere behind
the Iron Curtain, a person with the self-given code name of "Heckenschuetze" shipped the CIA more than two thousand microfilms
of Communist intelligence secrets. He, or she, was a sensation of the
Western chancelleries. He or she never sent over so much as a
trace of signature or other handwriting. ("Heckenschuetze" exposed more than two hundred KGB operatives in the West, major
and minor. During that close-to-three-year period, both American
and Red agencies were trying desperately to learn who "Heckenschuetze" was.)

The suspense ended for the Americans in December 1960. Shortly
before Christmas, a man's voice rumbled onto the phone switchboard at the U.S. consulate in West Berlin. He spoke both German
and English. He announced that he was "Heckenschuetze." He
said his life was in danger. He asked for asylum. He said he needed
security for himself, his wife, and a few others. He said he would
call back at a stated time the same day.

It strains the imagination to comprehend the dismay and confusion of the switchboard operator as she tried to find someone in
the consulate who could tell her whether the man was a nut or a

ten-strike in the Cold War. Finally she located someone high enough up to know the "Heckenschuetze" story. The caller was later given the answer—"Yes; all stipulations agreed to; come on over."

16 7429

On Christmas Day 1960, a man whose voice sounded like the one on the phone crossed into the American Zone in West Berlin. With him was an attractive brunette he described as his wife, Irmgard, and a handful of other persons. Blue-eyed, with a slightly drooping grenadier's moustache, "Heckenschuetze" was quick of step and imperious of manner. He looked to be in his late fifties. He carried a suitcase packed with microfilm and documents. He reiterated what he had announced on the phone—that he was "Heckenschuetze"—and he asked to see the credentials of the men who greeted him. When they identified themselves as CIA men, he looked shocked.

"I expected to be met by the FBI," he said. He was assured that he would meet FBI representatives in Frankfurt. This didn't prevent him from acting more perturbed by the moment. He pulled out of his pocket the identification papers of Lieutenant Colonel Michal Goleniewski of Polish Army Intelligence. He added, then, that he was in reality Alexei Nicholaevich Romanov, only son and heir of Czar Nicholas II.

The CIA men who welcomed Goleniewski to West Berlin soon learned something that only their superiors had known; that the "Heckenschuetze" network imagined it had been dealing in all those thirty-three months with FBI Director J. Edgar Hoover. Its messages had been addressed to Hoover via the U.S. embassy in Berne, Switzerland. The American responses had been signed "Hoover." The "Heckenschuetze" outfit had taken elaborate pains to bypass the CIA on the certain knowledge that it had been infiltrated by Russian agents. This trepidation proved to be well founded by the ultimate exposure of British SIS operatives Philby, Blake, and others.

When Goleniewski arrived in Frankfurt, he discovered that there were no FBI men to meet him there either—only CIA men. He then realized that the "Hoover" imprimatur on all those messages from the West had been fake. He realized that the "Heckenschuetzes" had been dealing with the CIA all along. He was suddenly afraid that he had jumped from the frying pan into the fire. He could be in grave danger. The trauma of this rude awakening, coming at the very moment of his "safe delivery" in the Free World, may be responsible for much of his truculent behavior on American soil.

He and Irmgard arrived in Washington on January 12, 1961, on a military flight from Germany. Whatever troubles he has had on this side of the Atlantic, he has attained a precious goal— he has survived. He lives in a well-buttressed and bolted Long Island apartment. That's where most of the known facts about Goleniewski end, and it's where most of the versions and uncertainties begin. It was to be another three years from the date of his arrival before a line about him or his defection was printed anywhere.

Freeze, for a minute, that Christmas-Day confrontation scene in West Berlin. Consider the dilemma into which Goleniewski's appearance plunged the Americans.

Was he really one of the "Heckenschuetzes," or was he a KGB stooge? (The word "Heckenschuetze" is German for "sniper" or "sharpshooter.") Had the Russians, in other words, tracked down and wiped out the real members of the "Heckenschuetze" ring and then been struck by a dazzling notion: since no one in the West knows that the "Heckenschuetzes" are no more, it can be exploited by sending over a Russian agent, who will claim to be one of the heroic "Heckenschuetzes." He'll be an agent who'll work for Russian causes. He'll cash in on the vast fund of credit the name has

already won him in Berne, Washington, London, Bonn, Copenhagen, Stockholm, Paris, Jerusalem, and Tel Aviv.

If so, the Americans had to ask themselves, what would Goleniewski's real mission be? Perhaps to feed us a little more useful information in order to gain enough confidence among American agencies to get possession of the names of our American operatives inside the Soviet Bloc.

Or perhaps that Romanov name-dropping was a desperate attempt to signal his potential pursuers that he had gone crazy and, therefore, needn't be stalked and squirted into eternity with a cyanide spray gun—the fate meted out to several other KGB turncoats.

Or perhaps the Russians had decided to use him for a pitch at Romanov money they couldn't get otherwise. Thus, they had found a man who was a double for the person Alexei[1] might have grown

---

[1] A number of skull measurements, and comparison of facial features, ears, relative distances between mouth, nose, eyebrow, forehead, etc. have been made of Goleniewski and compared with photographs and paintings of the young Czarevich Alexei. In general, they have turned out to be more affirmative than not.

Another doubt arose. Colonel Goleniewski appeared to be younger than the real Alexei would have been. The Colonel's explanation was that his growth was suspended by his childhood illness for many years and that he was a child "twice over." Hemophilia—the "Scourge of Royalty"—is a genetic, chronic disease whose cause and cure are unknown. It is an inherited blood-clotting deficiency, transmitted by females according to the sex-linked recessive pattern described by the Austrian botanist Gregor Johann Mendel. While females carry the defective genes, they hardly ever suffer from it. An emotionally tranquil patient has less bleeding difficulty than one emotionally distressed. The anxiety caused by the fear of bleeding may be dispelled through hypnosis. Bleeding in hemophiliacs can be prompted or influenced by emotional stress. When a hemophiliac is calm and relaxed, the tendency to hemorrhage greatly declines. Whether Rasputin practiced hypnosis on the Czarevich is not definitely known, although he certainly used all his powers of suggestion to calm the Czarevich and thereby caused the situation to stabilize and, in time, the bleeding to stop.

Although it is generally believed that hemophiliacs seldom reach maturity, this is contrary to the fact. For example, another hemophiliac, Prince Waldemar of Prussia, a first cousin of the Czarevich, died in 1945 at the age of fifty-six. His death was caused by his failure to receive the necessary number of blood transfusions required to restore his health. Colonel Goleniewski claims to be the Czarevich Alexei, age sixty-five, and is known to suffer from a blood-clotting deficiency. Colonel Goleniewski has been tested by Dr. Alexander S. Wiener, a co-discoverer of the Rh factor in blood, who found that the Colonel does indeed suffer from a blood disease, the main feature of which is slow blood coagulation.

23

up to be, complete with bad leg (which Alexei had) and the apparent aftereffects of hemophilia (which Goleniewski has and of which Alexei was also a victim) in order to lay claim to the personal wealth of the Czar that remains in Western hands. Obviously the Soviet government, Nicholas' slaughterer of record, could not seek this for itself. It would be far easier to have an "Alexei" do it, then hand over the loot.

Or was he a creation of the bankers? That is to say, was he a "new jockey" sent in to spur the horse of litigation over Nicholas' estate at a time when Anna Anderson's "Anastasia" suit was developing a game leg in the Hamburg court? For, as long as some form of legal action is in progress on the issue of Romanov inheritance, the bankers in some countries can hang onto the money on the grounds that "it's still in the courts."

These were some of the tough questions that Goleniewski's arrival posed in Washington when he came here more than eight years ago. Some, but not all, persist to this day. His total demolishment of Philby certainly added to his credit here, but it may also have added to his list of enemies. Britain's MI-5, which is roughly equivalent to our FBI, had been aware of Philby's treason for many months, but its efforts to force a showdown had been blocked by the branch of the Secret Intelligence Service for which Philby worked, MI-6, the branch roughly equivalent to our own CIA. It was MI-6 that induced Prime Minister Macmillan to defend Philby before the House of Commons and in so doing delayed his exposure.

If Goleniewski succeeded in doing what MI-5 couldn't—provide the clinching evidence against Philby—it can be presumed he aroused some implacable jealousies, and that new pressures were directed against him in the secret world of the agencies.

Philby escaped from Beirut, Lebanon, on January 23, 1963. He ducked from a taxi on his way to a dinner party in the house of Glen Balfour Paul, First Secretary of the British Embassy. He was a jump or two ahead of two trailing teams sent to Beirut to capture him. One was from SIS, the other from CIA.

On that last day in Beirut he had been in touch with his Russian controller every three hours. The pair won their last, little cat-and-mouse game with the Free World as they had won all the other, big ones in the years before. Philby surfaced in Moscow six months later.

His case is particularly galling to the CIA. He had helped the United States agency set up its own Soviet department in the early years of the Cold War. He had helped to staff it. He remained its liaison man with the British and was privy to all CIA operations in Europe.

Ever since the Philby getaway, many CIA staffers have felt that their London friends deliberately stalled his apprehension in Beirut, hoping he would flee to the Soviet Union and thereby save them from the further embarrassments sure to come in the long debriefing of him they would otherwise have had to conduct in the United Kingdom.

The fact that such a debriefing, which might have provided possible leads to other Russian stooges, never took place, still rankles many CIA executives in their headquarters in Langley, Virginia.

On the subject of the staggering casualties Philby had inflicted on the Western agencies, the authors of *Philby* write:

> The exact extent of the damage, then, may never be worked out. But there can be little doubt that in terms of international intelligence and espionage, Kim Philby's career in the West was a Soviet triumph of mighty proportions. It was well summed up, in slightly curious language, by a CIA man we talked to. "What it comes to," he said, "is that when you look at that whole period from 1944 to 1952—leaving out anything he picked up other times—the entire Western intelligence effort, which was pretty big, was what you might call a minus advantage. We'd have been better off doing nothing."

But even that is a deceptive understatement. It has come to light that Philby, right up to that last day in Beirut, was working for SIS as well as KGB in 1963. Were it not for Goleniewski, he could be doing so still.

Without taking into account all Goleniewski's other victims, it is very clear that the Polish defector, by bringing Philby down, saved the West an untold further loss of lives and millions of dollars.

There have been flurries of headlines about Goleniewski since his case first became public, in 1964. Twice he was subpoenaed for private questioning by the Senate Internal Security Subcommittee. Twice the sessions were called off. Twice, as though to make up for these defaults, Jay Sourwine, the SISS counsel, questioned witnesses from the State Department and brought out the invariable accuracy and importance of information Goleniewski had supplied. This was done during the grilling of William J. Crockett, Deputy Under Secretary of State for Administration, and John R. Norpel, Jr., of the State Department's Bureau of Inter-American Affairs, in matters pertaining to the Otto Otepka case. Their questioning took place on May 4, 1965. The testimony wasn't released for eight months. Their tributes to Goleniewski's intelligence data were unrestrained.

Jay Sourwine stated that the reason Goleniewski wasn't questioned directly was that he insisted on testifying first about his Romanov connections and their pertinence in the Soviet Bloc's anti-Communist underground. The senators, said the spokesman, decided this wouldn't be "appropriate."

I believe that counsel Sourwine has been eager for more than two years to get Goleniewski under oath for executive questioning but has, for some reason, been balked by the senators.

The subcommittee's rejection had a measurable effect on the moody Goleniewski. It made him as sour on the government's legislative branch as he had been on the executive branch for refusing to bring him into Hoover's presence. He began to isolate

PLATE 1: The Czar Nicholas II, 1896.

PLATE 2: The Czarevich Nicholas at the age of twenty, circa 1888.

PLATE 3: The Czarevich Nicholas and his fiancée, the Princess Alice of Hesse, on a visit to England, 1894. This was taken almost five months before their wedding day.

PLATE 4: The Imperial family on board their yacht *Standart*, circa 1911. The
Czarina Alexandra is holding the Czarevich Alexei on her lap. The Czar
Nicholas II is standing with, from left to right, the Grand Duchesses Maria,
Olga, Tatiana, and Anastasia.

PLATE 5: The Imperial family, 1913. Seated are the Grand Duchess Olga, the Czar Nicholas II, the Czarevich Alexei, and the Grand Duchess Tatiana. Standing are the Grand Duchess Maria, the Czarina Alexandra, and the Grand Duchess Anastasia.

PLATE 6: The Imperial family on a visit to Denmark, 1893. The Czar Alexander III and the Czarina Marie are seated in chairs. Their youngest son, the Grand Duke Michael, is seated on the ground. Their other children are standing—from left to right, the Czarevich Nicholas, the Grand Duke George, the Grand Duchess Olga, and the Grand Duchess Xenia.

himself. He "dismissed" (one of his favorite words) most of his American advisers and associates.

For most of 1968, on the visible surface at least, his case seemed becalmed.

All that changed in a matter of days when Robert Samborski's report from Chicago in November traveled around the Three G circuit. The disciples of the mystery were told about a letter Goleniewski had sent to the Justice Department; about the rare and enigmatic book *Rescuing the Czar,* about its narrative of a secret operative named "Fox," and Fox's part in the liberation of the Romanovs.

Thereupon began a sleuthing operation by a rather remarkable team in New York, Washington, Chicago, Saint Louis, San Francisco, Shickshinny, Pennsylvania, and Mendocino, California.

Mendocino is a coastal town 128 miles north of the Golden Gate. It's in redwood and lumbering country. The book contains a teasing reference to it and a man named—"Fox," of course.

The more reports that flowed back from the precincts the more it was evident that we should give higher priority to the following considerations:

If vital aspects of the Goleniewski case concerned a struggle for what remained of the Czar's once-great fortune, was there, in fact, enough left to make the struggle worth while?

If so, where was it? Who were the people after it?

IV

Where Did All the Czar's Money Go?

Wrap all the legends together—the search for Moby Dick, the Holy Grail, the Golden Fleece, King Solomon's Mines, and the Bluebird of Happiness. They add up to a total far short of the different tales about the wealth of the Czar and what happened to it. From one person or story you hear that it dwarfed all the kings' fortunes combined since the days of the Old Testament. From other sources you hear that, big as it was, it started to go into hock before World War I, and what with the seizure of Romanov property, gold, jewels, and palaces by the Bolsheviks, there is nothing much left. One point stands unchallenged: for abrupt change in fiscal status, the case of Nicholas Romanov must have established some kind of record. It is a rags-to-riches story in reverse.

In 1913 he was undoubtedly the richest man in the world. His trade-in value was somewhere between $20 and 30 billion. That topped the worth of Rockefeller, Morgan, Henry Ford, and the Rothschilds added together. He had the largest gold reserve in existence, amounting to more than $1 billion in bullion and coin. He owned palaces, mines, and great agricultural estates, and held in his own name more than 150 million acres of land. As head of the Russian Orthodox Church he owned all its property in the realm, too. In his dominion was one sixth of the earth's land surface.

Five years later he was in desperate straits. As a prisoner of the state in Tobolsk and Ekaterinburg, he was short of food and pressed for cash. His future was precarious. His credit was questionable. Not many great financial empires have undergone such a Humpty-Dumpty fall from the heights.

In the puritanic tradition of the Western Hemisphere, it is not hard to sympathize with the view that all the wealth, property, palaces, and jewels of the Czar really belonged to the Russian people, and that after he lost the job he was entitled to little more than a pension.

Strike out the pension, and that was the view of the Soviet government. Everything the Romanovs possessed, according to the Bolsheviks, they had obtained through robbery and plunder. The view was advanced with partial success to the governments of all countries that had any Russian assets. The United States, for instance, in the Roosevelt-Litvinov Agreements of 1933–34, decided to recognize the claims of the Soviet government to money and property in this country that clearly had belonged to the Imperial Russian Government rather than to Nicholas or to any of the Romanovs personally.

How much did that leave over?

That is an exceptionally interesting question that has a great deal of bearing on the Goleniewski case, for one thing, and on his affiliation with the Heckenschuetze network, for another.

I made a survey of my many personal contacts in the banking community, and was given to believe that there is nothing much left in the United States of the deposits and investments made here by Nicholas II.

What wasn't handed over to the Soviet government in accord with the Roosevelt-Litvinov Agreements, you are given to understand, amounted to a paltry figure. Most of that, you're told, has probably reverted to the State of New York in compliance with the laws applying to inactive and/or unclaimed accounts.

One must dig much deeper to learn that this "impression" is a smoke screen thrown out to discourage treasure-hunt fever. It falls in the category of those woeful protestations of bad luck made by a gold prospector who has struck it rich seven miles up the canyon but doesn't want a soul to know.

Hard-bitten prospectors, banking officials, and lawyers in charge of old trust accounts have many things in common. They like to hang on to a good thing. Secrecy is a common tool of their trades. And to make secrecy all the more available for the bankers, they are protected by law in refusing to answer an outsider's questions about one of their trust or depositor's accounts.

The search for the pot of gold under the Romanov rainbow has revealed that the treasure is not as staggering as some legends would have it; but its non-existence, by other reports, hints, and informal statements, is false.

There are at least several millions of dollars of the Czar's fortune in the West. He is not yet legally dead. His demise has not yet been established in any U.S. court of competent jurisdiction; so, of course, no heirs have been legally accredited.

There should be one slight proviso added to the statement about those millions. They are there if they haven't been filched or unlawfully sequestered. This is a highly sensitive issue on the banker-attorney-trustee circuit, for a scandal in one place could start a hue and cry in several others. It is one of the reasons why those believed to be custodians of Romanov assets will do their best to change the subject whenever it is brought up.

Expressions of doubt about the existence of substantial funds come from time to time from one or another of the forty-odd Romanov relatives around the world—and they are roughly assorted into six cliques—often motivated by the same sentiments as the custodians. They don't want to say anything that would provide helpful hints to others.

It is also true that if a reporter keeps badgering enough professionals in the field of estate management he will find that any experienced banker, lawyer, or trustee has learned how to keep unclaimed funds "with a prospect of litigation" from being impounded under the state's escheat laws. These are laws providing that land and property revert to the state if no legally qualified person claims the right of inheritance.

The gist of the anti-escheat technique is secrecy—letting as few persons as possible, including public officials, know of administrative activity, letters of inquiry, etc., designed to show that ultimate settlement or court controversy is inevitable. This file is ready to be shown, but only when necessary, to a challenging official. Such a challenge might come, for example, during one of the periodic audits.

Meantime, a sleeping fund like this, as long as it can be quietly nursed along, is the answer to a custodian's prayers. On the other hand, from a custodian's viewpoint, he has to fight to stretch out the keeping time. Otherwise he runs the risk of being sued by a rightful claimant on the ground that no diligent search has been made for the heirs. That's another way of spelling out the idea of concealment—an ugly word in the financial district. It is curious that it should be. Bankers and trustees are heavily fortified with legal rights to deny information about funds and deposits to all except those who can prove their qualifications to have the information. That can develop into a process as long-drawn-out as the suit over a bitterly disputed will.

At this juncture it should hardly be necessary to point out what a rich lode for custodians is a fund belonging to a man like Nicholas Romanov, who hasn't asked for a cent in more than fifty years but whose death has not yet been established in surrogate's court.

31

Those with the money have not even been given responsibility to search for legal heirs and heiresses.

For our study, the Romanov fortune should be viewed through trifocal glasses: as a source of some of the pressures behind the scenes of the Goleniewski case, as a possible explanation of Colonel Goleniewski's curious actions, and as a reason why the Heckenschuetze ring chose him as the emissary to the West most likely to receive the princely riches of the Romanov fortune.

Two broad evaluations of Nicholas' wealth and its whereabouts have been published since World War I. Ironically enough, one was written a few months before the stock market crash of 1929, when some readers may have felt that their finances were as secure as those of the Czar before the Revolution; the other appeared a few months after the crash, when many readers must have felt as bleak as Nicholas did near its end. One was in the New York *Times* of July 30, 1929. The other was in the March 1, 1930, edition of the French magazine *Revue Mondiale*. It was entitled "La Lutte pour les millions du tsar [The Fight for the Czar's Millions]." The French editors may have thought that the story of the loss of a multibillion-dollar empire, and the fight among the heirs, would provide timely therapy to the victims of a shrunken Paris Bourse.

Both articles sharply refuted the report of an anonymous British Red Cross official in his *The Russian Diary of an Englishman, Petrograd, 1915–1917*. In this book, published in New York in 1919 by R. M. McBride, the author records that as early as April 1917 Nicholas had no more funds left in foreign banks.

Both articles named banks and the size of the Czar's deposits in each. Both referred to investigations being conducted by Nicholas' heirs and heiresses preliminary to legal moves that have not yet materialized. Neither touch on certain areas we have explored. Nowhere do the findings of all three surveys reach greater common agreement than in the main facts about the starting point—

the fantastic riches amassed by Nicholas before war and revolution began to erode them.

The bare outline is unbelievable, especially to most young people. Few can imagine that anywhere in the world, in this century, and not yet sixty years ago, men and women could single out one of their number for such semidivine homage; lavish on him such a large portion of the national treasure; revere and fear his authority with such ritualistic awe; concede him both temporal and spiritual majesty; endow him with so many infallibilities and privileges; inundate him with as many jewels, palatial homes, goods, services, and servants. To most young moderns, when they start to hear about the Czar, it seems that they are hearing about one of the ancient pharaohs—not about a man who was alive when telephones and automobiles already were in common use.

He had scores of palaces and royal residences. Not even the Russians knew the names of half of them. A number were regarded by the members of the Imperial Family as mere camps or shooting lodges, but each required a retinue of servants, Cossacks, and members of the Imperial Guard. And some of the camps or shooting lodges were larger than the Metropolitan Museum of Art in New York.

Among the better known were the great Winter Palace, in Saint Petersburg; the flamboyant Catherine Palace, at Tsarskoe Selo, which, with its two hundred rooms, was designed to outdazzle Versailles; the smaller Alexander Palace, at Tsarskoe Selo, where Nicholas lived when in residence; Spala, deep in the Polish forest; Peterhof, on the Gulf of Finland, which, though basically a summer place, was so overawing with its fountains and statuary that the younger Romanovs preferred to stay in a smaller seaside villa; and Livadia, at Yalta, in the Crimea, a columned structure of white limestone built in the Italian style on a cliff overlooking the Black Sea.

That leaves a number of run-of-the-mill or less-publicized edifices, like the Nicholas Palace, in Moscow; the Anitchkov Palace, on the Nevsky Prospekt of Saint Petersburg, which was cozy enough to suit Nicholas' father, Alexander III, who positively refused to live in the big Winter Palace; and the palace at Gatchina, twenty-five miles southwest of Saint Petersburg. It was at Gatchina that the hard-working Alexander liked to conduct the business of his empire, while his gayer, Danish-bred Empress, Marie, Nicholas' mother, stayed in town and presided over the winter social season of the court.

There were thirty thousand servants, attendants, and gardeners assigned to this network of households. Each was protected by detachments of the Imperial Guard, Cossacks of The Konvoy, and agents of the Okhrana.

The Czar had an Imperial Train. It had enough cars to accommodate a full entourage, down to a pastry cook. When it made the long trip to Livadia, on the Black Sea, its entire route was protected by members of the Railway Regiment.

Scattered around the Czar's estates were five hundred automobiles and six thousand horses.

The Czar had two ocean-going yachts. His favorite, the clipper-bowed, two-stack *Standart,* was a black-hulled craft as big as a light cruiser (4500 tons). It had been specially built, with mahogany-paneled dining saloon, in a Danish shipyard. He used the *Standart* and let his mother, the Dowager Empress Marie, use the other, the *Polar Star,* which was only a little less ostentatious.

When a ball or a state dinner was held in one of the northern palaces, shipments of Crimean flowers, fruit, and vegetables were rushed up by rail from the Livadia region.

In addition to the more prosaic timber and mining activities conducted on the Czar's properties, he had his own gold mines. They contributed heavily to the stacked rows of bullion and coin in his $1-billion personal gold reserve, of which the greater part was stored in the vaults of the Imperial Bank Building in Moscow.

The New York *Times,* in its 1929 article, which, rather oddly, considering its scope, carried no by-line, estimated Nicholas' income in the days before World War I as around "$1,000,000 a day."

This scale of living, this tenacious hold on gold, real estate, business enterprises, and luxurious furnishings, might suggest that the Romanovs were Sybarites or greedy reincarnations of the Midas family. Certainly no one could charge them with being unworldly. Yet inside those ramparts of material splendor there was more than a touch of the Spartan way of life. Nicholas' father, Alexander III, was an early-rising work horse. He was also a martinet who believed in bringing up his three sons and two daughters in the same hard school that he prescribed for all his ministers, generals, and admirals. Nicholas, in rearing his own children, followed his father's example. So the Russian empire's last two generations of Romanov fledglings were exposed to austerities from the time they left the cradle.

They had to study hard. They were trained in manners and rehearsed for court functions by disciplinarians. (With mixed success, apparently; Gleb Botkin reports that the manners of the children, Alexei especially, were none too good.) Tutors, language readers, governesses, and bodyguards fluttered around them. Cold baths and porridge breakfasts in the English style were part of their regimen, and when the Imperial Family traveled from Tsarskoe Selo to one of the other palaces, the children often slept on camp beds and thin mattresses in rooms almost bare of furniture and decoration.

But there was nothing Spartan about the Romanovs' reaction to jewels. Few of the dynasty's women, and not many of its men, were spared the special sense of excitement, the mysterious and irrational allure, brought by the "starlight of the gods" that they saw shining from the crowns, scepters, tiaras, diadems, brooches, and necklaces passed down from czars and czarinas long since dead. The imperial bijouterie must have quelled for the Romanovs the feeling of insecurity that came from the ever-more-menacing outside world. It was said of them that they didn't look at their jewels as others might, but inhaled them with their eyes, gaining from the process the sensation of renewal and invigoration that a hungry peasant gets from a hearty meal.

Over the years, that kind of built-in reverence for jewels influenced the accumulation of a great collection.

Before World War I, the world's gem experts didn't vary much in rating the value of the Romanov collection between $450 million and $510 million. Some of the more famous baubles were: The Czar's Crown—appraised at $75 million, it weighed in at five pounds of gold and gems, including 32,000 carats of diamonds, of which there were fifty especially large crystals; towering over the matrix of the crown was the 389-carat Balal ruby, which came from seventeenth-century Peking. Catherine's Scepter—a golden rod nearly three feet long that lodges the Orlov diamond; this blue-white stone of 200 carats is reputedly the "Grand Mogul," which vanished long ago from Delhi, supposedly stolen by a French soldier from the eye of a Hindu idol, restolen by a sea captain, and bought in 1722 by Prince Orlov as a gift for Catherine the Great; it is valued around $11 million. The Shah diamond—marked with Arabic inscriptions and dating back to the year 1000, it is an inch and a quarter long. The Gold Ball—a golden trinket six inches in diameter that comes to a crest in a sapphire of 100 carats; the sapphire is, in turn, fixed in a circlet of large diamonds. Diadem of the Dowager Empress—a double row of pearls of robin's-egg size and a necklace of gold and platinum in which nestle eleven emeralds. The Diamond Mirror—a mirror, the size of a wrist watch, that was cut from a single diamond.

Of all the Romanovs, the Dowager Empress Marie, who was able to make a leisurely escape from the Bolsheviks by way of the Crimea, probably managed to carry off the largest part of her gem collection. Other members of the family are believed to have made getaways with the smaller and more concealable stones, pins, brooches, and necklaces.

The Soviets seized the bulk of the Czar's jewels. Some have been sold and some put on exhibit. The bulkier and more valuable items are reported to be kept in strongboxes in one of the Kremlin's secret rooms.

One might imagine that by the eve of the 1970s the mesmeric influence of the jewels would have long since ceased to exert itself on the Romanov clan, but that is not the case. The process of perpetuating the divisive power of the Imperial gems—some might prefer to call it a curse—was clearly illustrated in the bickering that followed the death in Denmark of the Dowager Empress Marie on October 13, 1928. It was displayed again thirty-one years later, after the death of Marie's elder daughter, Xenia, in London, on April 20, 1960. In both instances, there were post-mortem to-dos over cherished treasures of the departed. These feuds have relevance to the current division among the Romanov cliques.

To follow this continuing drama of a historic fortune, we should start at Yalta, in the Crimea. It is April 1919. As long as there was a chance that the White Army might prevail against the Bolsheviks in Russia's southern quadrant, the Dowager Empress Marie lingered in the Crimea with a sizable retinue. She had taken pains to see that her jewel box lingered with her. From the memoirs of her younger daughter, Olga, *The Last Grand Duchess* (New York: Charles Scribner's Sons, 1964), we learn that at least two kings were keeping their eyes as closely focused on that jewel box as royal etiquette allowed. Both kings were Marie's nephews. One was George V of England. The other was Christian X of Denmark. Both invited her to stay in their respective countries, and though she first made a brief trip to England, she settled finally in Denmark. Both kings, to no avail, strongly recommended that she put the contents of her jewel box for safekeeping in a vault or turn them over to a trusted agent in their realms.

Marie, who finally accepted King Christian's invitation to reside in Denmark, died in 1928. Thereupon Xenia arranged to have the box whisked out of Denmark to London and opened in Buckingham Palace; then the reasons for all the royal interest became more apparent.

In it were what Sir Frederick Ponsonby, the appraiser, described as "ropes of the most wondrous pearls . . . all graduated, the largest being the size of a big cherry." There was also a collection of Fabergé's famous Easter eggs, Cabuchon emeralds, large rubies and sapphires, and several big pieces that the Dowager Empress had inherited from her sister, the Dowager Queen Alexandra of England, George V's mother, who died at Sandringham in 1925. Sir Peter Bark, the former Russian Finance Minister, who had moved to England and been knighted there, valued the collection at half a million pounds, or roughly $2.5 million.

Ponsonby reported that the collection eventually "fetched 350,000 pounds." Sir Edward Peacock, a Canadian-born director of the Bank of England, whom George V had asked to look after the business affairs of Marie's two daughters, is quoted by Olga's literary collaborator, Ian Vorres, as saying that 60,000 pounds went to Xenia and 40,000 pounds to Olga.

That left a discrepancy of 250,000 pounds. Since Olga claimed she had hardly been consulted in the matter, and many details were left up in the air, her inheritance was pervaded by a bitter aftertaste. Vorres writes:

"Soon after the sale, some of the more important pieces in the collection appeared in Queen Mary's possession, as the Grand Duchess told me, adding that Lady Bark had also acquired a Romanov jewel."

He quoted Olga further: "Yes, indeed, there are certain aspects in this affair which I could never understand, and I have tried not to think about it too much. I know that May (Queen Mary) was passionately fond of fine jewelry."

Then and there the gems became bricks in the rising walls separating one clique of Romanov relatives from another—Olga's branch from Xenia's branch, and Olga's branch from the Windsor-Mountbatten branch, etc. The stage for the schisms began to be prepared as far back as April 1919, in the Crimea. That was the time the small, lively, dark-haired Dowager Empress got ready to leave Russia forever. The war had gone against the White Army. In the spirited bidding between King George and King Christian for the presence of Marie and her jewels, Whitehall had won the first round by virtue of the Royal Navy's dominance in the Mediterranean and the Black Sea and its pre-eminence in the sort of stylish modes of transportation befitting the mother of an ex-czar and the aunt of two reigning kings. The one assigned was HMS *Marlborough,* a famous capital ship of the Iron Duke class, with a crew of 942, ten 13.5-inch guns, a top speed of 21.25 knots, and a rakish over-all length of 622 feet.

The *Marlborough* was a distinguished veteran of the Battle of Jutland, May 31–June 1, 1916. She had been scarred by the Kaiser's guns in the First Battle Squadron of the Grand Fleet under Vice Admiral Sir Cecil Burney. She had been torpedoed amidships, in the engine room, on the evening of May 31, but she had managed to keep firing until 2 A.M. the next day, then limped into Immingham with a heavy list to starboard. She had been refitted for the glorious occasion of the German surrender.

The *Marlborough*'s royal ferrying mission from the Crimea was more than a symbol of Britain's naval supremacy over Germany's High Seas Fleet. It was a mark of King George V's ultimate supremacy over Prime Minister David Lloyd George in a family matter.

King George had promised his "Cousin Nicky" (Czar Nicholas II) that he would send a naval vessel to the Baltic or some North Russian port to evacuate the Imperial Family in late 1917 or early

1918—a promise that Lloyd George absolutely refused to honor.

There is a rather unusual pattern of agreement among the Romanov cliques about George V's rescue promise. Only the date of delivery is in dispute. Some contend that it was scheduled for the end of 1917; others insist it was for early 1918. Lloyd George's objections reportedly were not based on the menace of German submarines or on that of the mines (one of which cost the life of Britain's great War Minister, Earl Kitchener). The British Prime Minister's opposition to naval evacuation of the Romanovs was, according to several historians, linked to political considerations inside the Allied coalition. The withering away of the Russian Army had set in motion the release of two million German troops from the Eastern to the Western front. The renewed pressure on the Western Front was a grave threat. Lloyd George was said to be fearful of the reactions from democratic partners like France and the United States if it appeared that his nation was willing to risk valuable ships and men in an adventure that might be interpreted as an attempt to save czarism from its rightful demise.

King George was furious[1] that he had been prevented from keeping his promise. Whatever the reasons, the British failure to send a ship certainly aggravated the growing bitterness between the members of Nicholas' family and their relatives in England.

But in April 1919, five months after the Armistice, the scent of victory had softened hearts. A spirit of forgiveness abounded and so did a feeling of penitence. Britain had come in for a certain amount of lambasting for having done so little for the Romanovs, and now there were other reasons to make a grand gesture on

[1] Some scholars sustain this Romanov version of King George's attitude, but it is probably an oversimplification. There is ample evidence that both the King and Lloyd George changed their minds after agreeing to offer asylum to the Imperial Family in the early days of Prince Lvov's Provisional Government in 1917. The news leaked out. It brought an outpouring of protests from British leftists. Thereafter, for the failure of the plan, the King may have been glad to have the chance to pin the blame elsewhere. See *King George V* by Harold Nicolson [London: Constable, 1952] pp. 300-2.

their behalf. Lloyd George, architect of the nation's war effort, was shuttling between England and France. He was busy conferring with Clemenceau and Woodrow Wilson on a draft of the Treaty of Versailles that would be acceptable to all, including the Germans. He was only too happy to have the Royal Navy redeem King George's broken promise.

Reared by an impoverished widow, and forced to go to work at the age of fourteen, Lloyd George's sense of the value of a farthing had made him Chancellor of the Exchequer before he attained the premiership. Looking ahead to postwar financial problems, he must have been as aware as King George of the advantages of bringing the Dowager Empress of Russia to England, along with her jewels and the Czar's sister Xenia. (Nicholas' other sister, the Grand Duchess Olga, then married to a commoner, was still somewhere in the Caucasus.) Such a move could presage the transfer of still more Romanov gold from French to British banks. There were already some Russian deposits in London. Marie's presence in England could be insurance against their withdrawal and helpful in the game of getting the gold from France.

The *Marlborough* was converted into the biggest yacht in the world. Her recessional from Yalta was a British naval triumph.

The details have been passed down by Vice-Admiral Sir Francis Pridham, K.B.E., C.B. Though only a lieutenant commander at the time, he was an eyewitness to breaches of many hallowed naval traditions—parlor maids in the fo'c'sle, ladies in waiting on the flying bridge, landlubber Russian princes gazing in pale puzzlement at the fluttering signal pennants. The strange cruise of the *Marlborough* is described in Admiral Pridham's book *Close of a Dynasty*.

That voyage, over fifty years ago, would hardly be worth our attention were it not for what happened at Malta. Marie's stopover gives the first evidence of an enduring Romanov characteristic— the habit of denying that there was an assassination at Ekaterinburg when talking in confidence, but affirming the massacre of the Imperial Family when speaking in public.

This symptom is a start toward better acquaintance with the ways of a clan whose vanity, intelligence, courage, waspish feuds, amazingly fast evasive tactics, and myna-bird skill in speaking with several voices present a special problem in communication.

For the embarking operation at Yalta, the *Marlborough*'s chief carpenter had directed the construction of a special gangway and loading platform. On it, before the sailing hour, were piled seven hundred pieces of luggage weighing more than twenty tons. Members of the crew stowed the luggage below while more than one hundred Russian men and women, many of them titled personages, many more secretaries, attendants, and servants, were ushered into the quarters readied for them. In all the excitement, according to Admiral Pridham, the watch officer forgot to notify the captain when the Dowager Czarina (Marie) arrived on board, and she strode up to that mortified British naval veteran unannounced.

The *Marlborough* stopped at Constantinople. There, a few Russians got off and a lot more got on. The Yalta-to-Malta leg of the voyage ended on April 21. Marie and her party moved ashore and took over the San Antonio Palace. It was at a luncheon in her honor on April 27, attended by twenty-two persons, that a British Army lieutenant, Robert Ingham, heard a snatch of conversation that prompted him to make a record of it.

Ingham was assigned to dance attendance on Marie at the luncheon. He was seated on her right. He wrote:

"Her Majesty chatted freely with me during the luncheon and talked about her relatives and the awful time they had in Russia. On my right I had Princess Yusupov, the Grand Duchess Xenia's daughter (Irina) and wife of the Prince Yusupov. Prince Yusupov himself was sitting two away from me.

"It was a generally accepted fact that the Czar, Czarina, and the two daughters had been murdered by the Bolsheviks, so I was rather surprised when Her Majesty began to talk about her son— the Czar—and told me that she was careful not to let others know, but that she knew where he was. H.I.M. was fully convinced that he had escaped and was in hiding at a certain place."

In 1919, it seems, Ingham wasn't aware that there were four daughters, not two. His account was found more than twenty years ago in the archives of the Knights of Malta. The then Captain Ingham was located in England and was asked to verify his words. He did.

One might dismiss Marie's remarks in Malta as the wishful thinking of a bereaved mother if there weren't abundant evidence that she and her daughters, throughout their lives, had been given secret assurance that Nicholas and his family had been spared—an assurance they expressed only to those very close to them or to carefully selected acquaintances.

Their obstinate faith was a source of exasperation to one of Marie's sons-in-law, the Grand Duke Alexander. This sporty, bearded, high-domed father of Xenia's six sons and a daughter mentioned what he found to be their maddening certainty about the matter several times in his book *Always a Grand Duke* (London : Cassell, 1934). In one passage he writes. ". . . For the past six months I have been exhausting my supply of logic and patience in talking to my wife, my sister-in-law, and my mother-in-law, who maintained with all the fervor of real devotion that their brother and son Nicky had been 'rescued by the Almighty' from the hands of the Bolshevik executioners in Siberia."

Alexander was the fourth son of the Grand Duke Michael, the youngest brother of Czar Alexander II. He was not on the *Marlborough*. He left Russia ahead of Xenia. Eventually he became estranged from her. He lived in Paris, where he indulged his fancy for English blondes and took time in his memoirs to lavish particular praise on a lady he called "the woman of Biarritz" because

43

"she appealed to my adventurous spirit. She awakened in me my original self—a boy who dreaded to be a Grand Duke."

But he averred that he never forgot Xenia, a tiny, gray-eyed brunette whose sculptured beauty was the object of wide notice on the *Marlborough* and elsewhere. To Alexander, "she radiated security and personified the established order of things."

Alexander was brutally frank about himself. "I never had a job," he wrote, "and whatever I did was done badly." He died in 1933 at the age of sixty-six, shortly before his last book was published. The book was one thing he didn't do badly.

Never had he been able to crack the secret of why Marie, Xenia, and Olga were so certain that there had been no Romanov massacre at Ekaterinburg. One possibility is that if they spelled out their reasons more clearly, they believed, it might jeopardize the security of those in hiding.

Marie, her party, and her jewel box transferred at Malta to a slightly older and slower battleship, HMS *Lord Nelson,* for the last leg—to England. But already in her days of banishment at sea and ashore, her jewels had begun their controversial role. She didn't mind giving away an emerald or a ruby or two to those who pleased her, but she refused to sell any to help defray her expenses. This attitude tormented some relatives.

She made handsome presents to the officers of the *Marlborough* and the *Lord Nelson*. Commander Pridham, for instance, received a pair of diamond-and-ruby cuff links. He thought they were far too fancy to wear. He had them converted for his wife into a brooch and another ornament.

The arrival of the Romanov cavalcade aboard the *Lord Nelson* was a British propaganda triumph. With the battleship's 12-inch guns in the background, it had just about everything, including the victor of Trafalgar. Pictures of the royal greeting circuited the world.

There was no question about the cordiality of Marie's reception in the nation of which her sister had once been queen, but the warmth did not quiet her restlessness. All the blandishments of King George and Queen Mary, and all the pleas of her sister, the Dowager Queen Alexandra, couldn't end her yearning for her native Denmark.

By 1920 she had switched her court in exile to one of the wings of the Danish castle of Amalienborg. She found herself living under the watchful eyes of her rather niggardly nephew, King Christian X. Glad as he was to get her and her jewels away from England, it was only a matter of weeks before Christian became shocked by her extravagances and her bills, and began to reprove her.

So, two new Romanov feuds were brewing. On Good Friday 1920, Marie was joined at Amalienborg by her daughter Olga. Because she was plain, outdoorsy, and wore any old dress that came to hand, Olga was the Cinderella of the family. By the time of her second marriage, to an untitled guards officer, she had accustomed herself to imperial disfavor. It was most unfortunate for some of the Romanovs, therefore, that she happened to be a woman of great character who was almost indispensable in a crisis.

Her mother constantly demanded Olga's service—but that didn't mean mother had to be nice to Olga's husband.

With Olga were her two sons, one a newborn infant, and her commoner spouse, Colonel Nicholas Koulikovsky. The Koulikovskys had made harrowing escapes from Red troops in the Caucasus and the Crimea before finding a way out of the port of Novorossiysk on a British merchantman. They reached Denmark by way of Constantinople and Belgrade.

Life in the castle became an ordeal of nerves. Marie nagged the colonel. She, in turn, was nagged by King Christian about her expenditures. He sent emissaries to demand that unnecessary lights be turned off in order to reduce the utility bills. Marie, in response, ordered all the lights in her wing to be set ablaze so that the whole building glowed like the Winter Palace at Saint Petersburg on the night of a ball. He suggested that Marie sell some jewels to foot the bills. She refused.

This feuding moved the King's wife, Queen Alexandrina, to tears. The Grand Duchess Xenia found she couldn't stand it. She fled to London, taking her children with her.

Marie retreated into the less-spacious confines of Hvidore—a small palace she owned jointly with her two sisters, Alexandra and Thyra, the Duchess of Cumberland. It put several more miles between her and King Christian. He couldn't see the lights from his bedroom window.

At Hvidore, however, the financial situation didn't improve. The bills kept piling up. And despite the greater range, King Christian kept lobbing over complaints about the indebtednesses, and strong hints that Marie put some of her gems on the market.

Finally Marie's other nephew, King George V, came to her rescue for the second time since the Armistice. He settled on his "Dear Aunt Minnie" an annual pension of ten thousand pounds: a point to remember when we come to the day of Marie's death (October 13, 1928) and the Big Jewel Raid.

Playing Lady Bountiful, on the one hand, to Russian refugees who came to pay homage, and Lady Abominable, on the other hand, to Olga's husband, Marie in the last years of her life at Hvidore could see the postwar Romanov cliques forming and hardening all over the world.

There was Xenia in London melding slowly into the Windsor-Mountbatten subsuzerainty. In various parts of Europe, groups were forming behind such contenders for succession to head the House of Romanov as the Grand Duke Nicholas, the Grand Duke Cyril, and the Grand Duke Dimitri. Their fans deluged her with letters asking for her support. She ignored them.

A Battenberg scion who was to have his name changed to Mountbatten visited her at Hvidore at the age of six, with his grandmother.

This was Prince Philip, grandson of Queen Olga of Greece. He, too, was fated to pass into the British orbit, as the Duke of Edinburgh, consort of Queen Elizabeth II. Queen Olga had made a special trip from her exile in Italy to pay her respects, and to see Grand Duchess Olga, her goddaughter. At tea, young Prince Philip gobbled Danish cookies like a hungry puppy.

For three years after the death of her sister Alexandra in 1925, Marie's health deteriorated until she became a feeble and eccentric recluse. She had her famous jewel box placed under her bed. King George heard about it and wrote to her. He urged her to send the treasure-trove to a British bank. She would have none of it.

Early in October 1928 her condition worsened. Xenia came over from England. She and Olga kept a bedside vigil for three days and nights as their eighty-year-old mother passed into a coma from which she never emerged. Representatives of every royal house in Europe attended the state funeral.

Olga had an uncharacteristic indifference to jewelry. She didn't dote on her mother's fabulous collection, so she was inclined to blame herself for the success of the closely timed British commando operation that swept the gems to London within hours of her mother's death. At least, that is the interpretation of the traumatic event given by Olga's chosen biographer, Ian Vorres.

The first time she thought about the matter, Vorres wrote, was "two or three days after the funeral," when King Christian called on Olga "for the sole purpose" of determining whether the jewels were still at Hvidore.

Olga was "appalled." She checked up. She found that Xenia had approved all the arrangements for the removal of the box to London, with the help of the British legation in Copenhagen, and she was given to understand that the matter didn't concern her very closely "because I had a commoner for a husband."

Vorres concludes: "The matter of the jewel box had obviously made a gulf between the sisters." It also cost Olga all semblance of accord with King Christian. She was asked to leave Amalienborg, to which she and her family had moved before her mother's death.

The Koulikovskys shifted to the estate of a Danish millionaire, where Colonel Koulikovsky took care of the horses. In 1932 the Koulikovskys were able to sell their equity in Hvidore and buy a Danish farm. In 1948 they moved to Ontario. Xenia and Olga died in 1960 within a few months of each other, an ocean apart, Xenia at eighty-five, Olga at seventy-eight.

So much for the jewels, the havoc they wrought, and the cliques they helped to foster. But cliques are as dear to the hearts of the Romanovs as the breath of life. Or as jewels.

Let us consider less-ethereal items of Romanov worth, like gold and cash. In the days before and after the early weeks of World War I, Czar Nicholas made a number of financial moves that were duly recorded in the New York *Times, Revue Mondiale,* and other publications. He withdrew several million dollars from one of his accounts in the Mendelsohn Bank in Berlin and turned it over to the Russian Red Cross. He sent new gold from his own mines to a number of foreign capitals. Shortly after the start of hostilities, two British warships slipped into the port of Archangel in time to escape the winter freeze and to rendezvous with lighters laden with gold bars. When the Royal Navy's vessels headed out into the Arctic Ocean, they were weighted down with the first shipment of Czarist bullion, intended to establish a war chest in London. The sum was ultimately reported to have reached $2.7 billion, for the purchase of munitions and war materials on the world market.

Other such shipments went by rail and water to Sweden, Vladivostok, Japan, France, and the United States. The gold helped to keep the Russian Empire's credit in the triple-A category until 1917. It became the subject of dispute after the armistice. Creditors of the Czar's government lodged suits in several cities, claiming that the gold was security for loans advanced. Soon Soviet officials added their own claims to the others. They contended that the precious metal was all part of their nation's gold reserve.

Those intergovernmental negotiations dragged on for years. Meanwhile, various Romanov spokesmen argued that the funds really were held in trust for the Czar and should go to his heirs. Oddly enough, those undisputed heirs of Nicholas should the entire Imperial Family have been wiped out—relatives such as Nicholas' mother, two sisters, eight nephews, and a niece—never entered a claim in any court for their share of the inheritance. Only one suit has ever materialized, the one started in the 1920s by Mrs. Anna Anderson. Finally, in 1967, after years of litigation, a German court rejected her claim to be the Grand Duchess Anastasia, Nicholas' youngest daughter.

The reluctance of the others to file their claims tends to bear out Colonel Goleniewski's story that the Czar's close relatives were secretly informed of the Imperial Family's escape and survival undercover.

The Soviets definitely gained the bulk of Nicholas' wealth that hadn't been exported. On the night of November 6, 1917, most of the imperial jewel collection and about $700 million in the Czar's gold reserve lay in storage in the Imperial Bank Building in Moscow. At 2 A.M. a motor truck drew up to the door. A dozen Red guards, the militia of the Bolsheviks' new military revolutionary committee, climbed down and took up positions behind their commander.

He quietly addressed the captain of the guard:

"We are taking possession in the name of the people."

That's all there was to it. There was no shooting or resistance to defend gold and jewels worth a great deal more than a billion dollars. The Reds found more gold in the Czar's Imperial Bank and in his mines.

It was the greatest—and probably the easiest—looting operation in history. Especially if you add two items: the Czar's own gold mines and his personal 150 million acres of land. On the other hand, from the Reds' viewpoint, it was nothing compared to what the Romanovs had been up to for three centuries.

As to Nicholas' wealth in the United States, the New York *Times* agreed with the *Revue Mondiale* that there was money in the Guaranty Trust Company of New York. The *Times* put the figure at $5 million, and added that $1 million was in the National City Bank (now First National City Bank).

The *Revue Mondiale* boosted the National City figure to $5 million. It listed the value of the Russian Embassy in Washington at $1 million. It asserted that the Czar had $1 million in a "railroad business" over here and "important deposits" in other banks, which it didn't name, and estimated the worth of his personal American investments at 250 million francs (then about $10 million).

According to Colonel Goleniewski, these figures are extremely conservative when arrayed against those listed on Nicholas' portfolio in his last will and testament. Six New York banks alone, starting in 1905, received about $400 million in deposits from the Czar. Goleniewski named the Chase, National City, Guaranty, J. P. Morgan & Co., Hanover, and Manufacturers Trust. (The number of banks has been reduced to four through mergers.)

The same portfolio, according to Goleniewski, puts more than $115 million in four English banks—the Bank of England, $35–50 million; Baring Brothers & Co., Ltd., $25 million; Barclays Bank, $25 million, and Lloyds Bank, $30 million. It puts $180 million in two French institutions—$100 million in the Bank of France and $80 million in the Rothschild Bank of Paris. It puts $132 million in the Mendelsohn Bank of Berlin.

In addition it lists many millions of dollars more of Nicholas' funds in the Pennsylvania Railroad, U. S. Steel Corporation, Metropolitan Life, and New York subways (Hudson-Manhattan Tubes).

It gives Nicholas' real estate holdings in New York City and smaller deposits in banks in Switzerland, Italy, Spain, Belgium, and Holland.

This much-closer look at the financial bill of particulars was obtained in 1965, when a man named Kyril de Shishmarev, who was on cordial terms with Colonel Goleniewski, volunteered to make some inquiries in Europe.

Mr. de Shishmarev is one of several persons in the United States who knew the real Alexei N. Romanov, the Czarevich, before the Russian Revolution and had frequent contact with him.

Mr. de Shishmarev's father, Colonel Feodor Ivanovich Shishmarev, commanded a regiment of the Imperial Guard, the "Tirailleurs de Sa Majesté", and was killed in the Revolution. His wife was American. The Shishmarevs lived at Tsarskoe Selo, and the young Kyril was one of Alexei's playmates. Kyril left Russia with his mother and younger brother on one of the last trains to reach Vladivostok before the Trans-Siberian route became a bone of contention in the fighting between the Reds and the Whites.

With a heritage one half American, Mr. de Shishmarev is quite content with the appellation of "Mister." Like many well-born Russians, however, he doesn't forget his other titles—Count Rohan-Chandor, Knight Grand Cross of Justice of the Sovereign Order of St. John of Jerusalem, Knights of Malta, and the order's Associate Security General.

"It started quite informally," Mr. de Shishmarev told me. "I mentioned going abroad, and he became enthusiastic about the idea of my doing some scouting for him, since he couldn't make the trip himself. I had friends in Paris whom I knew well enough to be sure I would get straight answers.

"Colonel Goleniewski pulled out some papers and gave me the figures [quoted above]. I made two pages of notes. . . . He said the amounts were tabulated in 1951 and placed by Nicholas himself in his last will and testament made just prior to his death near Poznan, Poland, in 1952."

Mr. de Shishmarev agreed with me that a sharp downward revision of the figures could be in order on two counts. One was that Nicholas, if he had lived until 1952, might not have been up to date on the amount of his funds awarded to the Soviet Government by foreign governments and court orders in accord with such pacts as the Roosevelt-Litvinov Agreements. The other was the possibility that he had not been able to take into account the bankruptcies and defalcations that had shrunk the value of his real estate holdings, subway and railroad bonds, etc. On the other hand, we also agreed, the inventory undoubtedly had been aided by the findings of agents of the Heckenschuetze organization, whose record of errors was extremely low.

The fact that the list was far from mythical was established by a sampling made by Mr. de Shishmarev, as soon as he got to France.

"The heads of two large French banking institutions confirmed that they had sizable deposits by Nicholas II, awaiting proper claimants."

Their responses came as a result of confidential inquiries he made on Colonel Goleniewski's behalf. One of the bankers told him that he had already sent word to the same effect to "His Imperial Highness" (Goleniewski).

Both the publishers and author of this book have the names of the bankers. Because of the confidential nature of the questions put to them, and the answers given, it was agreed to withhold their identities. The first will be called "Monsieur X"—the second "Monsieur Y."

"When I got to France I was able to reach Monsieur X on the phone," said Mr. de Shishmarev. "I had met him once socially, but I told him I represented the Grand Duke Alexei Nicholaevich Romanov.

"He was very polite. He said he supposed I had credentials. I said I was acting in the matter as the Grand Duke's ADC.

"He said he would be glad to meet me and talk over the matter of the Romanov money in his bank. Then he added: 'I want you to know that I have already sent word to His Imperial Highness (Goleniewski) that there is money here and we are ready to serve him as soon as he wants to present his credentials and go through the formalities.'

"I thanked him and told him he would hear from me as soon as I was able to get in touch with the Grand Duke.

"My next move was to Monsieur Y. My inquiry to him was made through my friend Vicomte Yves de Pontfarcy. We were having lunch at Neuilly. I told the Vicomte my problem. I knew he was a good friend of Monseiur Y. He handled the matter.

"He got in touch with Monsieur Y and reported back that this distinguished banker, who has since become one of his country's most influential political figures, was very surprised. After expressing his surprise, however, he said, yes, he knew all about the Czar's account and would be glad to talk to me if I brought the proper credentials.

"I also made a similar tentative appointment with the then Finance Minister of Switzerland through an old friend and retired banker, Rudolph Iselin, of Basle.

"Then I cabled Colonel Goleniewski and gave him a report. I said that if he wanted me to press the matter further he should airmail me a duly signed accreditation as his ADC. I had other business in Europe. I guess I was there two months or so after I sent the cable, but I never got any further word from the Colonel. When I came home and talked to him I never got any satisfactory answer as to why I hadn't heard from him. Obviously something had happened to deter his plans at the time."

Mr. de Shishmarev was asked in 1969 if he had since gained any clearer insight into Colonel Goleniewski's reluctance to follow up his spadework in Europe.

"Well, that was four years ago," Mr. de Shishmarev replied.

"Knowing the man's temperament, I can't say I was greatly surprised at the time. I thought it might be due to some procedural question, perhaps something to do with a lawyer or banker.

"But as the months went by I became positive it was all the result of some kind of pressure to delay his identity claims. You can take your choice of what the reasons might be—political, or pertaining to espionage, or what. It may be the CIA and it may not be. God knows the CIA doesn't need any more bad publicity. Maybe the CIA wants to hide its own errors. It may be his own fear. As he steps to the verge of full exposure, it may be he finds he isn't quite ready to come out the tunnel and into the light and into the limelight of history once more. After all, if he files a suit in surrogate's court, he knows he will have to make an appearance— probably several appearances. He may be frightened of all the enemies he has acquired. They include a number of Russians, Poles, Romanov factions; probably some persons in the CIA and State Department. He must often think of that death sentence[1] pronounced on him by the military court in Warsaw. His view of the tunnel must be a bit chilling. He may be going out of his way quite unconsciously to find excuses to delay the awful moment. Certainly one good excuse is his failure to get his sisters to work with him. But I don't know. He has proved himself to be a very brave man.

"Once Americans understand that a thorough fumigation of the Goleniewski case is the way we can repair our connections with the Heckenschuetzes, I think we'll get more action in Washington. Just imagine, if the situation was reversed, how long the Reds would sleep on a similar opportunity to be kept posted on all our secrets. About five seconds flat!"

Mr. de Shishmarev was asked if he thought there was any chance that Colonel Goleniewski had failed to push his claims in court because he thought he would be exposed as a fraud.

[1] The Polish government sentenced Goleniewski to death when news of his work for the United States became known.

"Of course not," Mr. de Shishmarev said. "I know he's trying very hard to get the CIA and the British to release certain documents about his identity. That may be what's delaying him. He claims the agencies won't release them. But I haven't the slightest doubt about the validity of his claim. Remember, this man is not a new acquaintance of mine. I've know him since we were kids together at Tsarskoe Selo."[2]

I asked Mr. de Shishmarev why Colonel Goleniewski deputized him to make such highly personal inquiries among the French bankers. Mr. de Shishmarev explained that Colonel Goleniewski at about that time sought his advice on all kinds of matters—on the average of several days a week; that Goleniewski felt "like a prisoner" because of his personal security problem; that he couldn't make such a trip himself and was only too glad to have Mr. de Shishmarev represent him, especially since his old friend happened to know the bankers, or those close to them, personally.

For "inexplicable reasons," said Mr. de Shishmarev, he is no longer in contact with Colonel Goleniewski. Any idea that he (Mr. de Shishmarev) hopes, or ever hoped, for a share in the Romanov inheritance he described as "laughable." He said his continued interest in the case is rooted only to the fact that "I am an American and a former Army intelligence officer. I think I know something about what's in the national interest. I think I know something about an important historical story and when it has been too long suppressed."

At this stage of the hunt, thanks to books, libraries, newspaper files, and people like Mr. de Shishmarev, we had acquired more data about the Romanov fortune than we had about Fox, Smythe, Aughinbaugh, Ekaterinburg, *Rescuing,* the "Heckenschuetzes" and all the numerous other parts of the story.

2 See "The English Baby," Chapter XVI, for more on Mr. de Shishmarev and his connection with Alexei and Tsarskoe Selo.

V

The Scouts Fan Out

The coast-to-coast dragnet went on for weeks, taking us through bound volumes of the New York Times Index for the 1920s and 1930s. We dipped into newspaper libraries, back issues of Who's Who, publishers' lists, archives of bar associations, old phone books, diplomatic registers, rosters of lapsed memberships in the National Press Club, magazine files, records of medical societies, archive of the Explorers Club in New York, and the libraries of a number of universities.

The breakthrough with Mr. Haskin came with an assist from the San Francisco phone book. That trusty reporter's weapon showed that the California Printing Company was still in business at 269 Eighth Street. Unfortunately, however, we found that its elderly founder had left for an extended vacation in Palm Springs.

We had to bide our time before we got his phone number. The information he provided about Romanovsky was priceless in establishing the backing behind the book. But it also provided the new problem of running out an investigation of Romanovsky. We also received the distressing news that Haskin hadn't the faintest idea where to look for anyone the book names.

Flushed up were dozens of Aughinbaughs (the name of the foreword's author), droves of Romanovskys, coveys of Smythes, and fieldsful of Foxes. The winnowing-out process first hit the right Aughinbaugh (pronounced "Awn-baw") with the help of an old Who's Who and a column-length obituary in the New York *Times* on December 18, 1940.

It was in the San Francisco Public Library that an exciting gain was scored by a very persevering amateur digger, Charles J. Rapp, a retired fire department lieutenant with an interest in books and a flair for picking profitable growth stocks in the securities markets.

He had been unable to find a copy of *Rescuing* anywhere in the western Bay Area. As a last resort, before trying further afield, he decided to go back to the San Francisco Public Library and look at the duplicate catalogue maintained there of the principal volumes in the library of the University of California at Berkeley.

He was happily rewarded—or so he thought.

On the card bearing James P. Smythe's name as author of *Rescuing the Czar* was a printed note reading:

> In addition to the works of this author entered in the public catalogue, certain of his writings because of bibliography rarity or for other reasons are withdrawn from public use. Registered students having need to consult them in connection with university work are required to present a statement to that effect from the instructor in charge of such work. For further information inquire at the Reference Desk.

Here—unless there was some unforeseen obstacle—was what looked like a direct link to the men behind the book, or to their widows and relatives, and to a copy of the elusive volume itself.

Mr. Rapp lost no time in addressing a letter of inquiry to the librarian at Berkeley.

"I knew there might be a little delay," he said, "because things were a bit disrupted at Berkeley. Some of the student rioting was taking place right outside the library. But I expected an answer within the week. I was ready to drive over on short notice."

SAN FRANCISCO—Charles J. Rapp finds a copy of *Rescuing* in an old bookstore. Then he spots an article in a 1919 edition of the San Francisco *Examiner* that has the name of a wounded U. S. Army officer who could have been the source of the "Fox" and "Alexei" diaries in the book. (See Chapter VI, "The Actors Step Out of Costume.") The book's preamble mentions, but doesn't name, the officer who reportedly acquired the "begrimed and blood-smeared" documents in Siberia. It describes him only as hospitalized and as "a young commissioned officer who was having an artificial jaw supplied to replace the one shot off in a Bolshevik encounter." Rapp finds his name in the news story, "Lieutenant Lawrence D. Butler, of Company M, 31st Infantry Division." This was a unit in Major General William S. Graves's Siberian Expeditionary Force (1918–20). Rapp says that story didn't give Lieutenant Butler's home address and that Butler had his jaw shot off; he will try to track him down.

MENDOCINO, CALIFORNIA—Postmaster Don Burleson reports receipt from Sutro Library, San Francisco, of a digest of old news stories on Russian Consul General George S. Romanovsky. They show that Romanovsky was still alive in 1921. A most useful record is the diplomat's marriage, on December 30, 1917, to the former Frances G. Biankini, of Chicago.

CHICAGO—Samborski finds an old Yugoslavian friend and travel agent, Maro Guggic, who knew Frances Biankini. Says she was "dark-haired, very beautiful, but unfortunately became paralyzed after she married Romanovsky; they became separated, she went back to Zagreb and died a few years ago after a long illness. I know someone who knew Romanovsky well. I'll try to find out what happened to him."

ST. LOUIS—Attorney John Fred Schlafly completes arrangements with the Missouri Historical Society for a researcher to go over the private papers of David Rowland Francis, American ambassador to Russia 1916–18.

NEW YORK—Find column-length obit of William E. Aughinbaugh in December 18, 1940, edition of New York *Times*. Sources at New York University, Explorers, Adventurers, Circumnavigators Clubs, etc., affirm him as "versatile," "talented" man of highest integrity. He is author of the widely read memoirs, *I Swear by Apollo* (Gollancz, 1939).

WASHINGTON—Herman Kimsey traces Lieutenant Butler's widow, with the help of the Army, to Santa Cruz, California. He gets Mrs. Sylva Butler on the long-distance phone and finds that Butler kept a diary of his military experiences in Siberia. She has never read it, but still has it. She agrees to mail it to Kimsey. Kimsey is former CIA physical identification expert who worked on facets of Goleniewski case.

NEW YORK—Jon Speller, of Robert Speller & Sons, publishers of *Anastasia,* decides to read articles in the San Francisco *Examiner* published before and after the series on Lieutenant Butler's outfit in 1919. Speller sees an intriguing short clip in the issue of October 16, 1919. It announces that a "Colonel Nicholas Romanoff" has arrived in San Francisco from Siberia to confer with several persons including David Prescott Barrows, then Dean of the University of California at Berkeley. Barrows (soon to be made President of the University of California) had just returned from active duty in Siberia as Major General Graves's chief of intelligence. The *Examiner* took pains to state that Colonel Romanoff was "no relation to the Czar."

This was a beguiling morsel for several reasons. While working on the Goleniewski case in 1964 and 1965, we had received reports that Nicholas II himself, under the name of Raymond Turynski or Michal Goleniewski, had arrived incognito, in 1920, on the West Coast. There's a clouded but significant hint along these lines in a book by Czar Nicholas' brother-in-law, the Grand Duke Alexander (husband of Nicholas' sister Xenia), *Once a Grand Duke* (London: Cassell, 1932). In it Alexander alludes to the disappearance of a hefty portion of 650 million gold rubles once in the possession of Admiral Alexander V. Kolchak's White Army in Siberia:

> Until this day, the participants in the Siberian epic, the Bolsheviks as well as their adversaries, are trying to ascertain the identity of the persons who helped themselves to a portion of the six hundred and fifty million gold rubles of Kolchak. The Soviet rulers claim to have been cheated out of some ninety millions. Winston Churchill [then in charge of Britain's forces in Russia—ed.] believes that a mysterious deposit was made in one of the San Francisco banks during the summer of 1920 by a group of individuals who spoke English with a strong foreign accent."

Those three words, then, "Colonel Nicholas Romanoff," were pregnant with suggestiveness.

Just as Napoleon and Hitler favored themselves with the rank of corporal, Nicholas frequently called himself colonel. He never elevated himself any higher in the military pecking order. As a colonel he was proud of his status as commander of his own regiment. His role as commander in chief of the armed forces he regarded as an imperial rather than a military one.

Had a perverse whim struck Nicholas in the free and bracing air of San Francisco? Had he decided to become Colonel Nicholas Romanoff again? And under no thicker mantle of security than that provided by the phrase, "but no relation to the Czar"?

It was a fascinating thought. Speller plunged right into the task of running it out. He found that Barrows as well as his son were dead. Then he learned that the elder Barrows' daughter, Mrs. Gerald Hagar, was alive and in excellent health in Berkeley. He got her on the phone. Yes, she said, her father had kept a diary. It covered his months in Siberia and afterward. It was locked up in the Bancroft Collection of the University of California Library in Berkeley, but she said she would make arrangements for us to look at it.

SAN FRANCISCO—Charles Rapp is briefed by Speller on the Barrows papers, then by Mrs. Hagar. He makes plans for a trip to Berkeley. Just before he leaves, he receives a long-delayed reply to his previously written inquiry about the Berkeley library's catalogue card on *Rescuing the Czar* and its arranger and translator, James P. Smythe. "Unfortunately," writes Mrs. Margaret D. Uridge, head of the general reference service, "our copy of the book *Rescuing the Czar* by James P. Smythe cannot be located. It was in a collection that was transferred years ago to our Bancroft Library, but which never arrived with the rest of the collection. The reference card which you quote from our printed catalogue refers only to that title [and not to Smythe, as Rapp had hoped—ed.] It was a "form" card. . . ." Charles is disappointed, but expresses hope that the Bancroft Library jinx has not enveloped the Barrows papers, too.

CHICAGO—Samborski reports receiving an airmail letter from Sir Thomas Preston, 83, British consul at Ekaterinburg in 1918. Writing from his family home, Beeston Hall, Norfolk, England, Sir Thomas states he "never heard" of the Imperial Family's escape via a cistern tunnel to the British consulate. He gives his opinion of the report as "nonsense." The book, of course, doesn't say it was the British consulate but "foreign consulate" with a room displaying Union Jack and "steel engraving of King George of England." It could be an agent's room in a number of different structures.

WASHINGTON—Herman Kimsey tracks down a retired U.S. diplomat who is "sure he was shown" authoritative documents on escape of the Imperial Family. The papers were in the hands of a member of Nicholas II's entourage. They were in German and Russian. The diplomat, Joseph I. Touchette, understands German well, and had a chance to make extensive notes. Kimsey arranges for three-man interview at a later date.

NEW YORK—Candidates for the role of "Fox" in *Rescuing the Czar* narrow to two. One is Charles James Fox, former editor of the *North China Star,* in Tientsin, China.[1] He died in La Jolla, California, in 1963, at the age of eighty-six. Educated at Heidelberg, he had military background, National Guard experience, and adventurous nature. He spoke English, French, German, some Russian, and a smattering of Chinese. He had lots of friends in Kaiser's officer corps. He handled certain transactions for the United States during early part of World War I and later. When the guns of August sounded, in 1914, he returned from France to Tientsin via Trans-Siberian Railway. It would not have been hard for him to get back to London later. He was tall, dark, and distinguished-looking. Had a bushy moustache. In almost every way, he fitted description of the Fox who greeted Haskin, in 1919, in San Francisco's Post Office Building.

The other likely prospect is Edward Lyell Fox, a Rutgers University graduate who became a well-known war correspondent and author. He covered the German Army campaigns in Europe before U.S. entered the war. He wrote the books *Behind the Scenes in Warring Germany* (McBride, Nast & Co., 1915), *William Hohenzollern & Co.* and *The New Gethsemane* (New York: R. M. McBride). When U.S. declared war on Germany, he was commissioned an Army captain and assigned to intelligence. He spoke German fluently and had many friends in German Army as a result of his 1914–16 assignments in the battle zones. He was in his late twenties during the war. He would have been ideal for "Fox" assignment. Died only fourteen months after Armistice, on January 29, 1920. Married a Hackensack girl. Had a son. But Rutgers alumni office has lost all trace of his family. So has Hackensack Library.

Our researchers formulate a plan to find all Fox survivors in the families of both prospects.

---

[1] For an interview with James Marston Fox, Charles James Fox's son, see pp. 92–93.

CHEVY CHASE, MD.—Isabel Fox, niece of Charles James Fox, says story of *Rescuing the Czar* is all news to her. Never heard her uncle say anything about it. Doesn't think it can be her late father, Albert W. Fox, either. Ventures the opinion that Charles J. was pretty closemouthed about his personal affairs. When he stayed with brother Albert, she had a hard time getting him to say when he'd be home for meals. Referred us to Charles J.'s son in San Diego.

SAN DIEGO—James Marston Fox says the story doesn't sound like his late father, but is willing to do some checking. His father never talked much about the Czar. He, James, who was then just a boy spent some of the summer of 1918 in Japan. Believed his father was in Tientsin at the time of the Ekaterinburg crisis— but there, again, will check. Refers to a lady in Jamaica Plain, Massachusetts, who's an authority on the American clans of Fox.

NEW YORK—Files of New York *Times* disgorge one rather mystifying review of *Rescuing the Czar,* which appeared on Sunday, September 5, 1920. Authored by Herman Bernstein, foreign correspondent of the New York *Herald* and one of the founders and editors of the *Jewish Day*. He was born in Russia. Well versed in the language, Bernstein accompanied the *Times'* special correspondent, Carl W. Ackerman (later Dean of Columbia's School of Journalism) on a visit to Ekaterinburg in August 1918. That was shortly after the reported murder of the Romanovs. In his review of *Rescuing,* Bernstein gives much space to describing his own experiences in Ekaterinburg. There, he writes, he heard all kinds of versions about the fate of the Imperial Family. He expresses doubt that the diaries in *Rescuing* are, as offered, "authentic," but makes no effort to poke into the background of the book. Says nothing about calling the publisher for information. He concludes it doesn't really matter much whether the Czar is dead or alive because "czarism is dead" anyway.

PALM SPRINGS, CALIFORNIA—Henry Haskin, publisher of

Rescuing, reaffirms that no phone call or letter of inquiry was received from Bernstein or the New York *Times* in 1920. Has no idea how the *Times* got the book. Says he never heard about the review in the *Times* or anywhere else.

NEW YORK—In his Riverside Drive apartment, slim, gray-haired Carl W. Ackerman, seventy-nine, changes easily from the posture of a reporter to that of a professor. For years he was both. His eyes are bright. His mind is restless and incisive. It shows no effects of the arthritis that plagues him from time to time and cuts down the walks he likes to take along the Hudson. He has written five books. For many years he was Dean of the School of Journalism at Columbia. As Herman Bernstein's traveling companion on the long trip from Vladivostok to Ekaterinburg in 1918, he expressed surprise that Bernstein had never told him about his review of *Rescuing* or about the book itself. He, Ackerman, might have been traveling when the review came out in September 1920. Had heard nothing before of the review or book. He'd added he wouldn't be surprised if it turned out that the Imperial Family escaped. He had made that point not only in his dispatches filed in 1918 to the *Times,* but in the book he wrote afterward, *Trailing the Bolsheviki* (New York: Charles Scribner's Sons, 1919). In his chapter on the Czar's fate, he expressed great doubt that the Romanovs had been killed, and quoted several sources in support of his opinion. Said all witnesses he interviewed at Ekaterinburg were the same people Bernstein interviewed. Said he would be glad to search in a trunk for his original notes. He was asked to look particularly for notes on a source widely quoted in his stories—Parfin Dominin. This man was quoted as believing that most of Imperial Family escaped.

Dominin, the sixty-year-old Russian whom Ackerman described as having been in Nicholas' service for twenty-two years as "major-domo" and personal aide, presented a challenging piece of detective work. To the best of our researchers' knowledge, the only other mention of Dominin in all the other books and stories on the last months of the Imperial Family in Siberia was in *Rescuing*. Could Dominin have been "invented" by the White Russian military officials to provide the world with a cover story?

Our probe, four months after starting, had delved into nooks and crannies all the way from Norfolk, England, to Berkeley, California, but still there was a lot of work to be done.

VI

The Actors Step Out of Costume

In the preamble to *Rescuing the Czar,* he was shunted aside as
a hospitalized but unnamed Army captain. A few paragraphs were
enough for him. He was little more than a pretext, a mere
narrator's peg on which to hang the discovery of the agents' diaries.

After poking through fifty-year layers of dust, however, we found
that he was a very real and vivid personage—a genuine military
hero. His name was Lawrence D. Butler. He was born in Texas
but moved to Oklahoma. He was an up-from-the-ranks platoon
commander, and a natural troop leader. In slack moments he was
easygoing, with a sunny disposition and plenty of time to hear the
beefs and troubles of his men and tales of their home towns
on the other side of the world. But when the shooting started,
it changed Lawrence Butler into a man to remember. Though badly
wounded, he led his riflemen of Company A, 31st Infantry, so
valiantly in a counterattack against the Bolsheviks at Romanovka,
near Vladivostok, Siberia, in the dawn of June 25, 1919, that he
received citations and/or decorations from the United States, England, France, Italy, and Japan.

That day he was a lieutenant. He was quickly promoted to
captain. The Bolsheviks, in their surprise attack, hoped to capture

the arms and weapons of Butler's company. They never made it. Eighteen Americans were killed and twenty-four wounded. Butler's face was so disfigured by enemy fire that one of his men looked at the bloody mop between his shoulders and observed in hushed astonishment:

"You are dead, Lieutenant."

The battle lasted from 5 to 11 A.M. When Sergeant Sylvester B. Moore of K Company arrived on a relief train with sixteen men, he found the virtually featureless Butler the next thing to a living corpse. But Butler was miraculously still on his feet. He kept insisting that he join Moore and his men in scaling a hill in pursuit of the retreating Bolsheviks. Instead, horrified at the very thought of it, they forced him onto a litter and sent him back to the base hospital. Then Moore and his men took after the Reds.

Butler was evacuated to San Francisco. He endured a long series of operations to restore his torso, face, jaw, and lips. He married a girl who wrote to him from Zanesville, Ohio, after reading of his exploits, Sylva Irene Bower, and they had two sons. Butler died on January 14, 1940, at the age of fifty-three. He died just as his great love, the Army, in which he had enlisted on May 11, 1911, was getting ready for its second world war. Mrs. Butler, now seventy-five, lives in Santa Cruz, California, with her memories of the hero of Romanovka.

Butler was dismissed in *Rescuing,* without being identified, with a few casual comments like these:

> The soldier was a young commissioned officer who was having an artificial jaw supplied to replace the one shot off in a Bolshevik encounter. . . .
>
> The nurse brought in an old leather bag, from which the Captain extracted two begrimed and blood-smeared rolls written in a very small but strong and vigorous hand.

That's how the two diaries in the book are represented to have found their way to San Francisco.

True or false? Was it Butler who carried the diaries from Siberia to the United States? This issue will be examined in due course.

The Butler saga was exhumed by Jon Speller, who picked up the trail by poring over editions of the San Francisco papers for the summer and fall of 1919.

The story of the Oklahoman on Russian soil is a refreshing example of the rewards that came from dredging in the past. The operation worked both ways, however. It put the glow of life on misty figures, but others who had loomed large at the outset and promised to grow even larger were doomed to fade as our inquiry gained momentum. A few became so diaphanous that they were, in the end, scarcely more than ghosts. Such a fate befell James P. Smythe, A.M., Ph.D.

He is billed on the cover of *Rescuing* as the arranger and translator. In 1920, in the process of copyrighting the volume, his address was given to the Library of Congress as 320 Mills Building, San Francisco. Our search of the old records of the Mills Building (still one of the city's largest commercial structures), for the years 1919, 1920, and all the years since, showed no trace of a James P. Smythe in room 320 or anywhere else.

For the last half of 1919 and the first of 1920, the records showed, room 320 was rented to a John A. Clecak, a real-estate operator. He had rooms 318 and 319 also.

Henry Haskin, publisher of *Rescuing,* said he had never heard of Smythe and doubted if he existed, at least in connection with the book's production. None of the big California libraries and universities had ever listed James P. Smythe as a writer or scholar.

All this seemed to indicate that Smythe was fast stepping out of his costume as an actor in the mystery and heading for oblivion. For several months we mourned his departure. Then, lo and behold, a new actor stepped into the Smythe role. Within a day or two it was clear that the evaporation of Smythe into thin air was small loss, indeed, compared to what we had acquired in return—

a man with a whole galaxy of talents, a man by the name of William Rutledge McGarry. McGarry was not only a remarkably learned man, but his various interests and tireless energy had taken him all over the world. He put what he learned into action.

He is one of the most versatile men of whom I have ever heard —intelligence agent, lawyer, writer, linguist, corporation executive, and foreign-trade expert.

The find that led to the discovery of McGarry's role in *Rescuing* was made by Jon Speller on the third floor of the Library of Congress Annex, in Washington. It came through McGarry's signature on a letter written in the early 1930s. That's all—just his signature. There was no mention of the book.

But the signature jibed with the initials "WRM," which, as we shall see, we had long known as the key that might turn the most complex lock in the riddle. We needed the name for which those initials stood. It had eluded us for seven months.

From the moment Jon Speller phoned from Washington, only a few hours were required, in New York, to confirm that Mr. McGarry—who died in 1942—could be the "Smythe" we had been vainly seeking. It was an important landmark in the progress of the hunt. It was also the source of a pleasant surprise. McGarry turned out to be a three-in-one discovery. For different reasons, we had been searching for three unrelated individuals, never suspecting they could fuse. They were:

The man who had forwarded to Boris Brasol blueprints of the "My Dear Fox" letters—one signed by "Wilhelm," the other by "Nicolas";

The "James P. Smythe" of the book;

The representative of the U. S. Secret Service or Intelligence Branch of the State Department who had been covertly assigned to the case of the Romanovs in 1918.

Two days after Jon Speller's strike in the Library of Congress

Annex it was abundantly clear that McGarry was all three of the above, and then some.

The search for McGarry really began fifteen years ago. It was started by a New York private investigator with an Army background. He asked that I withhold his name, although, he said, he would be glad to identify himself and make himself available in any official investigation. Let's call him Joseph Stapleton. He began his sleuthing career as a volunteer in the Swedish language division of an Army Specialized Training Program, an intelligence project of World War II vintage. The results of his work, after the war, were put to use by a number of Congressional committees. Then he went into business for himself.

In 1954, in New York, a retired colonel of Army Engineers called Mr. Stapleton to his home for a conference. It was a man Mr. Stapleton had met and befriended during one of the Congressional probes. The older man told the younger that he was afraid he would not live much longer and that the time had come for him to turn over certain important documents, letters, and files to one who would be most likely to appreciate their continuing importance.

"I accepted them," Mr. Stapleton told me. "My friend had no wife or interested heirs. I regret to say his hunch was correct. He passed away a short time later.

"It took me a while to study the files he handed over and sort out what I thought was important. Among the things that caught my full attention were the 'My Dear Fox' letters from the two emperors. They were on blueprints. Attached were copies of two letters addressed to Boris Brasol. One referred to the 'Fox' letters.

"I thought," Mr. Stapleton continued, "I had better talk with Mr. Brasol about all the material in the files that pertained to him. I called him and we made a date and I went over to see him. I brought the papers with me.

"He seemed to be very pleased that I had come. He was one of the most delightful and cultivated persons I ever met. He really wanted all the material back, and as I pulled each item out, we went over it and I then gave it to him. But when we came to the 'Fox' letters I hung onto them. Also the unsigned copies of two letters addressed to Mr. Brasol, dated in 1931. One refers in some detail to the 'Fox' letters from the emperors. I asked him whom they were from. He said he couldn't tell me. He said it was a matter of honor and a promise he made. I didn't want to lose those letters. I asked him if he really thought they were from the Kaiser and the Czar. He said he was sure they were and that some day they would prove to be of great historical importance. I said I thought that was all the more reason why a younger man like myself should keep them and have all the information about them he could get hold of.

"I suggested he get in touch with whomever had the originals and obtain a release from the promise so that I could act as a safe custodian who knew also what the documents meant. But Brasol shook his head. No, he couldn't do it, he said. He had lost touch with the man who had sent him the 'Fox' blueprints. He didn't say what we now know to be true—that the man (William Rutledge McGarry) had died. He just said he had lost touch. Though I still hadn't learned from Mr. Brasol the source of the blueprints and the letter about 'Fox' and the other unsigned letter, I knew I had a key to work with. I never could get any more help from him on this matter. And for six years after his death I still could never make the key work, either. But I've always known it was there. I don't think Mr. Brasol realized I had it.

"The key is on the lower left-hand corner of the last page of the four-page letter of March 16, 1931, to Brasol—one of the two unsigned ones. The key is the stenographer's slug—'WRM:OB.' In standard office procedure, that meant it was dictated by someone with the initials 'WRM' to someone with the initials 'OB.' You don't have to be a genius to know that.

"Where the genius would have come in handy was finding, out of

Brasol's hundreds of friends and acquaintances, the right 'WRM.' I know I tried. There were no letters from any other 'WRM' in the files I turned over to him. But if you'll remember, I told you that was the key. I suggested you go through those many cartons of his papers in the Library of Congress and see if you could find the right 'WRM.'"

Mr. Stapleton spoke the truth. After learning that *Rescuing* was getting involved in the Goleniewski case, I got in touch with Mr. Stapleton late in 1968. I thought he might provide a lead to "Fox." I had heard he owned blueprints of the "My Dear Fox" letters. It was then that he told me of the possible usefulness of the stenographer's slug on the last page of one of those unsigned copies, the one dated March 16, 1931.

The tip sounded helpful, but only remotely so. One of the members of the Three Gs had spent two weeks, only a short time before, going through those fifty-seven cartons of Brasol papers in the Library of Congress. He had found nothing new about the happenings at Ekaterinburg. In hindsight, when asked, he could recall nothing from or about a person with the initials "WRM."

So we put the Stapleton idea down as something to follow up later—preferably when it was fortified by something that turned up elsewhere.

But in the weeks following, I thought many times of that teasing and tantalizing "WRM:OB." It winked out in the mind, every now and then, taking little more space than an average small word, but having a much more relentless effect. Just three little components of the alphabet separated by a colon from two more. Yet it might be able to clarify a hundred puzzles.

Neither the city nor the state in which the letter was composed showed up on the carbon copy. The imagination could place that pair wherever in the world it wanted. It did so, on different days at different places. In the end, that only worsened the ague of not knowing.

It was addressed to Mr. Brasol at 612 West 144th Street, New York City. That was the one address that showed.

"My dear Mr. Brasol": it began. "I am so deeply indebted to you for so many poetic and philosophical excursions that I scarcely know where to begin in making my feeble acknowledgements, while yet under the sway of such luminous thoughts as flash from your last intellectual gems."

Actually, in that one paragraph, WRM gives away quite a little information about himself—that he likes "excursions," likes to be "swayed," and has a propensity for "luminous thoughts." And OB also left a trace in that one paragraph. It was a comma that she or he forgot to put in after "acknowledgements." She or he had to go back and insert it in squeezed space before the "while." It's a human touch that seems far, far below the altitude in which the thoughts of WRM were flying, at the moment.

The letter went on for four more pages but no more typographical blunders. It devoted a number of paragraphs to express doubt that the newly announced "Anastasia" (Mrs. Tchaikovsky, who later changed her name to Mrs. Anna Anderson) was who she claimed to be. But there was nothing about "Fox."

It was a warm, literary letter. It had orchidaceous phrases here and there, such as, "Really, my dear Brasol, you have the divine afflatus of a Poe," and it dropped a few foreign expressions like *"C'est très!"* It also made a sarcastic reference to the sulphuric acid that reportedly made the bodies of the Romanovs disappear so quickly. But it submitted no new facts about the assassination story.

On the other hand, the style and tone of this March 16, 1931, letter to Brasol suggested that it could have been written by the same person who wrote him the letter of March 20, 1931. The second mentioned "Fox," but the carbon, at least, showed no stenographer's slug and no signature.

73

There was another link between the letters. The first mentioned a book that hadn't arrived. The second letter said it had arrived. If both came from the same person, as it seemed, there were interesting implications. They meant that the same person could have written *Rescuing the Czar*. There were similarities of sentence structure among all three productions—the book and the two letters. There were recurring allusions that appeared in the book and the letters. One was a reference to *The Man in the Iron Mask,* which novel by Dumas père the writer attributes to Victor Hugo. Another was to Lycurgus.

The March 20 letter was especially rich in the promise of significance:

> . . . What would you say if I told you there was a document in existence, dated 6 JANUARY 1919, signed NICOLAS, thanking someone for "CONSUMMATING MY ESCAPE"? As a student of literature you might say it could be Nicholas Nickleby; but it isn't.
>
> I am enclosing you a blue-print in strictest confidence as an off-set to this Sokolov invention.
>
> You will notice at the bottom of this little note a "box" enclosing some typewritten matter that does not appear distinctly in this blueprint. The wording on the document from which this blue-print is taken is as follows, "The foregoing has been inked over the original penciled note to make certain of its preservation. C.J.F." [1]
>
> If you have any of the Emperor's handwriting near you, it might be well to compare this with it to see if you can discover any CHARACTERISTIC which appears NATURAL to both. I do not happen to have anything with me to make the comparison. But there is no mistaking those *I*s and *J*s and *Y*s, and the way the *T*s are crossed, for anything else but a *characteristic* of the author of this document. While a signature may be counterfeited easily enough by a practiced hand, the SPEED indicated in this writing seems too natural to its author to be spurious.
>
> But who is Fox?

[1] See pp. 15–16 for the entire text of the "Nicolas" letter.

Perhaps the blue-print[2] which accompanys the other, may throw some light on that question. It is not dated, and seems to be written on a piece of leather or cardboard, so that the text is greatly obscured. But it is signed by the German Kaiser, apparently, and reads as follows:

"My dear Fox—

I am profoundly pleased to learn that G_____ has so good an opinion of my efforts in that matter. It strikes me—with such eminent support you cannot fail to *fulfill* your arduous task with the very best results . . . *Pense à bien—*

Wilhelm."

The inference is permissible that Fox was known to both; and the "G_____" above referred to could easily have been George V, or Galitzin. And the *"ardous task"* Fox had in hand, the result of which Wilhelm advises him to "think for the best" in executing, could certainly NOT HAVE BEEN TO ALLOW THE BOLSHEVIKI TO ASSASSINATE the Kaiser's blood kin and, thus, prepare the way for a general collapse of MONARCHY. And if Lenin and Trotsky were the Kaiser's agents, the Czar's SAFETY must have been CERTAIN when the treaty of Brest-Litovsk was signed or both Trotsky and Lenin would have been shot by the victorious Germans who regarded the EMPRESS with the liveliest feelings of affection.

Let me have your criticism of this phase of the question; for, some day, I may imitate Victor Hugo's "Man in the Iron Mask" and startle my countrymen.

Sincerely yours, . . .

Most intriguing, indeed, was the author's hint that he might startle his countrymen with another "Man in the Iron Mask." More discouraging was his posing the question "But who is Fox?" That sounded as if he didn't have the faintest idea.

And finally, to diminish further the urgency of searching for WRM, his or her imprimatur didn't garnish the copy of the last

---

[2] This same letter appears on p. 15, but for the reader's convenience is reproduced here.

page of the March 20 letter, the one that mentioned "Fox" and the emperors' letters to him.

Though the tone and the typing were similar to the WRM:OB creation, carbons, as far as typewriter identification is concerned, are so often deceiving. The March 20 letter to Brasol could have been the work of an entirely different person. It was notable, too, that neither letter displayed any knowledge of the existence of *Rescuing the Czar,* a book published eleven years before the letters were written.

All these reasons postponed our ultimate combing through the Brasol collection of papers in the Library of Congress. By the end of May 1969, however, the time had come. We had done everything else that had to be done. Unfortunately, no more helpful leads to WRM had come to us.

Jon Speller was tapped for the mission in Washington. He arrived there on May 26 and went to the Library of Congress Annex the next morning.

Jon Speller is a vice-president of Robert Speller & Sons. Jon and his brother, Robert, Jr., are a practiced pair of archivists. Both have many outside interests, Jon in research and writing, Robert in genealogy, but both have rummaged in the library catacombs for years. It was Robert who translated large sections of Joseph Lasies's book from the French to help this investigation. (See Chapter X.)

Lithe, tallish, bright, and impatient, Jon has a sense of humor that has wreathed his features into a gaily sardonic expression. As in the case of Joe Stapleton, his fast reflexes and high I.Q. constantly outrace all the rest of him in the struggle to meet deadlines. They lend him the same incongruous air that Stapleton has of someone who is far ahead of everyone else, but, at the same time, badly delayed and desperately late. Each is a past master at devising short-cuts to a main objective, and this was the problem that engrossed Jon Speller on the third floor of the Library of Congress Annex, on Capitol Hill.

"I must say, I was feeling a bit grim about the job ahead of me," he declared. "I looked at the index which Mr. Brasol prepared so carefully for all those fifty-seven boxes. All were clearly titled according to subject matter—Russian foreign policy, the Pushkin Society, criminology, and so forth.

"There was nothing in the catalogue card about the Brasol papers' being restricted. There was simply a notice that all the material was to be made available to Professor Leonid Strakhovsky, the library's Slavonic expert.

"Considering that all the cases earmarked with those heavy subjects had been examined before, I cast my eyes around for a less clearly defined title to gamble on—you know, something that might cross boundaries. I decided it might be the one entitled 'Miscellaneous Correspondence.' I made out a requisition slip for that one. I filled out an alternate slip for the one marked 'Russian Foreign Policy.' I turned in the 'Miscellaneous' slip first and held onto the second. I thought I'd try the second if the first didn't work.

"Pretty soon the attendant delivered 'Miscellaneous Correspondence' to me. It was a greenish carton of heavy cardboard, or something like cardboard. About a foot and a half high, I'd say, and two feet long or more. There were documents in it—also some big envelopes and folders. There was a big packet of letters. I went for them. I opened a lot and put them back. None was from any WRM. I guess an hour and a half went by. I was down near the bottom of the packet. Then I hit it. It was the original of that March 16, 1931, letter to Mr. Brasol. Printed on the Page One letterhead was 'William Rutledge McGarry.' On the bottom of the fourth page was the inked signature, clear as anything—'William R. McGarry.' The first page showed it was written in Washington, D.C. That's something, as you know very well, you couldn't see on the carbon. That's when I went to the nearest booth in the building and phoned New York."

Nowhere in "Miscellaneous Correspondence" was the original

or duplicate of the March 20, 1931, letter to Mr. Brasol. Nowhere were the originals or blueprints of the "My Dear Fox" letters.

Mr. Speller's phone call from Washington was quite a jolt. William Rutledge McGarry was indeed the man for whom we had been waiting.

I hurried to the New York Public Library. First I checked in the master file on the authors of books, on the third floor. No luck. There was no card for him. Then I tried in the north reading room in three or four volumes of Who Was Who, chosen at random. That's the handy compilation of the more important biographies of men and women who have appeared in past Who's Whos and then been dropped.

Nothing in any of them. The New York Public Library, whose efficiency is one of the great consolations for living in range of it, keeps all old copies of Who's Who in America.

I tried to find William Rutledge McGarry in four or five more Who's Whos from the late thirties and early forties. There was nothing.

By this time it must be painfully clear that our search would have been months longer were it not for the resources of the New York Public Library (including two copies of *Rescuing the Czar*) and its imaginative staff—to say nothing of Who's Who in America and an exceptional reference volume, The National Cyclopedia of American Biography.

With a mounting sense of frustration I looked at the long line of Who's Who in America on different shelves, all crimson but all blacker and grimier, the older they were. The prospects were dismal. I reached into the 1920s and picked one. I couldn't tell the year from the cover. The lettering was too faded. It didn't seem to make any difference, anyway. Either my man was in it or he wasn't. I never did look for the date on the frontispiece.

I flipped the pages to the Ms, then to a McAdoo, then to a

"McGarrah, Gates W., banker. . . ." In a twinkle, from the right side of Page 1314, it leapt out—

McGARRY, William Rutledge, foreign trade counsel; *b.* N.Y. City, Apr. 29, 1872; *s.* James Adams and Catherine (Rutledge) M.; U. of Minn., 1889–93, later studied at U. of Paris, and in France, Germany, Russia, Asia Minor and Far East; *m.* Margaret Hoche Doscher, of London, Eng., 1894 . . .

It was that schooling record that stopped me—that restless pilgrimage in search of knowledge through France, Germany, Russia, Asia Minor, and the Far East.

My spirits picked up. My eyes jumped over clusters of type until they reached something Mr. McGarry had done in "1922–24." It had to do with "foreign trade." This was discouraging. There was something missing. There was no mention of World War I.

No Army, no Navy, no government service, no diplomatic activity, in those tumultuous years when a great war was convulsing all those countries in which Mr. McGarry had studied? Had he been content to sit in his office in all those years, driving international business deals?

It didn't add up, I thought. It probably wasn't the right man at all. Yet it was a William Rutledge McGarry, and he had been to Germany and Russia. It was certainly progress. Maybe his family could help us get to the right McGarry—and here I took note that this man had had addresses in New York, San Francisco, and Paris. They all could be leads.

I read no more. It was now early evening. The print was small and the light was poor at the shelves. I knew the library's Xerox room would soon close, and rather than waste any more time taking the volume into a better light at the reading desk, I decided I should get the necessary permission to remove it from the stacks, carry it to the reproduction room, and have copies made. These I could bring home, and there I could ponder the next move.

In the reproduction room of the library I handed over the Who's Who in America with the page marked for copying. I got it back quickly. The attendant gave me the three Xerox sheets and a yellow folder to carry them in. I put the sheets in the folder. Not five minutes later I was on my way home after returning the weighty volume to its place on the shelf of the north reading room.

Outside on the streets I found myself in the last stages of the evening rush hour. I was soon a squeezed straphanger for the two-station subway trip to Lexington Avenue and Fifty-ninth Street. I was aware that my yellow folder under the strap-free arm had had a mauling on the journey, so when I climbed to the sidewalk and into the dusk brightened by a brilliant street lamp, I stopped to inspect my prize package—the yellow folder. I pulled out one of the Xeroxes to make sure it was all right. There, under the kind of illumination that rendered every tiny letter of type legible, I read the McGarry piece from start to finish, line by line, for the first time.

I came close to the end with no undue emotion. I was glad to see the sheet was unwrinkled. Then I reached the line with the word "Author." Just a few words more—and that was enough. Suddenly I was struck by something. It could have been a truck, a bomb, or a heart attack. It would have made no difference. Here's what I read:

McGARRY, William Rutledge, foreign trade counsel; *b.* N.Y. City, Apr. 29, 1872; *s.* James Adams and Catherine (Rutledge) M.; U. of Minn., 1889–93, later studied at U. of Paris, and in France, Germany, Russia, Asia Minor and Far East; *m.* Margaret Hoche Doscher, of London, Eng., 1894 (died 1906); children—James Giles (dec.), Ruth Elaine (Mrs. William C. Tesche), Mark Rutledge; *m.* 2d, Emily Graves, of Los Angeles, Calif., 1919. Ry. service until 1904; pres. Chetlo Harbor (Wash.) Packing Co., 1906–10; chmn. bd. Federal Gas Co., Mackie Steel Tube Works, 1905–07; traveled widely abroad in interest of Am. foreign trade, touring world, 1922–24, making survey of polit. and economic possibilities of principal commercial nations; active in promotion of interest in Nicaraguan and Panama Canal projects, deepening of rivers and harbors, Am. merchant marine, Cape Cod Ship Canal, development of Gogebic and Messaba iron fields. Drafted plan for stabilizing finances in Nicaragua, first plan for selection of U.S. senator by popular vote, in Ore.; counsel in case of Hibbard vs. Belding, controversy over boundary line between N.C. and Tenn., etc. Mem. Am. Bar Assn., Pan Pacific Union, Am. Asiatic Assn., Japan Soc., Latin Am. Assn., Foreign Legion, etc. Mason, K.P., Red Man, Woodman. *Clubs:* Commercial, Foreign Trade. *Author:* From Berlin to Bagdad, 1914; **Rescuing the Czar, 1919.**[3] Contbr. numerous articles on foreign trade to mags. *Home:* 588 West End Av., New York, N.Y. *Address:* 1155 Jones St., San Francisco, Calif. (also 52 rue François 1er, Paris, France).

At last the fabulous book had come out of the crepuscule to roost on a visible perch! But it was anything but a bold emergence. The perch was about as conspicuous as a leaf in a maple grove.

It would be trite to say I was elated. The reaction was deeper than that. One of the most elusive quarries I had ever pursued was beginning to show through the underbrush. From here on, it seemed, the hunt would become progressively easier. Whether or not Mr. McGarry was still alive at ninety-seven, the names of his son and daughter were listed. There were definite addresses in New York, San Francisco, and Paris. With leads like that, the rest was child's play—something for a freshman class in journalism.

Seven hours later, however, all cause for optimism had gone. After passing the whole evening on the telephone with information operators, the distressing truth was spelled out by scrawled notes all over a check-off pad. There were no listings for William Rutledge

[3] The publisher, Henry Haskin, claims the book was published in 1920, not 1919. The author uses the publisher's date rather than McGarry's. The bold-face type is not in the original, and is used here merely for the reader's convenience.

McGarry, or his wife, or his son, Mark R., or his daughter, Mrs. William C. Tesche, in the five boroughs of New York City, or on Long Island, or in Connecticut, or in New Jersey's north counties, or in Westchester, or in San Francisco, or in the six main regional areas of metropolitan Los Angeles.

It required lengthy chats with different operators, until way past midnight, to attain this rather gloomy but conclusive estimate of the situation. One could imagine that the whole McGarry clan had been wiped out in a common disaster. None were in their old haunts.

True, Paris remained—that suite or little *pied à terre* at 52 rue François 1er. I could make a last stab there the next morning. And, true, the McGarrys could have moved to any of a thousand different places. But one could grow old, white, and senile at the telephone trying information in every city and town of the United States, inquiring about the presence of a McGarry with the right first name and middle initial, and about Mrs. William C. Tesche.

All in one day the trail had turned from cold to warm to cold. I went to bed late and my mind kept churning up my mistakes. I was extremely angry at myself for not having taken note of the exact year in the 1920s represented by my Who's Who in America Xeroxes. That was plain stupid. I could be tossing around names and addresses up to forty-eight years stale.

I returned to the library early the next day. I determined very quickly that the volume from which I had made copies was the 1926–27 book. I examined editions for years before and after. I discovered that Mr. McGarry made his debut in the reference book early in the twenties; that the first entries had no mention of *Rescuing the Czar,* but only named his work *From Berlin to Bagdad* (without listing the publisher); that *Rescuing* was entered for the first time in the 1926–27 edition; that it remained there until the whole McGarry biography washed out of Who's Who in America entirely in the early thirties to be replaced by a reference line to older volumes; that in a year or two more, even the reference line was dropped.

This was revealing. He had "sneaked" the book into his Who's Who in America write-up the same year it had been "sneaked" onto the shelves of the New York Public Library as a creation of "James P. Smythe" (1926). In both instances, apparently, he had been moved by the desire to get something onto the record, but in such a way that no one would notice it at the time. There would be no stir. There would be no one at the library aroused to the shattering conflict involved in having on its list of books a *Rescuing the Czar* with its authorship credited to "James P. Smythe" with, at the same time, in another room, in several editions of Who's Who in America, a *Rescuing the Czar* whose authorship was credited to "William Rutledge McGarry."

All the Who's Who in America write-ups omitted any reference to World War I. All gave the same addresses. There were no new ones, in other cities, to work on. And since his name hadn't been picked up by any of the editions of Who Was Who, I found I was really back where I'd started. I still didn't know if he was alive or, if not, when and where he died.

A real ordeal was in store. I would have to look through every New York *Times* yearly news index, starting with 1930 right on through 1968—a little matter of thirty-nine years. That meant searching through more than thirty-nine volumes, for some of those years were divided by the *Times* into two halves and two volumes. The job entailed looking for the name of William Rutledge Mc-Garry on the chance he had made some kind of news story or had died, and, therefore, an obituary had been published. But there was also the perfectly good chance that he hadn't died; also, that he had made no story. So the whole effort could be a wild-goose chase.

The feeling of victory that had come the day before with the discoveries in the Library of Congress in Washington and the library in New York began to slope down to the old, familiar sensation of being hemmed in by a wall.

Then, as on other occasions, I decided to seek the help of a man at the New York Public Library's reference-room information desk. My victim of the moment was Christopher Samuels, a wide-eyed, dark-haired, extremely perceptive young literary detective. I explained the whole problem. I tried to entice his curiosity as best I could.

"Have I no other recourse," I asked, "than going through all those New York Times Indexes?"

"In theory there are other recourses," he said. "But they may not pan out."

First he double-checked my report that there was no author's card for McGarry, not even for his other book, *From Berlin to Bagdad*. There was no card for that book by title, either. You have to be very sharp with the library's enormous number of file drawers on the "Macs" and "McCs" because they are all interwoven.

Mr. Samuels' findings were the same as mine: zero.

Then he led the way back to the central desk in the reference room. He tried one biographical index after another—some prepared by publishers, others by scientific and medical organizations, others by bar associations, others about authors, others about certain fields of public service. After all, from McGarry's record in *Who's Who,* he could qualify in any number of categories.

The pages rustled. The minutes dragged on. Mr. Samuels began to look as discouraged as I felt. My thoughts wandered toward the north reading room, where those *Times* news indexes were stacked row on row. It seemed as if I might as well prepare myself for the drudgery of going through them. It was a painful reflection, because I knew that it offered no assurance at all of finding a mention of that quintessential man of mystery, William Rutledge McGarry.

I heard a little growl of triumph. I looked at Mr. Samuels.

He's a very disciplined and decorous personage, and I suppose I shouldn't have expected anything louder. He was copying something on a pad from an open book in front of him.

"What's up?" I said.

"Something, at least," he said.

"About what?"

"About your friend Mr. McGarry. It's in The National Cyclopedia of American Biography."

He tore the sheet from the pad and read:

"Volume thirty-nine, page six hundred and nine. There's a sketch. Come on!"

He stomped through the gate of the pen that encloses the staff of the reference room. He led the way west, toward the two big reading rooms. I was right after him. We were in a foot race. I had to smile to myself about this resourceful young man's sudden gusto. He had learned just enough, apparently, he had been balked just enough, to have been made a member of the Three Gs without knowing it.

Under the big, wooden arch of the third floor's west wing, he wheeled smartly to the right. He entered the north reading room, with me after him. We turned right again. We climbed the two or three steps to the elongated platform with shelves on both sides that runs for most of the whole length of the reading room. It makes a narrow walk. One must go single file. Mr. Samuels' gait was close to a run, and I was fast falling behind because a few others who had made way for him bounced back in my path. But I never lost sight of Mr. Samuels.

He stopped halfway down the room, which is as long as a college dining hall. He crouched to inspect some big volumes on the shelves. He pulled one out and put it on top of the low, outside row of shelves. He consulted the slip of paper in his hand. He flipped a few pages, leaned closer. I drew up to him. He glanced up with a smile of victory.

"There's your Mr. McGarry," he said. "Good picture of him, too."

It was more than a good picture. It was a revelation. And no one could have been happier than I to view it at last, face to face. He was white-haired, with a narrow, white moustache. The hair was the only touch of antiquity. Everything else about his features was young and awake. His eyes searched up intensely, above the focus of the camera, with a note of poetic fervor, perhaps even religious. But this otherworldly effect was offset by the corners of the mouth, which seemed to be having a hard time looking solemn enough for the photographer. It was a massive head. The cheekbones were wide. The forehead was high—just a trifle too domelike. The total effect was something Rodin would have liked to work on—a good natured, brooding giant who did his best dreaming under maximum physical strain.

I kept looking at him, and he kept looking past me and over my head. Just once, and just for a moment, I had the illusion that he lowered his gaze and fixed his eyes on me and extended those mouth corners into a definite smile. I imagined I could hear his voice, saying:

"My word, son—I thought you'd never get here!"

Two minutes later I could better understand the message I had read from his face. The article Mr. Samuels had found in the 1954 (Volume 29) edition of The National Cyclopedia of American Biography was far more widely dimensioned than anything in Who's Who in America. And in a flash that fired right out of the lines of type, it solved the mystery of where this man had been in World War I.

"During the First World War," it stated, "McGarry did intelligence work in Paris, France, for the U. S. Department of State."

Then, elsewhere, it added:

"Throughout his career he traveled widely abroad, and at different times he was U.S. embassy attaché in London, Berlin, and Russia."

Not until fourteen years after his death were these apocalyptic sentences allowed to surface on his record. They were totally absent from Who's Who in America. They were not included in his obituary, which, I soon learned, the New York *Times* ran under a Redwood City, California, dateline on May 15, 1942—two days after his death.

It was now unmistakably clear that William Rutledge McGarry had been one of the earliest, and very few, secret agents who during wartime served the United States in several foreign countries. The "arranger and translator" of *Rescuing the Czar*—and perhaps its author—was very likely one of the men who participated in the rescue. With his hand in both the book and the operation it describes, William Rutledge McGarry was probably one of those who took pains to see that the book came as close to the truth as possible, but not close enough to violate security, and not close enough to jeopardize the lives of the beneficiaries.

By the book, by his letters to Brasol, by the blueprints of the "My Dear Fox" letters he had left around with trusted friends, the extraordinary Mr. McGarry had converted his own grave into a well-wired time charge. It was destined to explode years after his death—how many years after, he would have no way of knowing.

In his oblique and ingenious way he had tried to prod his talented friend Boris Brasol into making the discovery for himself. Those letters he wrote to Mr. Brasol now had a luminescence that an ordinary reader would miss.

"What would you say if I told you," he wrote to Brasol, "there was a document in existence, dated 6 January 1919, signed NICO-LAS, thanking someone for 'CONSUMMATING MY ESCAPE?' As a student of literature you might say it could be Nicholas Nickleby; but it isn't."

He derided the alleged destructive powers of the sulphuric acid at Ekaterinburg.

Some day, he wrote, "I may startle my countrymen."

Brasol wouldn't take the bait. Good writer that he was, good reporter, good criminologist, Mr. Brasol somehow was able to restrain himself on this issue. Perhaps he, too, was concerned about the security of the Romanovs in their hiding places using their cover names. But there is no evidence that Mr. Brasol didn't take McGarry's nudges very seriously. Otherwise why would he have been so careful to conceal the source of the "My Dear Fox" blueprints from Mr. Stapleton and others? Also Mr. McGarry's correspondence about the blueprints?

I thanked Mr. Samuels for his help. Rarely has an expression of gratitude been more genuine. I found Mr. McGarry's obituary in the New York *Times* of May 15, 1942, and had a copy made from the microfilm. The story from Redwood City, California, named his son and daughter among his survivors. It stated that his daughter, Mrs. William C. Tesche, lived in Glendale.

I thought the path was clear. I could picture the long-distance operators connecting me by phone, in a matter of minutes, with someone in the Clan McGarry between Redwood City and Glendale. But a few minutes after I reached home I was in trouble again. Neither in Glendale nor Redwood City was there a trace of any of the McGarrys. I spent a troubled half hour trying to figure out my next move. My best bet, I decided, was the publishers of The National Cyclopedia of American Biography, James T. White & Co. They were listed at 101 Fifth Avenue. A call soon established that they had moved recently to Clifton, New Jersey. (And a frail voice from my pessimistic side spoke up: "And have just jettisoned all their old files, I suppose.")

But it seemed to me there must be someone in the firm who could find an address of a McGarry back in 1953, possibly, when that

1954 article was being prepared. That would be eleven years more up-to-date than the obituary.

I phoned White & Co.'s Clifton headquarters. I explained what I wanted to Susan Samet, an editorial assistant. She was sympathetic but anything but hopeful.

"I'm afraid we throw out that kind of material," she said. "Particularly after all that time. We've just moved, you know. I don't think there's any chance we'd have an address."

"But would you give it a try?"

"Well, I'll see."

I left my number. Three hours later, when I was on the point of calling her, she called me.

"We looked," she said. "We looked long and hard, but what we've got doesn't look much good. It's the address of a Mrs. William C. Tesche. It says 2500 Ocean, Corona del Mar, California."

It sounded great to me.

"It's a pretty old address," she said. "Mrs. Tesche may have moved. She may not even be alive."

I learned that Miss Samet had not taken her lunch hour and had enlisted the help of her colleagues in combing through old files. I owe it to them both to introduce her to Mr. Samuels at the library. They should open a wayside inn for lost hunters.

She had broken the last barrier. The information operator found Mrs. Tesche in the Corona del Mar directory. My phone call caught Mrs. Tesche on her way out of the house to a luncheon for which she was already late. The sound of the ringing had brought her back.

She, too, was polite, but in no mood to be expansive. She referred to the widow of her brother, Mark, in Saint Petersburg, Florida, where she also had three nephews, one a circuit-court judge.

"All of my father's papers are down there," she said. "My brother

89

was working to get them in shape. He never finished before he died."

Her brother, Mark R. McGarry, had recently died, I learned, after making a preliminary effort to arrange and appraise his father's vast collection of letters, documents, personal papers, manuscripts, and business records. Obviously our long search was nearing an end.

For several days there were calls back and forth between New York and Corona del Mar and between New York and Saint Petersburg. I spoke at various times with Judge Mark R. McGarry, Jr., his wife, and his mother, Mrs. Mark R. McGarry, who was the daughter-in-law of the World War I secret agent. These points began to emerge:

The members of the family knew that William Rutledge McGarry regarded *Rescuing the Czar* as mostly a true story. Not all of them had read it, because most of them believed they had heard more about the real truth than the book could tell them. They were aware also that William Rutledge McGarry believed it "would all come out some day, at the proper time," and that, until then, it was not for him to make the first moves.

Mrs. Tesche, the daughter of the great man, said she regarded herself as "getting too old to be of much help—I wouldn't remember as much as I should. You should put most of your questions to my sister-in-law in Florida."

She gave me good advice. The sister-in-law, Mrs. Mark R. McGarry, mother of the judge and his two brothers, has a vivid memory of the author, engineer, lawyer, secret agent, linguist, and promoter of public works.

Mrs. McGarry is a New Yorker. She spoke with a well-bred accent that would sound at home at the Colony Club.

"William Rutledge McGarry was a genius," she said. "He was a great man and one of the most well-rounded I have ever known.

Plate 10: Charles James Fox, a "rescuer" of the Czar and the Imperial family.

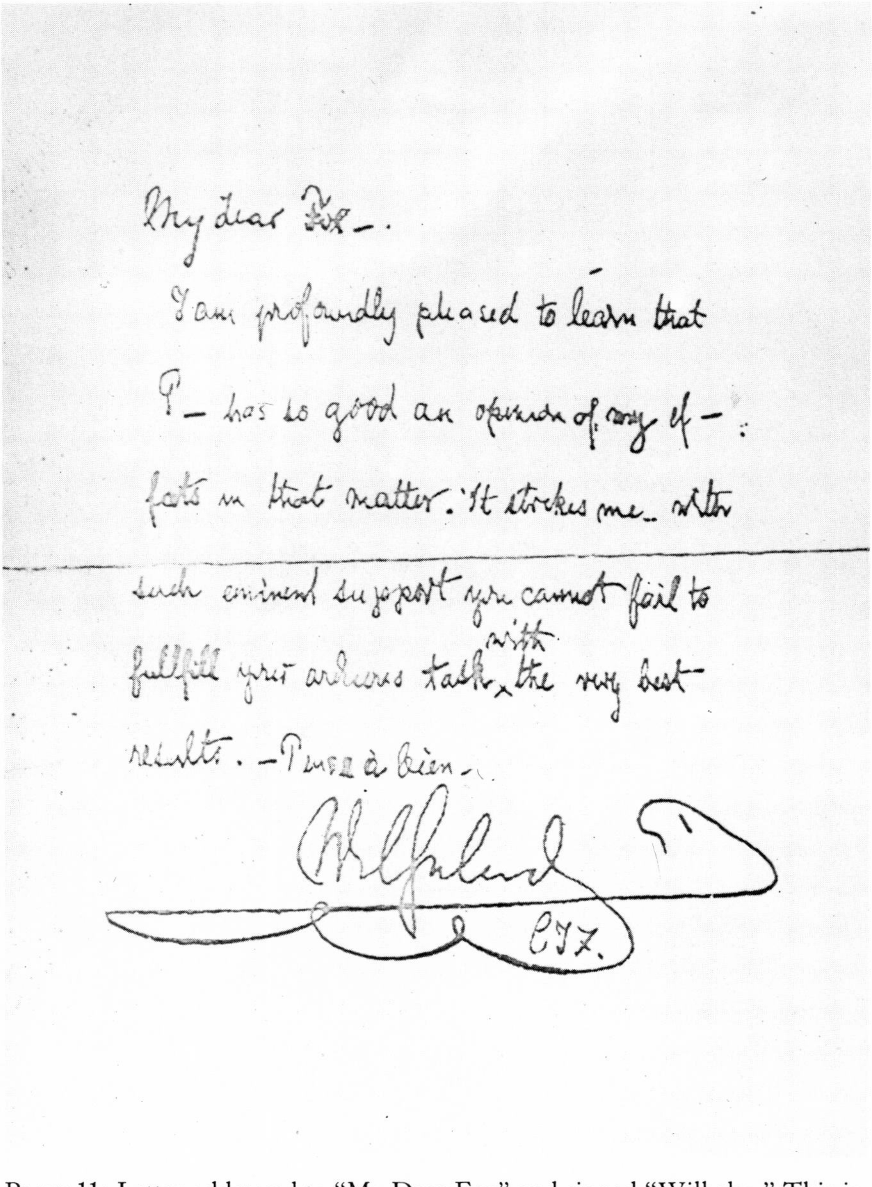

My dear Fox—.

I am profoundly pleased to learn that

P— has so good an opinion of any ef—:

forts in that matter. It strikes me— with

such eminent support you cannot fail to

fullfill your arduous task, with the very best

results. — Pense à bien—.

Wilhelm
CJF.

PLATE 11: Letter addressed to "My Dear Fox" and signed "Wilhelm." This is addressed to Charles James Fox and is supposedly signed by the German Kaiser Wilhelm II. Note the initials "CJF." (Charles James Fox?) in the loop of Wilhelm's signature.

My dear *Fox*, Lio – Jan'y '19

I need not tell you how I feel indebted for all that you have ~~done towards accommodating my escape.~~

I feel that you will do all you can to maintain my State secret.

Believe me sincerely
Nicolas

PLATE 12: Letter addressed to "My Dear Fox" and signed "Nicolas." This is addressed to Charles James Fox and is supposedly signed by the Czar Nicholas II, 1919.

PLATE 13: The German Kaiser Wilhelm II, 1905. Compare Wilhelm's signature with that in the "My Dear Fox" letter, plate 11.

PLATE 14: The English King George V on his wedding day, taken in 1893, when he was twenty-eight. Compare with the photograph of Nicholas taken in 1896, when he was 28, plate 1.

PLATE 15: The Grand Duke Michael, a brother of the Czar, is seated in the foreground with his wife, the Countess Nathalia Brassova. The Grand Duchess Olga is seated in the background with her second husband, Colonel Nicholas Kulikovsky. This was photographed while the Grand Duchess Olga was still married to her first husband, the Duke Peter of Oldenburg, to whom the Colonel was an aide-de-camp. Circa 1914.

PLATE 16: The exterior of the Ipatiev House, Ekaterinburg, where the Imperial family was imprisoned, 1918.

PLATE 17: The room where the Imperial family was allegedly massacred, 1918.

PLATE 18: Joseph Lasies, a French official who assisted in gathering material concerning the disappearance of the Czar. He believed that they all escaped.

PLATE 19: Robert Wilton, a special correspondent of The Times of London sent to Russia to assist in research on the disappearance. He supported the assassination story.

PLATE 20: Trio of investigators at the Ipatiev House, Ekaterinburg, 1919. Seated is General Michael Dieterichs, standing and pointing is Nicholas Sokolov, and listening is Inspector Magnitsky.

He spoke seven languages. There was almost nothing he wasn't good at.

"He was a short man, you know. He had five brothers, I think it was, all six feet two or over. I suppose that had an effect when he was growing up. He seemed to do everything more intensely than anyone else.

"I think it was hard on my husband to hear that his father was always right about everything, or almost everything. Sometimes Mark would want to dismiss his advice. I wouldn't object if the matter didn't affect our lives directly, but when it did, I learned to heed my father-in-law's advice. Before the stock market crash of 1929, for instance, he advised us to sell everything. He thought securities were priced too high and a day of reckoning was coming. My husband didn't want to sell, but I insisted. Well, we did sell. I've always thanked my father-in-law for it. If we hadn't acted on his advice, we'd be far from well off today."

Mrs. McGarry said there were twenty or thirty cabinets and suitcases in her home, crammed with her father-in-law's papers, and she invited us down to inspect them. Our acceptance was instantaneous.

So William Rutledge McGarry, who certainly had been in a position to know, upheld the story told by *Rescuing* as being mostly true.

I had long been prepared for such a finding, but it left a haunting amount of unfinished business. Which portions recorded the real sequence of events? Which were pure decoration? Which were the diversions thrown in to put the hounds off the scent and thus preserve the security of five Romanov women, a man, and a boy?

As far as the principal figures are concerned, the grand design of the shrouded and complicated maneuver was clearly beginning to protrude through the sands that had buried it.

An interest in foreign trade was one great common denominator that undoubtedly made at least three of the Americans known to each other before the start of World War I. Among a great many other things, William Rutledge McGarry was an expert on foreign trade. So was Dr. William E. Aughinbaugh. So was Charles James Fox, the editor of the *North China Star,* in Tientsin. All had written articles on the subject for magazines specializing in international commerce.

There was another bond. All three were writers, and good ones. There was another bond between McGarry and Fox. Both had attended the Sorbonne, in Paris. Both had gained further education in Germany. Though McGarry was nearly five years older than Fox, it is unlikely that their paths didn't cross somewhere in Europe during their student days, for McGarry continued his quest for knowledge in "Russia, Asia Minor and the Far East," during which period he was in and out of Paris, Berlin, and London.

A quick check of the McGarry papers in Saint Petersburg established the presence of a long-time correspondence between William Rutledge McGarry, on the one hand, and both Fox and Aughinbaugh, on the other.

James Marston Fox, of Alexandria, Louisiana, the son of Charles James Fox, said the name of McGarry only vaguely rang a bell and he wouldn't swear that his recollection was significant.

"At the time of the Ekaterinburg crisis, during the summer of 1918," he said, "I thought my father was in Tientsin. My mother and I were in Japan for the summer. If he was in Siberia at the time, I think he got back to Tientsin by August 18. I bought a share of stock in the paper from him, and it was a big event in my financial history as a boy, and I remember it. The stock certificate is dated August 18.

"It is perfectly possible, however, that my father was in Siberia in July and the early part of August."

The assassination of the Romanovs is supposed to have taken place the night of July 16–17, 1918.

James Marston Fox, who is now living in the Louisiana town

where he met his wife during World War II, when he was an Army officer, then added an interesting thought:

"When we lived near Washington, before we moved to China, my father was a great friend of William Arnold Landvoight of the United States Secret Service. I remember that Mr. Landvoight was at the house many times—probably as often as once a week."

One of Mr. Landvoight's principal tasks, under President Wilson, was to safeguard visiting foreign dignitaries. In the spring of 1917, for example, Mr. Landvoight was one of the Secret Servicemen assigned to protect a Russian military delegation headed by Lieutenant General Roop. It included members of the War Ministry.

Mr. Landvoight, now in his nineties, lives in Washington. He confirmed his friendship with Charles James Fox, thought long and hard before venturing the opinion that the name of McGarry meant nothing to him, and seemed inclined to want to duck any further questions about those old security matters. He said, finally: "Well, I hope you boys get what you're after."

Though Mr. Landvoight probably didn't leave the United States in the 1917–18 period, it is probable that he and the Secret Service lent their hands to McGarry and the State Department during the planning phase of the Romanov operation. And both he and Mr. McGarry must have known that Charles James Fox, who was a linguist like McGarry, was in a key spot, Tientsin. A few days' trip on the Trans-Siberian Railway could have put Mr. Fox close to, or in, Ekaterinburg; or gotten him to London and/or Berlin and back via the Scandinavian countries. One can take his speculation from here in a hundred directions.

Then there's the question of the diaries in *Rescuing*. Did they really ever exist as diaries or were they among the many subterfuges used to disguise the realities?

If we are to follow the scenario of *Rescuing,* Captain Lawrence Butler, the hero of Romanovka, is supposed to have brought them to San Francisco from Siberia (though *Rescuing* doesn't mention Butler by name). Did he really do so?

Herman Kimsey, one of the scouts of the Three Gs in Washington, tracked down Butler's survivors through the Army and the Veterans Administration. He talked to Mrs. Sylva Butler in Santa Cruz, California, and she was quick to reply that "Larry never mentioned bringing any diaries home with him. He kept his own record, though. I'll be glad to send it to you."

Larry Butler's son, Bruce J. Butler, of San Francisco, said he had never heard his father speak of any diaries such as Mr. Kimsey described.

His mother was as good as her word. She forwarded a long chronicle that her late husband had kept on his Siberian experiences. There is no reference to finding two diaries of secret agents, but enclosed in its pages is a minuscule clue to what might have happened if the diaries weren't a literary contrivance (a much likelier theory).

In the pages of Butler's chronicle was an old calling card. It bears the inscription:

Ernest Lloyd Harris
Consul General of the United States

On the back of it, in Sylva Butler's handwriting, is the notation, "Gave Larry long ivory cigarette holder, en route home from Siberia."

This visit and gift was probably given to the wounded Butler in the base hospital at Vladivostok. That the senior United States diplomat in Siberia should make the presentation is most unusual. Generals and colonels might have dropped in, but a busy senior diplomat?

We know now that Mr. Harris was strongly anti-Bolshevik and opposed to the tepid role United States troops were playing under their War Department orders. It is not at all inconceivable that

Mr. Harris planted the diaries—or purported diaries—on the homeward-bound Army officer as a way of getting them to San Francisco outside of the regular channels.

What might be taken as corroboration of Butler's role in carrying the diaries to San Francisco bobs up in the San Francisco *Examiner* series on Captain Butler. In the fourth installment of the series of interviews with Butler, while he is still hospitalized, he says:

"I never heard an expression of sympathy or pity for the fate of the Czar and his family from any one of the Siberians to whom the dead ruler had once been known as the 'Little Father.'

"And I found that the idea was predominant among them that none of the Czar's family was really dead and that in any case the Czarevitch is still alive to be produced as a trump card by the Bolsheviki whenever their interest demands it."

Would a young platoon commander, with wounds to worry about, with memories mostly at the tactical level of a rifle company, be talking about the international situation like a statesman or foreign correspondent unless someone he respected had "briefed" him?

The reader should weigh that one for himself.

VII

The Most Eloquent Secret Agent

In the long history of international secret agents, who perfected such marvels as the microdot message, the microfilm camera, and the cyanide spray gun, William Rutledge McGarry probably was the first of the big-time operators to learn how to disable his opposite numbers with timely outpourings from the classics—Greek classics, Roman, French, Persian, Celtic, English, Russian, or Scandinavian; it made no difference. He used them all.

He was at his best in the first quarter of this century. It was a period in which American operatives were not expected to be as smoothly cultured as he was. His impact around the foreign capitals and courts was considerable. Anyone as learned as he, his amazed rivals surmised, must have connections of incalculable power and importance.

They were right. He certainly did. One of Mr. McGarry's long-time friends was Myron T. Herrick, the urbane former Ohio governor who served twice as a much-beloved American ambassador to France. Another close acquaintance was David R. Francis, a former mayor of Saint Louis, a former governor of Missouri, who was our last ambassador to Czarist Russia. Still another powerhouse with whom Mr. McGarry became acquainted after World War

I was James A. ("Jim") Farley, now Chairman of the Coca-Cola Export Corp. Such contacts not only provided Mr. McGarry with circuitous channels to the White House. They led through devious loops and conduits to several European heads of state.

The story of McGarry's personal mixture of charm, culture, and malarkey, and the effects of this mixture abroad during the late stages of the Edwardian era undoubtedly are worth a book of their own.

Even in this day and age it is impossible to read any of Mr. McGarry's reports, letters, or books without being impressed by the baroque eloquence of his style. Qualified witnesses say that when these words were being delivered in his own voice, McGarry achieved total fascination.

To have imagined McGarry as a supercilious cultural dilettante, however, who exerted little force on his life and times, was to have made a mistake of large proportions. But it is a mistake he seemed to have encouraged many persons to make. Some of his major accomplishments are only now coming to light twenty-eight years after his death. For, what is rare in men with his innate sense of showmanship, he preferred the background to the foreground. He liked to exclude all but a few from his most cherished secrets. He was short (his daughter, daughter-in-law, and grandchildren can't agree on his height, but it must have been somewhere between five three and five seven), but handsome, astute, imaginative, dogged in the pursuit of a goal, a scholar of history, and attractive to both men and women.

Were it not for the self-dramatic touch in McGarry's record, historians could be more securely astonished by a narrative found in June 1969 among his cabinets of personal papers by investigators Jon Speller and Herman Kimsey. It's a carbon copy of a letter McGarry wrote to a friend in May 1928. It was unostentatiously stacked away with hundreds of other documents in the Saint Petersburg, Florida, garage of McGarry's daughter-in-law, Mrs. Mark R. McGarry.

The letter describes McGarry's meeting in 1923 with the allegedly dead Nicholas and Alexandra, the ex-Czar and ex-Czarina, while McGarry and his wife were walking in the French city of Marseilles. The date checks with Colonel Goleniewski's claim that the Empress Alexandra lived until 1924.

Other papers in his files confirm that he and Mrs. McGarry were in France's great southern port in 1923. No assessment of the extraordinary passage, however, should be made without judging it along with four other considerations: one, his known tendency to melodrama; two, his record of being scrupulously truthful on matters he considered serious; three, his complete avoidance, from 1918 until his death, of any frivolous remarks about the Imperial Family, and four, his unwavering assurance to members of his own family, and a few others, that he happened to know that all the Romanovs escaped from Ekaterinburg and that it would "all come out some day."

Here's the passage that starts on the third page of a letter to his friend John Waldron, of Washington, D.C.:

When I met Nicholas and his wife at Marseilles in 1923, we, naturally, did not discuss so painful a subject [the "fiction" of the Czar's murder mentioned earlier in the letter], as our meeting was quite accidental and brief: As my wife and I plodded slowly up the steep incline to the *basilique de Notre-Dame de la Garde,* after alighting from the *escalier* far down below us, a tall, soldierly man with gray, pointed beard strode slowly down with a lady gowned in black clinging tightly to his arm. At a distance of about twenty feet from me, they stopped abruptly and gazed at me momentarily. As I drew closer, he spoke to me in French. His voice sounded like the voice one sometimes hears in dreams when, like a flash, the Past flits by and clothes the vision with the pageantry of years.

"Ah! Mon vieux!" (Ah! My dear chap), he exclaimed, extending his hand, "comment vas-tu? Je suis enchanté de te voir." (How are you? I'm delighted to see you.)

We clasped hands. "Merci, mon cher, c'est un bonheur de te revoir. Come tu es pâle! Qu'as-tu?" (Thank you, my dear friend, it's good to see you again. You look pale. What's the trouble?) I replied.

"Je ne me sens pas bien" (I don't feel very well), he rejoined, as his eyes wandered off in the direction of the Chateau d'If and his voice fell into a whisper. Then pressing my hand tightly once more, he saluted and strode silently down the walk until he entered the funicular and vanished like a wraith.

Thus the Xenophon of the Carpathians passed into the penumbra of a tragic panorama which linked the Present with the Past. And I thought of Baoth and ancient Scythia, of Phoeneas and of crumbling Shinaar and of the wreck of Empire in the days of Priam as I stood out upon the lofty parapet where once paused Hannibal, and, like him, gazed down in reverie upon the ancient mart where Homer sat as he charted his deathless requiem to departed pomp and power. Thus faded the stalwart form of that modern Scyth as faded Magog when the world was young when he carried into tongueless silence the Empire of his Noetic fathers on his back!

And now, like another Justin, another Herodotus, a more eloquent Diodorus, comes Father Walsh [Father Edmund A. Walsh, S.J., Ph.D., of Georgetown University, whose book *Fall of the Russian Empire* was mentioned in the first paragraphs of the letter], with flaming pen and prophetic glance; and with magic strokes he causes the Future to rise up like an aura of disembodied grandeur and march forward with the steady tramp of purified and rejuvenated Power!

This flowery flight of multiloquence is larded with McGarry-isms. It shows how much McGarry's imagination could be stirred by very little. It betrays his deep inner vanity. Notice, by his account, that it is the two dethroned Romanovs who recognize *him* first and stop. It is Nicholas who speaks first. It is Nicholas who first extends his hand. As the former autocrat of the world's largest nation breaks silence on the heights overlooking the old port, he uses, to McGarry, the more intimate "tu" rather than the more formal "vous." Thereafter one must take heed of how quickly the two wives and all other living persons disappear from the scene in McGarry's mind. That comes after "they" stopped and looked at "me." All who remain are the two titans of history, Nicholas and McGarry, closing for the momentous encounter, like Grant and Lee at Appomattox.

There is another McGarry hallmark preserved in this forty-two-year-old epistle. The reason he seemed so elusive to so many of his contemporaries is undoubtedly because he was so busy brooding over the romantic past, off by himself somewhere. Here in his own words are a couple of samples. In writing overburdened with adjectives and ancient names (that was partly the style in those days, though a modern editor would annihilate three quarters of it) we find him gazing down like "Hannibal" on the "ancient mart" and charting the "departed pomp and power" as no one less than "Homer" had. Mr. McGarry never in his most charitable moments is found equating himself with mice, rats, slaves, servants, or assistants.

There is also a McGarry touch in the letter that is more cogent—a sense of history-in-the-making, for which he had a real flair. Elsewhere in the same letter he writes:

> I believe that every statesman will admit that IF it were KNOWN generally among the old RUSSIAN people that there were an HEIR to the Throne ALIVE, and capable of being brought to Moscow, the present regime would be overthrown by a popular uprising. And I happen to know, personally, from the lips of both John Reed and Trotsky, that this belief was fully shared by them.
>
> So it is not an unreasonable supposition to assume that Lenin, Kamenef, and Bukharin held similar beliefs. Indeed, it is certain they did; and knowing the Russian PEOPLE as they did, they conspired to remove, OFFICIALLY, this obstacle to the perpetuity of their

power. Hence the *'official'* execution which supplies the place of a *physical* execution in creating the lingering ILLUSION of the Royal Family's murder in *thirty-six* different ways!

Many would debate Mr. McGarry's contention that a resurrected Czarevich would create a popular uprising that could overthrow the Bolshevik regime, but in the context of the time of his letter (1928), and his specific reference to the "old RUSSIAN people," he may have been accurate in putting his finger on a real phobia of the Reds in the twenties. He closes out this subject, in his letter to Mr. Waldron, with a few more paragraphs:

> With the whole Family in their power, they could have been shot openly, could they not? Then why this elaborate preparation to kill them in so many different and opposite ways? Why this "proof" of such a *necessary* killing by introducing evidence that six CORSET STAYS became the mute accusers of murderers who gloried in the ferocity of their immortal deed? Anastasia and Maria never wore a corset in their lives. So this disposes of the "proof" *du linge de dessous*. And though it was necessary to convince the Russians that the whole Family WAS dead, the "proof" is that the executioners took pains to blot out the evidence of such proof. . . .
>
> This is proving too much!
>
> The evidence offered . . . would not be admitted before a coroner's jury, or in any civilian tribunal, as a basis for accusing a bandit of murder.

Here, as in so much of what Mr. McGarry wrote about the doings at Ekaterinburg, he seems to be leading from strength; to know more than he can tell; but to be annoyed with others for not seeing for themselves the simple verities to which he has led them by the nose.

But returning to that meeting at Marseilles, how about the "tall, soldierly man with gray, pointed beard"? Nicholas' height was between five seven and five eight. Alexandra was just a little more than an inch taller. To a man of McGarry's diminutive size the ex-Czar may have seemed "tall," but the word would hardly be applied to Nicholas by a trained reporter unless in comparison with someone else. On the other hand, Nicholas may have found a shoemaker in Marseilles who had learned how to boost him up a few inches. Furthermore, the Romanovs were "up" the incline, the McGarrys "down." The former could have loomed larger than they were.

How about the "tu"? Could Nicholas have known McGarry that well? And recognized him that quickly from a modest distance?

It is by no means impossible. From the trove of McGarry documents in Saint Petersburg, Florida, it is clear that he was in and out of Moscow and Saint Petersburg, Russia (There is, indeed, irony, in the name of the American city where McGarry's documents are now stored) before and during World War I. He could have met the Czar and Czarina many times. His social sponsorship in Imperial Russia was at the highest levels. Again, he could have been in contact with Nicholas in 1917 and 1918 at Tsarskoe Selo, Tobolsk, and Ekaterinburg.

It seems possible now that McGarry was the American coordinator and field supervisor for the Romanovs' escape, in which Germans, Britons, and Japanese probably were involved. It also now seems possible that he met Nicholas again in Vladivostok, Manila, or San Francisco, and possibly in all three cities, in the 1918–20 period. There is a suggestion that the dethroned monarch visited one or all of these cities under an assumed name and conferred with McGarry and George S. Romanovsky on the manuscript of *Rescuing*. That conference might have coincided with the big infusion of Russian gold, at the time, into California banks, as reported by Winston Churchill.

How about the over-all credibility of the Marseilles anecdote? Of Mr. McGarry himself? The resolution of those questions poses the same kind of problem faced by McGarry's two children, Ruth Elaine and Mark Rutledge, when they wondered about their fascinating but sometimes hard-to-believe father. He was away a great deal in their infancy and adolescence, but when he was home his stories kept them spellbound. They held conferences about those stories, and once they decided they must be about "half true." Later, as they grew up and became students at the University of California at Berkeley, met people from all over the world who had known their father in Russia, Germany, France, England, Turkey, etc., and heard independent testimony about his achievements, they decided to revise their estimate of his veracity higher and higher.

Interviewed by phone at her home in Corona del Mar, California, McGarry's daughter, Mrs. William C. Tesche, said:

My father was a natural spinner of yarns, and Mark and I were always charmed with him and his stories.

They were often about places we had never been to. We had no way of knowing how true they were. That's how we worked out the half-and-half formula.

I must say, the older we grew, the more he seemed to be right about everything. I think it annoyed Mark to be the son of such a genius and a man who spoke six or seven languages—not a linguist, you know—but a working knowledge of all those languages.

Well, father was traveling a lot, and Mark and I were away at school and college, and then I got married quite young, and Mark moved to New York, and that half-and-half business didn't come to a head in the family until just before the stock market crash in 1929.

A few months before the crash, my father passed the word around the family to sell out everything. Securities and everything were much too high, he said. There was going to be a day of reckoning, and it was coming fast.

Mark wasn't so sure. He thought he knew a thing or two about finance. He didn't believe father was that right about it. We talked it over, and Mark talked it over with his wife. Finally, with his wife more inclined to believe my father than Mark, they decided to follow the old formula—half-and-half. Mark agreed to sell half of everything he had. He did, too. He made out very well.

It can be presumed safely that Mark soon wished he had followed the paternal counsel one hundred per cent.

With a wife from Brooklyn and an interest in finance, Mark made his home in New York and settled down to a Wall Street career as a broker. He was busy in the thirties raising a family of three sons. He and his father frequently crossed the continent to visit each other. For a few years, the elder McGarry lived in Scarsdale, between many trips elsewhere, to see more of his son, daughter-in-law, and grandsons. Little by little, Mark got a better fill-in about the facts of his father's days in Europe and Asia, and his World War I experiences. But it was all very sketchy.

But New York served one purpose—in rendering William Rutledge McGarry's youth a little less hazy to his son. It's a crossroads city for travelers, and Mark kept meeting more and more older persons—many of them foreigners, who spoke of his father with awe—who seemed to know more about his father than he did.

It was not until his father's death, in 1942, that Mark realized the extent of the unfinished business ahead of him. It was measured by the boxes and cabinets of papers in the house at Redwood City and elsewhere. He found just enough on his first inspection of his father's wake of documents to realize it would take months, if not years, to make head or tail out of them, to marshal all the pertinent truths. One thing struck him immediately. It was the awareness that under the mantle of McGarry's charm there had been transpiring all the time transactions of great importance all over the world. Some had been solid successes. Some had been limp failures. Some had been enmeshed in rather bold adventures. Some were in the realm of confidences with men in various governments. Some were simple "excursions" of ideas with kindred spirits in private life and the universities. Like many a son before him, Mark McGarry came to realize that he had been guilty of failing to comprehend what a complex personality his parent had been.

The son's first move in the restitution process was aimed at The National Cyclopedia of American Biography. He and his sister, Ruth (Mrs. Tesche), collaborated in preparing the amplified sketch that appeared in the 1954 edition of the NCAB. It's the one that publicized for the first time William Rutledge McGarry's service to the State Department in England, France, Germany, and Russia. It's the one that first uncovered his affiliation with the intelligence branch.

The debut of that article was thirty-six years after Ekaterinburg, thirty-five years after the quiet printing of *Rescuing,* and twelve years after the death of William Rutledge McGarry.

Mark was determined to do much more with his father's papers. Several years ago, he retired from Wall Street and moved to Saint Petersburg. All the boxes and cabinets were shipped from California to the Florida city. Mark started to work on them in earnest. Then his health took a bad turn. He died in 1966.

Anyone who picks up where Mark leaves off is bound to discover what Mark himself did—that one of the unsung heroes behind William Rutledge McGarry was his father, James Adams McGarry.

James was a tall, husky, prosperous industrial engineer. He had operations all over the country directed from his Grand Rapids, Michigan, headquarters. He had four other sons, all six-footers plus, but he agreed with his wife, Catherine Rutledge McGarry, that there was something different about their smaller-sized progeny, Bill, that should be encouraged.

They paid for Bill's extensive travels. They were quite astonished and proud, according to the family folklore, about how quickly their investment in the youngster began to pay bizarre dividends. He had the faculty of arousing the interest of important people. He also had a keen nose for good business opportunities to be exploited either by his father's firm or by his father's friends.

Exactly how this worked out, however, on Bill's peregrinations through Europe and Asia, is still unclear to his descendants. Some day they hope to find the answer in one of those thirty cabinets and suitcases.

Another answer they will seek has to do with how he made all his money. Though his family undoubtedly gave him a good financial start, he seems to have made a lot more on his own efforts and invested it with all the prudence of those industrialists with whom he was on such good terms—indeed, with a better sense of timing than many of them.

The chances are that Mr. McGarry became a secret agent through a natural process of his own personality long before he knew what a secret agent was. He was curious about the inner workings of everything. His generous imagination naturally beguiled the attention of men who possessed crucial information and could be persuaded by McGarry to pass it on. He learned early in his life what many reporters take longer to discover. In order to get a good interview from an interesting man, you have to give *him* one.

Mr. McGarry's image as an adviser on "foreign trade" must have put a platinum lining around his other talents. In the big cities of Eurasia it would have made him a very welcome man; for, in the years before World War I, there were very few nations that were not putting time and energy into an effort to increase their exports into the world's richest market—McGarry's native land.

These virtues must have made McGarry's visits to Germany, France, Russia, England, and countries in the Near East lively and important. They probably figured in his decision to work with German officials on his novel, *From Berlin to Bagdad* (Portland, Oregon: International Publishers, 1914), a discreetly restrained glorification of the new German-sponsored railroad route to Old Testament countries, of which the Kaiser was very proud. McGarry had been outspoken against the machinations of British foreign policy. It's an open question whether this railroad book didn't represent the first phase of an attempt by the Wilhelmstrasse to recruit him as an agent.

The stars in McGarry's constellation—writing, business, finance, history, foreign trade, and culture—certainly played a role in Ambassador Herrick's interest in him. Mr. Herrick himself was exceptionally versatile. In addition to being a man of affairs who had risen to the highest elective office in Ohio, he was a writer, historian, and avid reader. He was also the founder of one of Cleveland's most successful savings institutions. The exciting and dangerous panorama of pre-World War I Europe would have provided these two with an endless source of conversation. The special-agent status that McGarry enjoyed in the intelligence branch of the State Department, under Mr. Herrick's tutelage in Paris, was given him by Mr. Herrick's successor, William G. Sharp. He took over at the end of 1914, shortly after the outbreak of World War I. Mr. Sharp was another Ohioan. He was another admirer of Mr. Herrick's.

It would be piquant as well as helpful if we knew all of McGarry's important intrigues at the moment he was dictating that letter to John Waldron on May 10, 1928. We can, at least, relate that moment in his life to some important events in it.

His friend Myron T. Herrick was on his second tour of duty as top man in the American legation in Paris. Ten days less than a year before, Charles A. Lindbergh had flown alone across the Atlantic to Le Bourget airfield and caused a tumultuous outpouring of Franco-American goodwill. Ambassador Herrick handled the laconic flier so well that France gained almost as much prestige from the event as the United States, and Herrick almost as much as Lindbergh.

The collapse of the stock market was brewing. We know from McGarry's family that its advent was preying on his mind. The Day of Judgment came the following year—1929.

Though Mr. McGarry escaped the stock market holocaust by

selling his holdings beforehand, the year was a black one on other counts. He saw a number of foreign-trade projects go down the drain. He lost one of his most influential friends: Myron Herrick died at his post in Paris. Few American diplomats have equaled Herrick's record of winning friends in a host nation. After his death, various French cities named streets after him and erected monuments to his memory. His passing probably cost McGarry his best pipeline to those Americans who help to fashion foreign policy.

VIII

The State Department's Hidden Romanov File

If William McGarry could have seen far into the future as he prepared that letter about Nicholas and Alexandra, in 1928, he could have taken satisfaction in something else. His preservation of the "state secret" of the Romanovs was to prove better than the State Department's. Beyond telling his two children that *Rescuing* was a true story, beyond informing them that the unidentified "Mr. Fox" was without any doubt whatever a "remarkable man," Mr. McGarry never gave out any more details about the case. Not even to John Waldron, to Boris Brasol, or to anyone else, it now appears, did he divulge any more factual information than that provided in the mysterious book published by the California Printing Company.

The State Department didn't do as well. Due to an error or two, apparently, several documents about the Romanov case have spilled out of classified files into the National Archives.

A departmental spokesman contends that State never had a Romanov file and, therefore, couldn't be hiding it.

The facts are in violent conflict with his statement. We found two sets of documents in the National Archives that bear heavily on the Romanov case. Both originated in the State Department. One clearly refers to the "Romanov File," and the other has a blurred inked inscription that could be the same thing. Both have been initialed by a number of officials in State. One bears the stamp and scrawl of an otherwise indecipherable "Chief Special Agent."

The first set of documents are stapled under a message from Rome, dated December 7, 1918, and addressed to the Secretary of State, Washington. It reads:

> For your confidential information, I learned that in highest quarters here it is believed that the Czar and his family are all alive. Paris informed. (signed) NELSON PAGE.

Attached to this telegram are a number of other messages querying other embassies about this report in the name of "The Division of Near Eastern Affairs." They are all splotched, pockmarked, and griddled with signatures. On the upper right-hand corner of the first sheet is a notice to the effect that the papers were declassified (and consequently sent to the National Archives) by authority of a letter of "1-8-58 FROM W. H. ANDERSON, STATE DEPARTMENT."

Thomas Nelson Page was United States Ambassador to Italy from June 21, 1913, until February 18, 1920. He had the reputation for being a resourceful gatherer of intelligence, and often his phrase "in highest quarters here" included not only the advices of the diplomatic corps accredited to Italy, but those of the wholly separate group assigned to the Vatican. When and if the two agreed on something, it was considered worthy of a high rating.

The second set is fatter than the first. It is built around a communication to the Secretary of State, dated August 25, 1927, from Sheldon Whitehouse, "Chargé d'Affaires ad interim" at the American Embassy in Paris. It is clearly slugged for reposition in the "Romanoff File." It, too, is bespotted with signatures of the executives who read it.

The message concerns the emergence in Poland of a young man whom several persons believed to be the Czarevich, Alexei N. Romanov. In many ways, the young man fits a description of what Colonel Michal Goleniewski might have looked like in 1927. Thus this 1927 report from Mr. Whitehouse could be, in effect, the first impact, though all unknowingly at the time, that the modern Goleniewski case had on those American officials who had no knowledge of the Romanovs' survival:

> Sir, I have the honor to enclose the text of an article by Henry de Korab, published in LE MATIN of August 24, 1927, discussing the case of a young Russian in Poland, calling himself Eugene Nicolaievitch Ivanoff, who is afflicted with hemophilia like Tsarevitch Alexis, and is believed by some persons to be the latter, escaped from the massacre at Ekaterinburg. . . ."

The De Korab article, in French, bears the two-column headline:

> LE TSAREVITCH ALEXIS DE RUSSIE EST-IL VIVANT?
> (IS CZAREVICH ALEXEI OF RUSSIA STILL LIVING?)

The French story is almost wholly adapted from one in the Polish newspaper *Express Poranny,* of Warsaw. It is accompanied by a full-figure picture of young "Eugene Ivanoff" (see photograph section following text page 146) in a military uniform, and it reads in part:

> It is a queer affair. . . . I (Henry de Korab) have heard on several occasions that the Grand Duke Alexis was a refugee in Pomerelia, at Bydgoszcz, or on the outskirts. But it is very difficult to have details. There is on this subject a little conspiracy of silence. The persons knowledgeable about the matter have, no doubt, interest in being silent, and only answer you by monosyllables.
>
> Today a Warsaw newspaper, the *Express Poranny,* gives the matter on the head of a pin, and the fuller particulars that it brings forth are of the kind likely to prick to the greatest degree the curiosity of the public.
>
> Eugene Nicolaievitch Ivanoff is exactly the same age as Alexis, he resembles him astonishingly, he suffers like him from hemophilia. How has he run aground in Pomerelia? He explains it himself thus:
>
> "I fled, accompanied by an old Cossack, through Siberia. There I

succeeded in penetrating into a camp of prisoners and German interns. I made myself pass for the compatriot of these people, which was easy for me, for I know the German language very well. I had been repatriated at Magdeburg, but in 1919 I proceeded to Poland, wanting to be nearer to Russia, for I was expecting events, changes in my country. . . ."

Curious phenomenon, since his arrival in Pomerelia, this little Russian, in appearance insignificant and anonymous, was taken under the protection of the Catholic clergy. During two years he was chambered by the abbot Bienarz, parish priest of Chelmno, who kept himself busy with him with an ardor that one would not know how to explain only by the Christian charity owed to an unfortunate refugee. Thus the young Eugene has been granted two tutors, one for French and the other for English. . . .

The abbot Bienarz is convinced that it is indeed the most authentic of the Czarevitches that he has, for several years, sheltered under his roof. . . .

"The child, although never having been to secondary school, spoke perfect English, German, and French, and if I gave him tutors, it was for the sake of completing his learning of literature.

"He was knowledgeable of the lesser details of the court of Russia. Timid and sick, he had nevertheless much difficulty in curbing violent attacks of authority [very typical of Michal Goleniewski], and I have seen him give peremptory orders to aged persons, only to apologize afterwards with tears in his eyes. One day he fled, encouraged by other protectors whom he had found in the Russian colony and who occupy themselves in concealing his existence. There is no doubt that many, among the Russians, believe him to be the genuine heir of the throne, for more than one time I have seen passers-by in the street bow deeply to him with a sort of mystical fervor."

M. de Korab turns from quoting the abbot to making a few final remarks of his own:

Presently, the alleged Grand Duke is in Bydgoszcz, guest of a Russian family of the name of Zuruk; he sews and embroiders, feminine craftsmanship that the authentic Czarevitch had picked up as a habit during his long illnesses. Although he never served in the military, on Sundays he used to dress in the uniform of an officer of the former Imperial Army, which explains the photo that we publish here.

The real Alexei, whether or not "Eugene Ivanoff" was he, was very fond of appearing in uniform by the side of his father as regiments of the Imperial Guard passed in review.

A more extensive search of the National Archives might uncover one or two more bundles of papers like this. But our own hunt managed to establish that there has been a "Romanov File" in the State Department; that it hasn't been declassified and isn't in the National Archives. For all this we are indebted either to an administrative error or to genuine innocence by some department officials. We believe that the "Romanov File" was sent to the CIA in 1960 or 1961, when the Goleniewski case first developed its Romanov colorations. We believe it is there now, with duplicates in the National Security Agency, along with a sizable folder of prints, handwriting specimens, skull measurements of the Romanovs, etc., forwarded by Britain's MI-6. The dental charts, once in Paris, may be there also.

It was at this turn of the road that I regretted more keenly than ever the recent death of Mr. Allen Dulles. As an American agent in Switzerland, during two world wars, Mr. Dulles had been able to obscure his own trail and demolish the very rumor of his existence with all the skill shown by William Rutledge McGarry. Mr. Dulles was director of the CIA at the time Colonel Goleniewski defected.

I had known Mr. Dulles for years, though only professionally, in my role as a newspaperman. In 1964 I asked Mr. Dulles about Goleniewski's various claims, and he told me in a telephone conversation, "I don't want to talk about it at all."

At different times in 1964 and 1965, to Herman Kimsey, and to the late Philippa Schuyler, a newspaper correspondent who had interviewed Goleniewski, Mr. Dulles gave the same rejoinder to the same questions:

"It may all be true and it may not. I just don't want to talk about it."

Goleniewski has this to say about his confrontation with Mr. Dulles about eight months after Goleniewski's arrival in the United States:

On September 30, 1961, I visited with Mr. Ronan and Mr. Slov (both CIA operatives) at the offices of Mr. Allen Dulles, then CIA director. The meeting took place in the old headquarters of the CIA.

Mr. Dulles took quite a little time in the early part of the conversation discussing his pipe collection and how he expected to have trouble, when he moved into his new office in Langley, finding a place to hang all of them.

At this time my status in the United States was illegal. After I deposited my Polish documents with the CIA, I received for the first time my immigration card. This was two months after my conference with Mr. Dulles.

Mr. Dulles was well informed, prior to my arrival in the United States, about my real identity. He knew also of the tests of my identity made in 1961 by the CIA. Likewise he was aware of my voluntary support of the United States for several years. Consequently I was expecting that Mr. Dulles would have many reasons to speak with me in an open and fair way. But his visit and conversation, which lasted about an hour, in the presence of Mr. Ronan and the Deputy of the CCI of the CIA, Mr. James Hunt, was very nice and very empty of results.

It was clear that Mr. Dulles was interested neither in disclosing that he knew my real identity nor in the support of my claims. He was more interested in preventing the proofs. For that reason also the CIA prevented me from visiting FBI Director Mr. J. Edgar Hoover. About my real identity, Mr. Dulles, as the chief of American intelligence, made only one digression. Before I left his office he said:

"You would look exactly like your father, if you had a beard and moustache."

Mr. Dulles had instructions from higher authority about the recognition of Goleniewski's claims, even if the CIA had run them out. But he was always honest with newspapermen. If he knew they had wrapped up most of a story they were working on and he couldn't affect the issue much one way or another, he was always helpful, either on or off the record. If I had brought in what we had gathered by July 1969, if I had spread the story before him of William Rutledge McGarry, whom he must have known very well, Mr. Dulles might have added a morsel or two.

It would have altered our inventory of gains and losses. We had learned a great deal. We had come face to face with the inimitable Mr. McGarry. But it was also true that we had found nothing in the National Archives or in McGarry's personal papers that added any new light to the strategic plan and scheme of maneuver given in *Rescuing*'s account of the flight from Ekaterinburg.

IX

Reappraising "Rescuing the Czar"

The time had come to reappraise *Rescuing the Czar* in conjunction with all we had found out about McGarry and other Allied agents in the Moscow-Ekaterinburg-Turkestan area, in the summer of 1918.

We noted that nowhere does McGarry claim to be "Fox." In fact he takes pains to indicate that "Fox" was another person. The "C.J.F." in the loop under Wilhelm's signature on one of the "My Dear Fox" letters points in that direction, too. Those three capitals are not similar to McGarry's handscript. Also, McGarry frequently alludes to Nicholas in various letters as "rescued by Fox."

That doesn't carry the implication of being "rescued by McGarry." There is no such thought in any of McGarry's Saint Petersburg notes, letters, and memoranda. It is not beyond McGarry to make his apparent disengagement from "Fox" part of the general obfuscation. But there is too much weighted against the idea.

There was a very real Charles James Fox whom the laws of probability favor as the Fox of *Rescuing*. He was at Tientsin, a few days' journey from Siberia. He was known in U.S. intelligence circles. He was a linguist. He had been a major in the National

Guard in the District of Columbia. He was also an inveterate hiker and much more of an athlete and outdoorsman than McGarry was. In fact, the chief objection to him is that he's *too* logical. It is uncertain also whether he knew enough Russian in 1918 to be able to do what "Fox" did in the last days at Ekaterinburg. So there is still the chance that we haven't brought the right Fox to bay. There were other Charles James Foxes in the United States at the time. One, long since dead, came from Pasadena. We never managed to pick up the trail of his descendants, if there are any. It is also worth considering the theory advanced by the son of Charles James Fox, James Marston Fox of Alexandria, Louisiana— that "Fox" was a code name for all the Americans assigned to the operation; that the name was used among them interchangeably.

At any rate, an electric sense of momentousness came over me during my rereading of "Fox's Diary" after I had found out about McGarry, Aughinbaugh, Ackerman, Lasies, "Ivanoff," De Shishmarev, Romanovsky, and the rest.

Important excerpts from the "Fox diary" appear in Chapter XVIII. They give the reader a chance to reach his own conclusions. My reactions were skepticism here, incredulity there, sometimes pique over the unabashed stripteasery used toward persons, places, and dates. Often in Fox's chronicle, with its schoolgirlish use of capitals to emphasize words, the reader is made to feel he is being gulled by a writer who is trying to pawn himself off as a combination of Dink Stover and Lawrence of Arabia. The two hardest lumps to swallow are the tunnel commentaries Fox attributes to Nicholas and the grand itinerary of the Romanovs' journey to Chungking. It seems hard to believe that Nicholas would choose moments in cramped surroundings, in darkness lit only by a flashlight, with the outlook still foreboding, to expatiate at such length on Rasputin and other figures from the past; or that Fox would be in the mood to put it all down in such detail. (Several other of "my prisoner's" speeches have been deleted from my excerpt.)

Likewise the chosen escape route seems improbably circuitous. Why go all the way to Chungking, and thence down the Yangtze to Woosung, when ports like Karachi and Bombay were hundreds of miles nearer? The crow-line distance from Ekaterinburg to Chungking is 2700 miles. According to Fox's account, that means the fugitives were going another 1400 miles down the river. Assuming they were on trucks, wagons, or horseback much of the way, that's quite a jaunt for a family of seven—particularly when the family includes an ailing Alexandra and a hemophilic Alexei.

There were nominal reasons for avoiding India. In 1918 resentment sprang up in some Indian cities against the incursions of Russian *émigrés*. But the Romanovs, *Rescuing* tells us, were disguised as Buddhist pilgrims for a part of their mileage in Asia. Why couldn't they stay in that disguise, or switch to Moslem dress and head for Karachi or Bombay?

There may have been other good reasons for their routing, and they will be mentioned. But Fox doesn't bother to explain them. Neither does the arranger and editor of the book, McGarry.

These objections amount to a criticism of the manner in which the story is presented. The coy embellishments and cloudy touches might suggest that the fine hand of some Romanov was applied to the manuscript after its first draft.

But the substance of the story related in the book is another matter. Clearly a great deal of thought went into what was to be omitted as well as what was to be included. As to the geographical path of the Imperial Family's flight, it doesn't vary greatly from the account given to me five years ago by Colonel Goleniewski. He didn't mention Tibet or Kashmir. I should think any young man who traversed that dramatic terrain would refer to it. There were a number of other matters about the trip, however, on which he didn't seem to want to dwell.

But the Romanovs' long swing east makes sense if Nicholas' ultimate destination was Vladivostok. It is more than possible that the family split up somewhere along the line to enable him to appear incognito in eastern Siberia preliminary to leaving for San Francisco. Reports of his being on the U. S. West Coast in the 1919–20 period would tie in with this nicely. He could have participated in preparing *Rescuing* for publication.

The trek from Ekaterinburg to safety would have been governed also by the military situation in the summer of 1918 and the dispersal of Allied agents to the south and east. Spread all over Russia were heavily subsidized sub-operatives of three British secret agents whose feats have become legendary: R. H. Bruce Lockhart, William Lequeux, and Captain Sidney George Reilly, alias M. Massino, alias Comrade Relinsky of the Cheka, alias Monsieur Constantine, quick-change artist and master of seven languages. He laid the groundwork for his personal intelligence service as a pre-war naval armaments representative of the Mandrochovitch and Count Tchubersky combine at Saint Petersburg. Before August 1914, he had enjoyed as many German contacts as Russian through his connection with the Hamburg shipyards of Bluhm and Voss. He had obligingly passed along to the British Admiralty valuable information about the Kaiser's submarine-construction program, and it was the Admiralty, having discovered his wily and extraordinary resources that eventually started him on his ascent to the post of director of British Secret Intelligence operations in Russia.

Reilly was a native of Czarist Russia. His father was an Irish sea captain, his mother a Russian. Having been reared in the Black Sea port of Odessa, his contacts in hostile Turkey were as good as they were anywhere else.

His courage and poker-faced gall enabled him to pull off one of the great coups of the war. In 1916 he entered Germany from Switzerland. He penetrated the German Admiralty by posing as a German naval officer. He was able to get a copy of the official

German Naval Intelligence Code and with it in tow to find his way back to London. This feat alone may have shaved months off the duration of hostilities.

Though Reilly was seeing plenty of action around Moscow at the time, it would be unlikely if he weren't a part of the alleged Ekaterinburg rescue operation.

South of Ekaterinburg, all in Russian Turkestan, was another trio of highly talented Britons. Lieutenant Colonel Percy T. Etherton had replaced British Consul General Sir George Macartney in Kashgar, Chinese Turkestan. As a military man, he moved with ease in and out of the adjacent Russian territory—the territory of an ally—so both Turkestans, for secret operations, were in his baili-wick.

Another agent in the area was a pioneer pilot, Major Latham Valentine Stewart Baker. In later years he was to be the first aviator to fly over Mount Everest. In 1922, four years after the name of Ekaterinburg was emblazoned in the history books, he wrote very cryptically:

"The time is not yet ripe for a full and complete description of the events of June, July, August, and September 1918 in Turkestan."

A third agent operating out of Tashkent, Russian Turkestan, was Lieutenant Colonel Frederick M. Bailey, explorer, naturalist, and master of disguise. In this ancient city, which dates back to the seventh century A.D., and which is frequently shaken by earthquakes, Colonel Bailey had to deal with a man who from the very onset of this investigation was a dark-horse candidate for the role of Fox in *Rescuing*. He is Roger C. Tredwell, a Yale graduate, and up to then the only American consul ever assigned to Tashkent. It was Tred-well's wife who brought a mild tremor to our researchers. Her maiden name was "Van Schaick Reed."

Recall the words of Fox, in his conversation with the Grand Duchess Maria: "When I informed her that my ancestors fought beside Kosciusko and Pulaski and that their names might be found on the muster rolls of the First Line Regiment of New York Colony and State, along with the names of Goose Van Schaick and Jeremiah Van Rensselaer, she burst her sides with laughter."

All the agents I mentioned are dead. The last to go was Roger Tredwell, Yale '07, who died in Ridgefield, Connecticut, July 12, 1961. According to the alumni records at New Haven, he outlived his wife.

Another who crossed Bailey's trail in Tashkent in 1918 was the confidant of Rasputin, Dr. Badmaev, the Buryat Mongol physician from Saint Petersburg. His presence in Tashkent at the time might arouse speculation that his mission was associated with one of the intrigues of Rasputin's son-in-law, Boris Soloviev, that were designed to free the Romanovs.

The Nipponese agents mentioned by Mr. de Shishmarev would have helped the most in the later stages of the push toward the Orient. From Tibet to the East China Sea, the farther they progressed, the more the Romanovs would have been treading ground where Japanese secret operatives had been playing the divisive game that the Mikado's ministers had found so effective in making sure that no one Chinese regional chieftain became strong enough, or angry enough, to block the island empire's long-range plans in Asia.

Another interesting personage on the general azimuth of the trip described in the book was General Dutov, a picturesque Cossack leader, and one of those reported by Mr. Carl Ackerman as a principal in the plans to liberate the Imperial Family.

General Dutov was Ataman (leader) of the Orenberg Cossacks. The Orenberg region adjoins Turkestan. Other than the forces of the Czechs and the Whites, General Dutov's Cossacks were the nearest military effectives to Ekaterinburg in July 1918, and it is quite reasonable to suppose that they could have escorted and protected the Romanovs.

Dutov's troops were defeated by the Reds in 1920. He managed

to escape to Chinese Turkestan with two thousand survivors, but in 1922, in Sinkiang, he was murdered by Bolshevik agents, who were able to make a getaway to Soviet territory.

Whatever moments William Rutledge McGarry shared with Nicholas in 1918, it is likely that the two parted company somewhere between Ekaterinburg and the China coast. But their separation may not have lasted longer than about a year. It now looks as if in autumn 1919 the two had a San Francisco reunion right under the noses of unsuspecting Americans.

Jon Speller was the first to spot this possibility when he was studying the files of the San Francisco *Examiner* and came across the report in the October 16, 1919, issue that "Captain N. T. Romanoff of the Kolchak forces in Eastern Siberia" was visiting Dean David P. Barrows.

The second article that drew Mr. Speller's attention was in the *Examiner* of July 26, 1920. It described how "Nicholas Romanoff, natural son of Grand Duke Nicholas Nicholaevitch, uncle of the late Czar and former commander in chief of the Russian armies, who won fame as an assistant to General Semonov and upon whose head a price was set because he opposed the policy of Japan in Siberia, may yet prove the savior of Japan in Siberia."

This article bore no wire-service imprimatur. It was offered as a local interpretation story. It said "young Romanoff" had fled to Manila. It quoted a background story in the Manila *Daily Bulletin* of June 12. It was accompanied by a picture of "Nicholas Romanoff," and Mr. Speller, after studying the picture, decided it resembled Nicholas II—brow, nose, bone structure, and ears, but minus beard.

Printed nine months apart, these two *Examiner* stories on "Nicholas Romanoff" are oddly in conflict. The first called him "no kin of" Nicholas II. The second had him a "natural son" of Nicholas' uncle. That's getting a lot closer to Nicholas.

The first billed him as a "captain" in the lead of the story and a "colonel" in the bank of the headline. The second gave him no military rank at all but called him "Romanoff" and "young

Romanoff." Yet, youthful as this second account made him seem, the accompanying picture was not of a very young man but of a person who could have been the fifty-two-year-old Nicholas.

The Cossack Ataman, General Grigori Semonov, received praise, direct and inferential, in both articles. Semonov was later to be called a "Jap puppet." At the time, however, in Siberia, he was not getting along well with the Japanese commander there.

There was a strong Royalist thrust to both stories. The second had a particularly fierce propagandist slant, and one sentence jarred Mr. Speller's credulity: ". . . he (Romanoff) has formulated plans to overthrow the Bolsheviki and restore the peace and order of the days of the Czar . . . [which] Russians now so ardently desire."

Was there really any such person as the "natural son" of the Grand Duke Nicholas Nicholaevitch? That was among the first questions Mr. Speller passed on to the Romanov experts in New York after he found the *Examiner* stories.

The Romanov scholars got busy. In a few days they sent back word to Mr. Speller that neither they nor any of the Russians consulted in New York had ever heard of this "natural son" of the Grand Duke before or since. Their consensus was that he was an invention.

Herman Kimsey checked the files of the Manila *Daily Bulletin* in the Library of Congress. Not in the June 12 issue, nor in any June issue or May issue, was there any story such as the one to which the *Examiner* alluded.

This gave the *Examiner*'s 1920 article a strong scent of contrivance. It looked like a plant inserted by someone who packed weight in the newspaper's editorial offices—someone like David Prescott Barrows.

It seemed to us that the motive for brandishing the Royalist banner was inspired by a desire to concoct a new cover for Nicholas and, for his personal safety, to put him in Manila, where he wasn't, rather than San Francisco, where he was.

Some papers found in Mr. McGarry's cabinets in Saint Petersburg may bear out this theory. There are copies and originals of letters between Mr. McGarry and George S. Romanovsky, the Russian Consul General in San Francisco. They deal with their plans to publish *Rescuing the Czar*. There is a copy of a contract drawn up between them on the subject of the book. There is even a document showing that the book had an alternate title, *Prisoners of Tobolsk*, and a line of subtitle: *Royalty Must Die in Order to Live*.

From the McGarry/Romanovsky exchanges, it is clear that they believed the manuscript had been made sufficiently vague and patchy so that a strong publicity and selling effort would not jeopardize "security." They planned a big merchandising program. A sale to the movies was made a part of the pact that, apparently, Romanovsky had drawn up and witnessed. All these roseate plans went awry.

There was no advertising, publicity, or marketing. Copies simply were "dropped off" at libraries and universities throughout the nation and in the British Museum as long as six years after publication date in 1920.

What went wrong? Did someone disagree with Messrs. McGarry and Romanovsky about the risk of their plans to "security"? Was that "someone" Nicholas himself? Was he, perhaps, not only the man who financed the book, not only the man who helped to write it, but also the "Man in the Other Room" whom Henry Haskin could never get a good look at but to whom George Romanovsky always deferred when a question came up between him and Haskin in those conferences in Romanovsky's office about typography, spacing, chapter headings, etc.? An affirmative answer to each of these questions would not be unreasonable.

The unfolding of later years added a small footnote to those *Examiner* stories that glorified General Semonov. The Cossack leader became friendly with ex-Chinese Emperor Hsüan T'ung, better known as Henry Pu-yi. In 1925 Semonov requested the aid of Chinese monarchists to help restore "the Russian Imperial

Family." Henry Pu-yi gave Semonov fifty thousand dollars. It is doubtful if he would have parted with the money unless he believed the Imperial Family was alive.

At the time he handed over the fifty thousand dollars, Henry Pu-yi was living in Tientsin, not far from the residence of Charles James Fox. The information about the gift to Semonov comes from Pu-yi's autobiography, published in Peking before his death in 1966.

General Semonov became very active in Manchuria. That rich and important territory had developed into a Japanese protectorate by 1932, under the name of Manchukuo. There Henry Pu-yi became chief of state under his old royalist name, Hsüan T'ung. In 1934 he became Emperor, and chose K'ang Tê as his reigning monicker. The Russians captured him in 1945. They extradited him to the Chinese Communists. He was maintained in considerable style and veneration for the rest of his life under the personal patronage of Mao Tse-tung.

General Semonov wasn't so lucky. The Russians seized him in Manchuria in 1945. He was taken back to the Soviet Union. In 1946 he was hanged.

Jon Speller found a footnote to this footnote. While trying to decode the meaning of those *Examiner* articles, he obtained permission from David Prescott Barrows' descendants to take a second look at Barrows' personal papers in the Bancroft Library of the University of California, in Berkeley. Charles Rapp got the assignment, and he came to a passport issued to "Nicholas Romanoff" by General Semonov. The passport had been used frequently. It bore stamps and signatures. How it found its way into those papers in the Bancroft Library is a mystery not unlike the one of how *Rescuing* found its way into all those other institutions.[1]

[1] A photograph of the "Nicholas Romanoff" passport appears in the photographic section following text page 146.

X

M. Lasies and the Buried Treasure
of Dr. Aughinbaugh's Foreword

As we knew by now, there had been an enormous amount of
human traffic and military movement in Siberia in 1918. Refugees
flocked through the cities. There were newspapermen from many
countries. This thought struck us:

Was the New York *Times*'s Carl W. Ackerman the only
journalist at Ekaterinburg to decide that official accounts of
the Romanovs' assassination were a cover story? Had no other
reporter gotten the same impression?

Indeed another had. He was French, and with a three-sided
personality. He was a cavalry major in the French Army Reserve.
He was a correspondent for *Le Matin* in Paris. He was a former
member of the French Chamber of Deputies. His name was Joseph
Lasies. Our route to him led directly from a few short sentences
in Dr. Aughinbaugh's foreword to *Rescuing the Czar*.

Few have lived so many lives in so many places as Dr.
William Edmund Aughinbaugh. He was a doctor, lawyer, educator,
writer, and explorer. A map of his peregrinations would require
most of the globe. His urge to visit out-of-the-way spots often
harmonized with his instinct to lend a hand to those whose luck
had run out in some kind of epidemic or catastrophe, and, at various times, he went to work for the lepers in Cuba and Puerto Rico,

for bubonic plague victims in India, for disease-ridden pariahs in the slums of Egyptian cities. In the later years of his life he became a writer and foreign-trade expert on the faculty of New York University. He also wrote a column, "The Doctor Tells the Story," for a newspaper syndicate.

Though he died, at the age of sixty-nine, in New York twenty-nine years ago, he is still remembered as one of the most distinguished members of three clubs devoted to outdoor adventure—the Explorers, Adventurers, and Circumnavigators.

Those who remember him most keenly seem to be men whose careers have been equally kaleidoscopic. Such a person is Dr. Carl von Hoffman, the anthropologist, explorer, and photographer. He was born in Czarist Russia, of German ancestry, in 1890. The excitement in Dr. von Hoffman's life began at an even younger age than it did for Aughinbaugh. As a mere cadet-mascot serving in Siberia, in the 17th Siberian Sharpshooters, which was commanded by his uncle, von Hoffman was wounded by Japanese shrapnel during the Russo-Japanese War. Then he came to the United States—the country that brought him and Aughinbaugh together.

At the age of seventy-nine, he is still chairman of two committees of the Explorers Club, of which he is a past director. Dr. von Hoffman has this to say about the friend he has outlived by almost a generation and a half:

"Aughinbaugh was not a warm, talkative character like some adventuresome types. He was a short, plump man. His manner was quite formal and detached until a subject came up in the conversation that caught his interest. Then he liked to dig right to the heart of it.

"He especially disliked frauds and frills. I'd say he had a particular interest in finding out the truth about things—all kinds of things—irrespective of whose toes were stepped on. He was also quite fussy about little things."

Dr. Aughinbaugh's memoirs, *I Swear by Apollo,* are populated with ornery, colorful people he met all the way from Mexico's mining country to India. The author pays frequent tribute to men and women whose convictions impelled them to run counter to conventionality.

He died on December 18, 1940. The New York *Times* gave him a column-long obituary topped by a photograph. He left no immediate survivors. However, we now know from McGarry's files in Saint Petersburg that he and Dr. Aughinbaugh were good friends. They corresponded frequently and it was at McGarry's urging that Aughinbaugh wrote the foreword to *Rescuing the Czar.* From their letters on the subject, the matter of the foreword was apparently settled in a series of conferences, so the letters refer largely to what was decided on in conference. It is not hard to surmise, however, that Aughinbaugh believed thoroughly in the principal theme of *Rescuing.*

In his foreword, Aughinbaugh praises *Rescuing* for the "preservation, discovery, and piecing together of the various scraps of first-hand information." He adds that if *Rescuing the Czar* does no more than set at rest the *fable* (the emphasis is his) of the "'Romanoff Execution,' it will have done its work by characterizing the source and methods and objects of its inspirations."

In his third paragraph, Dr. Aughinbaugh brushes past one of the richest sources of data on the anti-assassination side of the controversy, "M. Lasies." Under that name lies the buried treasure of Dr. Aughinbaugh's contribution.

FOREWORD
by
W. E. AUGHINBAUGH, M.D., LL.B., LL.M.

Is the former Czar and his Imperial family still alive? There are millions of people in Europe and America who are asking this question.

European governments have considered the question of sufficient interest to justify the investigation by official bodies of the alleged extinction of this ancient Royal Line. Millions have been expended for that purpose. Commissions have pretended to investigate the subject *after* the event. Volumes have been returned of a speculative nature to authenticate a mysterious *disappearance* that has never been explained.

April 5; the Universal Service carried a cable from Paris reading: "Czar Nicholas and all members of the Imperial family of Russia are still alive, according to M. Lasies, former member of the Chamber of Deputies, who has just returned from a mission to Russia." This was several weeks after the manuscript of the following account of the Czar's escape was in my possession (February 20, 1920). Yet this confirmation of the manuscript has not sufficiently overcome the universally persistent doubt that has grown out of many previous imposing reports.

There is however no further reference to Lasies in *Rescuing*'s 269 pages. The Frenchman arrives and departs in the same paragraph like a porpoise jumping through the surface of history only to plunge once more out of sight.

Dr. Aughinbaugh would never have let Lasies disappear if he had known as much about him as we do now. This stubborn, inquiring soldier-politician from the French provinces is an important figure in the assassination controversy.

Joseph Lasies was a wit, politician, newspaperman, cavalry officer, and gifted public speaker. He was drawn into the Romanov controversy quite by accident. He made a long study of it at Ipatiev House and elsewhere, and then he ran into another journalist, an Englishman, who had done the same. The force of their impact was felt strongly among Lasies's French readers.

The place was the platform of the Ekaterinburg railroad station. The date was May 18, 1919. The Englishman in question was Robert Wilton, correspondent of the London *Times*. His stories from Ekaterinburg were to gain a large audience in English-language newspapers. The dispatches of Marie Louis Joseph Lasies, correspondent of *Le Matin,* garnered a similarly large French readership.

For the French version of the meeting we have a supplementary report from another Frenchman, a friend of Lasies's, Commander Bolifraud, a member of the French Military Mission at Ekaterinburg. Lasies asked Bolifraud to write his account of the platform dialogue with Wilton, and the resultant letter from Bolifraud became the preface to Lasies's book *La Tragédie Sibérienne* (Paris: L'Edition Francaise Illustrée, 1920). It is not surprising that the Bolifraud treatment agrees with Lasies's, as given in the book's text. Essentially the following is Lasies's interpretation of what happened at Ekaterinburg:

Lasies and Bolifraud were talking on the station platform. Wilton joined them. The Romanov mystery soon became the subject of their conversation. Lasies expressed his many mental reservations about the claimed effects of the "inferno" that supposedly caused so many cadavers (those of the Romanovs and their aides) to vanish into thin air.

At this point Wilton remarked, "I shall have a clear mind about it. Wait for me a few minutes and I shall return."

He walked off and didn't come back for about half an hour. Returning, he was barely within earshot when he called out: "I have the explanation!"

When he rejoined the other two on the platform, he said:

"Here is what happened. The victims were burned with eleven carboys of sulphuric acid."

There followed, according to the Frenchmen, a discussion of the acid and its chemical properties, with Lasies questioning Wilton about the amount, the supplier, the containers, etc.

Then, after a moment of reflection, Lasies remarked:

"My dear Wilton, only English sulphuric acid *diplomatically* prepared can also produce magic effects. (The emphasis is Lasies's.)

"Moreover," Lasies continued, "your magistrate-instructor [at Ipatiev House] had discussed with us the matter for more than two hours and he did not speak to us, at any time, of sulphuric acid!"

Then Wilton lost patience. Addressing Lasies in a tone that both Frenchmen stated they long remembered, he said:

"Commander Lasies, even if the Czar and the Imperial Family are living, it is necessary to say that they are dead!"

At the conclusion of this exchange of thoughts at Ekaterinburg, Mr. Wilton's parting words were: "I am going to do articles in the *Times* to affirm the death of the Czar and of his family."

"Go to it, Wilton," said Lasies. "I shall do some articles in *Le Matin* to say that you know nothing about it, nor do I."

Both men lived up to their promises. Each wrote articles and a book to back up his contention. (Wilton's book was published in the United States as a collaborative effort, *The Last Days of the Romanovs,* by George Gustave Telberg and Robert Wilton (New York: George H. Doran & Co., 1920).

Almost a year later Lasies found himself unable to resist the temptation to expand the scope of his witticism about British diplomatic acid. The occasion was an April 22, 1920, Havas dispatch from New York that quoted reports that the Imperial Family was safe in England. Lasies concluded that British Government censors no longer had any objections to a Romanov resurrection. He was now convinced that the Whitehall brand of sulphuric was even more miraculous than he had given it credit for. It not only burns like any other acid, and causes bodies to vanish into thin air, but it can restore them "on command."

Mr. Wilton's articles and book were instrumental in the English-speaking world's readiness to believe in the Romanov assassination. But his remarks on the station platform at Ekaterinburg have been used over the years by the anti-assassinationists to reinforce their theory that British Foreign Office policy embraced the massacre version as a cover story to be followed devoutly regardless of the facts. Mr. Wilton's remarks are not the only grounds for this supposition. Others will be noted in this inquiry. It is far more than a coincidence that not so much as a line was printed in the British press about the Michal Goleniewski case at a time, in the winter and spring of 1964, that newspapers all over the world were running the story.

The views Lasies conveyed to Wilton were not frivolous after-thoughts to a bit of light conversation. He had done a lot of legwork on the case. He had reached his conclusions slowly and carefully.

Marie Louis Joseph Lasies, who used "Joseph Lasies" for his byline, was born at Houga, Gers, in 1862. He died at Bordeaux in 1927. He had thrice been elected to the Chamber of Deputies from Gers, town of Condom, and served from 1898 to 1911. That year he lost his race for re-election, but in 1914—the year of Sarajevo and the Marne—he won his campaign to become a deputy from Paris. He was fifty-two at the outbreak of World War I. In the Chamber he had established a reputation for caustic and sometimes comical interruptions of speakers whose views he scorned. He had also maintained his status as a cavalry officer in the French Army Reserve. He was on the editorial staff of the Paris daily, *Le Matin*.

As the result of France's heavy casualties on the Western Front, Lasies was called to active duty in the Army. In the spring of 1919, with the war in Europe over, he was assigned to Ekaterinburg, where the French already had a military mission, as commander of a cavalry squadron.

Lasies made his first visit to Ipatiev House on May 11, 1919. The magistrate-instructor gave him what was then the orthodox briefing on the last hours of the Romanovs, including the massacre in the basement, the burning of the bodies near the mine pit, etc., and though he had an open mind on the subject, his first reactions were: "I remained skeptical about the facts such as they were re-lated to me."

Revision of his skepticism toward outright disbelief began in conversations with Bolifraud, who had arrived in Ekaterinburg four months before Lasies. Bolifraud's disbelief had sprung, in turn, from conversations with a Russian general who had arrived long before Bolifraud—a general who had come to Ekaterinburg with the Reds and converted to the Whites when the Reds left.

In his published letter, Bolifraud covered all this.

I was especially shaken following a conversation with General Bogoskovski of the headquarters. General Bogoskovski had been in the service of the Bolsheviks since the *coup d'état* of November 1917, and held an important post in the war school of Petrograd. He had been transferred to Ekaterinburg by order of the Bolsheviks at the time of the German advance in March 1918.

General Bogoskovski thus was there at Ekaterinburg, carrying on official functions, when the (Romanov) drama was fulfilled. Upon the recapture of the city he took up service with the Czechs and became afterwards chief of headquarters of the Army of Siberia, which was commanded by General Gaida.

I saw General Bogoskovski daily, and each time that I tried to open a conversation on the fate of the Imperial Family he obstinately resisted all attempts at confidence. But one day, returning with him from the front, in the course of a lunch we took together in the train between Glosov and Perm, my having insisted again, General Bogoskovski, after a few moments of hesitation, almost whispered to me:

"I am convinced that His Majesty the Czar Nicholas is alive, as well as his whole family."

Since then, my doubts have only increased about the drama of Ekaterinburg, for General Bogoskovski, in his official position with the Bolsheviks, was probably aware of many of their secrets.

Lasies endorsed his friend's skepticism, but it was from two other Russian officers, first a lieutenant, and then a colonel, that Lasies gained persuasive intelligence that all the Romanovs had escaped and were alive and well just a few weeks prior to Lasies's arrival in Siberia.

On May 12, 1919, the day after his first visit to Ipatiev House, Lasies made a trip to General Pepelaev's headquarters at Berechagino. He talked with a lieutenant whom he refuses to name for security reasons; he calls him "Lieutenant X." The Lieutenant spoke French well and remarked:

"You doubt the reported fate of the Imperial Family? Perhaps you are right, for I, in particular, have serious reasons to believe in their survival."

The Lieutenant read to Lasies two letters from a member of his family who, he said, was an important functionary in the imperial regime. One of the passages he translated and dictated as Lasies made his notes,

"Letter of April 1919: 'The Emperor is here! How to understand it? I think that you will understand it as we have understood it ourselves. If that is confirmed, the festival of Christ [Easter] will be for us all bright and infinitely joyful.'"

"Lieutenant X" showed Lasies another letter from the same source, written a few days after the first. It read: "These last days we have received confirmation on the subject of the health of those whom we love. May God be praised!"

The lieutenant referred Lasies to a colonel in Perm who had gotten the same kind of information by mail. Passing through Perm, Lasies looked up this senior officer and was told by him that he had, indeed, received similar advices from those who ought to know.

Lasies appeals to the reader's intelligence to understand why he is concealing the identity of two officers and why he has not included in his book a copy of the photograph of "Lieutenant X" that that officer presented to him as a memento of their meeting.

Armed with a supply of tough questions to fire at the magistrate-instructor stationed at Ipatiev House, Lasies asked General Janin for permission to make a second visit. Janin passed on the request to General Gaida, who approved.

Lasies arrived for his second inspection of the mansion on May 15, 1919. This time not only was the magistrate-instructor present but several other persons, including the residence's wealthy merchant owner, N. N. Ipatiev, and his wife. Point by point, Lasies reports, he went over the official story of the Imperial Family's last day on the premises and listened to the magistrate-instructor, who "no longer believed with either his eyes or his ears."

Then he wrote an entry in his diary.

"Imperial Family has not been assassinated here, not as it has been told to us. At the very most, the Czar alone has been executed."

By the time Lasies's book was published, he had made it very clear that he had information that *none* of the Romanovs had been killed.

From the very moment of the Romanovs' disappearance, a contest for the world's belief was launched by the disciples of two schools of thought. One was embodied by the stories of Lasies and the Russian officers, to which Lasies and Bolifraud referred. It contended that there had been no mass murder of the Romanovs. The other was embodied by the dispatches of Robert Wilton and the later "findings" of Judge Nicholas A. Sokolov's investigation. Some of these "findings" were previewed in Wilton's stories. (See Chapter XV "Tie Score at Ekaterinburg.") Disciples of this school maintained that all members of Nicholas' family were killed.

That is the way the struggle for believers has ranged down the years.

Scorners of the assassination story believe that official British policy, as expounded by Wilton, complemented Nicholas' own "death" wishes, and made this version of the imperial fate capture the mind of the public. This would account for Sir Thomas Preston's "firming up" to orthodoxy after Carl W. Ackerman of the New

York *Times* found Preston as uncertain as everyone else about what had happened.

Ackerman arrived in Ekaterinburg only a few weeks after the Romanovs vanished. He was not a bit impressed with the murder story and found very few persons who were. He wrote:

> When I questioned the American [Palmer, now dead], British [Preston], and French consuls, who were in the city throughout the Bolshevik occupation, as to their opinions, they stated frankly that they did not know whether the Czar was dead or alive, and they are still conducting their investigation.

Suddenly, however, with no new facts at hand, the utterances of the Allied spokesmen on the subject changed from equivocation to certainty. This rather amused Mr. Ackerman. In his book *Trailing the Bolsheviki,* he expressed wonderment that, on returning to Vladivostok, more than thirty-five hundred miles by rail from Ekaterinburg, all the officials, who were so far from the scene, were so much more resolutely sure the Imperial Family had been brutally and bloodily wiped out than those who were on the scene at Ipatiev House. Obviously, someone had passed the word down the chain of command. Was it the same thought that Mr. Wilton expressed on the railroad platform? "Commander Lasies, even if the Czar and the Imperial Family are living, it is necessary to say they are dead!"

Considering the failure of the anti-assassination adherents to make their views prevail, it is interesting to note how much contemporary support they had.

In the New York *Times* alone, four dispatches appeared in 1918 and 1919 that supported Lasies's version. Here are the lead paragraphs:

> WARSAW, Dec. 16 [1918] (Associated Press)—The mother of former Emperor Nicholas, who is living near Livadia in the Crimea, has been receiving letters every ten days purported to come from the

former ruler, according to Polish officers who have arrived here from Sebastopol.

WARSAW, Dec. 24 [1918] (Associated Press)—"There is no doubt that the Czar and his entire family are alive. I am positive of this," was the declaration made to the correspondent today by Michael Chikhachev, a nephew of General Skoropadski, who has just escaped from the Ukraine after a recent trip to Petrograd, Dvinsk, Vilna, and Rovno.

"I cannot reveal where the Czar is, because he does not wish it," he added.

LONDON, Jan. 8 [1919] (British Wireless Service)—According to a story sent by a special correspondent of *The Morning Post* at Archangel—which it is necessary to treat with reserve—the former Emperor of Russia is still alive. The correspondent telegraphs:

"A friend of mine, Prince M_____, who has just arrived here from Petrograd, informed me that he had a long talk with Grand Duke Cyril on November 18. The Grand Duke told him that he had just received a letter from Grand Duchess Tatiana, daughter of the Emperor, who wrote that the Empress and her daughters were still alive and that the Emperor had not been shot."

ROME, March 14 [1919]—According to an interview with Stephania Turr, a daughter of a noted Hungarian general, printed today in the *Giornale d'Italia,* the belief still exists that Emperor Nicholas and his wife, as well as some of the Russian Grand Dukes, were not put to death by the Bolsheviki.

The interview quotes a conversation between Miss Turr and Prince Obolensky, former Captain of the Russian Imperial Guard, in which the Prince expressed his firm belief that the Russian Royal Family is still alive. He is reported to have refused to give any details as to the basis for his belief except that the former Emperor and Empress were, perhaps, hidden in Northern Russia.

After the denouncement at Ekaterinburg, the signals must have gotten snarled somewhere between the Bolshevik high command in Moscow and the lower echelons in Siberia; or perhaps Moscow had decided not to tell the underlings exactly what was going on. At any rate, there were alarms and excursions from western Siberia to the Pacific, which resulted in frantic searches for an "escaped Czarevich" and an "escaped Czar." As a result, a Socialist Finnish statesman, Oskari Tokoi, whose son bore some resemblance to Alexei Nicholaevich Romanov, came close to losing his boy to Red militiamen.

The incident took place in Siberia in the summer of 1918. Mr. Tokoi, who later became Premier of Finland, was homeward bound after a visit to Russia. He describes what happened in his book *Sisu: Even Through a Stone Wall:*

I almost lost my youngest son. Late in the night, beyond Perm, the train was stopped at some wayside station and surrounded by Red militia. They searched the train with great thoroughness. The passengers learned that they expected to find Czarevitch Alexei, the Czar's fourteen-year-old son, who had escaped from Ekaterinburg.

My son was sharing a compartment with our interpreter. As soon as the militia saw the boy, they pounced on him. He was the same age, and the same height, and—they declared—he looked the same as the Czarevitch, so he could be nobody else but the Czarevitch. The interpreter tried to assure them that the boy was Finnish and did not even speak a word of Russian, but no one would believe him. Finally the interpreter remembered that the Czarevitch was said to be lame, and he came up with the last trump. My son was marched up and down the corridor and everyone watched closely to see if he limped. When the militia were convinced he walked straight on his own two feet, they let him go.

Every compartment, every corner, of the train was searched, and the pillows and mattresses so thoroughly bayonetted that not a mouse could have remained alive in them. Perhaps the son of the Czar Nicholas succeeded in escaping. Perhaps he remained somewhere among the living when his family was executed behind the tall plank fence surrounding a villa in Ekaterinburg.

And while some Bolsheviks were looking for Alexei in the Perm-Ekaterinburg area, others were searching for his father, as late as 1920, the length and breadth of Siberia, if we are to believe the following story in the July 16, 1920, edition of the San Francisco *Examiner*:

LONDON, July 15 [1920]—The Soviet Government is offering a reward of 2,000,000 rubles for the head of a man claiming to be Czar Nicholas 2nd of Russia, according to information received by the Jewish Correspondence Bureau today. The advices say the claimant, who is in Siberia, has raised a considerable following. In accounting for his escape from the hands of the Bolsheviks, he asserts it was a servant impersonating the Czar who was killed at Ekaterinburg, where the Czar and his family are understood to have been executed.

Some reports of the escape of the Imperial Family were passed along furtively. One of these was current in the Black Sea sector. It is described by the White general, Baron Peter N. Wrangel, commander of the South Russian forces, in his book *Always with Honor*. Mentioning an event in the spring of 1920, he writes:

Another time the manager of an officers' co-operative society, an old retired colonel, was among the visitors. He explained the object of his visit very clearly and in great detail. I promised to help him, and as I was saying good-by I asked him where he had served previously.

"In the old days I was an instructor at a military school in Petrograd." He mentioned the name. "I had the good fortune to show the Czarevitch over our Museum." After a moment's silence, he leant over to me and continued in a mysterious manner. "How he has grown, Your Excellency! I would not have known him the last time I saw him: he is taller than I am. He is quite well and cheerful; the Czar and the Grand Duchesses are also well, thank God!"

"Where and when did you last see the Imperial Family?"

"Well, it was last year, at Rostov. I was walking along the Sadovia, when suddenly I saw the Czar in ordinary clothes. I scarcely recognized him. He greeted me, and later I called on him several times and saw him, the Czarina, and their children."

I had difficulty in changing the subject, but as soon as we began talking of something else, the colonel became perfectly normal again.

It was in the ambiance of this secrecy, confusion, and forgetfulness that time, applying its characteristic dosage of indifference, won an overwhelming victory in the court of public opinion for the "fact" of the Romanov massacre. And added to all the other factors, whenever doubters came forward, the persuasiveness of the very reasonable but unanswerable question was felt: If they survived, where have they been?

But a long-sustained absence of news and evidence does not serve as proof of a crime, and this is emphasized later in Dr. Aughinbaugh's foreword. He puts it this way:

In certain Royal quarters the anxiety to disseminate the "reports" of their Commissions is too apparent to authorize a judicial mind to accept their speculative guesswork as convincing evidence of a legal *corpus delicti* when no identified bodies have been produced. The eagerness to convince the world by substituting a mere *disappearance,* or the lack of evidence, for positive proof of the Royal assassination raises very naturally the presumption that certain circles are more interested in misleading than in satisfying the public mind.

XI

Life After Death

If all the recent claimants to the imperial inheritance were taken as seriously as those historians who believe in the Ekaterinburg massacre, most of the world's Romanov scholars would consider the assassination story a wide-open mystery.

Mrs. Eugenia Smith, a capersome soul who changed her story four times after delivering her *Anastasia* manuscript to the publisher, was "The Lady Who Came to Dinner" at the residence of Mrs. W. H. Emery, in Elmhurst, Illinois, in 1945. She stayed for seventeen years.

Another of the alleged Imperial sisters, the ex-Grand Duchess Maria, is now in Warsaw awaiting the approval of the Polish authorities to visit Goleniewski and her young niece (Goleniewski's daughter) Tatiana. A courier from the Three Gs has interviewed her several times in her modest Warsaw suite. She corroborates most of Goleniewski's story. We learned that Polish officials put her through an inquisition after Goleniewski defected. She had to move from a comfortable home to more frugal lodgings.

She seems to be the right age (seventy) and to have more or less the general appearance for the role of the real Maria. If she is, she's a woman of formidable character. She's the sister who took care of her parents and acted like a mother to her hemophilic brother. She's also the sister who parried with "Fox" in bursts of high-spirited banter on the long trip from Ekaterinburg eastward. "Fox," on various occasions, seemed quite smitten by her. (See the excerpts from "Fox's diary" in Chapter XVIII.)

There there's the "other Anastasia." She is the former Mrs. Anna Anderson, the former "Mrs. Tchaikovsky," the figure around whom all the legends of one daughter's solitary escape were started in 1920. She has become an American housewife in one of the most rank-conscious states of the Union—Virginia.

It must be said for this claimant that the public hue and cry about her being "Anastasia" was started by someone else. The real launcher of the tale was a German dressmaker who had once worked in Saint Petersburg, Russia. Both women were in a Berlin hospital in 1920. "Mrs. Tchaikovsky" was there because she had been rescued after what might have been a suicide attempt in a Berlin canal. The other patient in a neighboring bed—the dressmaker—decided that in "Mrs. Tchaikovsky" she recognized the Romanov features of Nicholas' youngest daughter. The story spread around the world.

It was a bewitching story. The world wanted to believe it. It was so appealing that it won powerful supporters, who attributed "Mrs. Tchaikovsky's" inability to speak Russian or English (the Romanov children could speak both), or to recognize the children's tutor, M. Pierre Gilliard, as among the amnesic effects induced by the shock of her near drowning. The Danish ambassador in Berlin was impressed. So was Prince Valdemar of Denmark, brother of the Dowager Empress Marie and uncle of Nicholas, Xenia, and Olga. Eventually the Grand Duchess Olga was persuaded to make a four-day visit to Berlin in order to examine the slow-to-recover patient. The real Anastasia was Olga's goddaughter as well as her niece. Olga returned to Denmark, reporting that she was unconvinced.

(Colonel Goleniewski disavowed Mrs. Anderson's claims. He sent a multipage affidavit to the German court asserting his reasons why she couldn't be one of his imperial sisters. Despite his estrangement from Mrs. Eugenia Smith, he has never wavered in his support of her as the "real Anastasia"—Ed.)

All this seemed to spur the believers in her authenticity as Anastasia to greater efforts. She changed her name to Mrs. Anna Anderson and launched what was to prove a marathon suit for recognition as Nicholas' daughter. It went on for years.

Many Romanov-watchers came to the conclusion that Mrs. Anderson's legal maneuvers, which must have cost a tidy sum, were backed by some persons only too happy to "keep the pot boiling in court" in order to put off the day of settlement. Though World War II interrupted the suit, it continued until the Hamburg court finally rejected it in February 1967.

One of her chief supporters throughout the years was Gleb Botkin, son of the Czar's doctor, Eugene Botkin. The physician was supposed to have been murdered at Ekaterinburg with the Romanovs. His son, Gleb, had seen a good deal of Nicholas' children.

Gleb Botkin gave interviews and composed articles in support of Mrs. Anderson's claims. He wrote two books about her and helped on another. He brought her to the United States when her appearance wasn't being required in the Hamburg court. When that court rejected her claims, Mr. Botkin showed a commendable determination not to abandon her.

He was on this side of the Atlantic. A jolly, round-cheeked, imaginative man, he had become a fine example of the process of rejuvenation that can overtake an aging writer who has been mixed up with the Romanov stories. He had moved to the lovely old college town of Charlottesville, Virginia. It was here that he transformed himself by a stroke of the pen into the "Archbishop of the Church of Aphrodite." The church and the title were created in the same spontaneous act of faith. The church is still a few centuries too young to provoke the protests and picketing of Virginia's anti-establishment students, but if anything is going to save it over the years it will be (1) because few, outside of the Archbishop, have ever heard of it, and (2) because its precepts appear to be closer to those of our swingingest hippies than to stuffy old institutions like Judaism, Christianity, Buddhism, Shintoism, and Existentialism.

Archbishop Botkin invited Mrs. Anderson to Charlottesville. She arrived from the debacle at Hamburg on a visitor's visa. Soon she was married to a former history professor, at least eighteen years her junior, Dr. John E. Manahan.

He appears in a picture sent out by the Associated Press on December 26, 1968. The picture was taken just before the wedding ceremony in Charlottesville. Seated and bent forward, in a fur cap and coat, is Mrs. Anderson. Standing and beaming behind her, which is not where an imminent bridegroom ought to be, is Dr. Manahan. Seated next to her, in what should have been the groom's position, is Archbishop Botkin. His expression is solemn, triumphant, and regal. His beard is just a little squarer at the bottom than the one made famous all over the world by Nicholas II.

Dr. Manahan gave his age as forty-nine. By her own calculations, the bride was sixty-seven on the nuptial day, but by the estimates of physicians who at the time of the canal incident, in 1920, estimated that she was in her late twenties, she must be well into her seventies.

The unrecognized Romanovs are a hardy breed. Snubs and reverses don't crush them. Otherwise they would not have been able to shift their center of gravity so persistently, if stealthily, into the Western Hemisphere.

If Maria visits Goleniewski; if Colonel Goleniewski patches things up with the CIA and Mrs. Eugenia Smith, whom he once hailed affectionately as his long-lost sister Anastasia; if Olga and Tatiana can be persuaded that the time is ripe to surface in Frankfurt and join the clan in America; if brother "Alexei" can learn to be less abrasive with his sisters; if Xenia's children can be lured from England and France, and Olga's sons can be brought down from Canada; if the Spanish branch of the Romanovs can make peace with the English branch, and the English branch with the German, then they may all wind up in New York. There is also no question that if these same assembled and reconciled Romanovs could summon the statesmanship needed, and bring the unrecognized children of Nicholas together with their more recognized and acknowledged cousins, and convince the latter that the "state secret" is out, and the need for "security" gone, a good deal of money could be coaxed out of the vaults by due process of law.

One of the most serious considerations in evaluating the Romanov case is whether it is possible to wash out the Romanov colors from the Goleniewski affair or from the Heckenschuetzes' reasons for sending him here. Are they separate dilemmas, or are they inseparable?

In order to prepare answers to those questions, let us turn back to July 16, 1918, the last day on which everyone agrees that the seven members of Nicholas' family were alive. We'll look at them as they were on that historic date, then at the versions of what happened as day turned into night and night turned into the years afterward.

Nicholas was fifty. He was in good health, though undoubtedly affected by the strain of imprisonment. We need no introduction to his widely advertised faults. Less known is the fact that he was a gentle man, a considerate father, an avid reader, an outdoorsman. Many said of him that he would have saved his empire if he had treated his subjects half as well as he treated his family.

Alexandra was forty-six. She was in poor health. A doting mother, her desperate struggle to ease the pains of her hemophilic son, Alexei, had left its toll on her nerves. She was overwrought; she was inclined to see divine omens in natural events. Her tendency to be oriented more to her family and friends than to the invisible Russian people had caused observers to remark that if her more dedicated older sister, the Grand Duchess Serge ("Aunt Ella"), had been the Empress "there would have been no revolution." This must have haunted her at Ekaterinburg.

The Grand Duchess Olga, oldest of the five children, was almost twenty-three. As befitted her seniority, she had a motherly attitude toward the others. She was her "father's child." She was as shy as he was. She was tenderly inclined to see things his way. She had greenish-blue eyes set in a broad, Slavic face. She struck others as being exceptionally sensitive and kind.

Tatiana was twenty-one. Her hair was auburn, her eyes dark gray, almost brown. She was fun-loving in an aristocratic sort of way, but she was disposed to be stiff on occasion, and some considered her snobbish. She favored her mother. She was a gifted pianist and quite a beauty. She was the most elegant of the sisters. She was her "mother's child"—as thoroughly regal as Alexandra.

Maria was nineteen. She was probably the prettiest of the lot. Her eyes were deep blue, her hair light brown. She was bubblingly gay and rather flirtatious, but of them all she had the most highly developed "team spirit" about the family. She preferred painting to music.

Anastasia was seventeen. She, too, had blue eyes, with a fleck of gold in one of them. She was the wit, wag, and wisecracker of the family. She was also a loner and a tomboy. Both her parents regarded her as the most daring of their daughters, but took comfort in the fact that she was self-reliant enough to wangle out of any scrape she got herself into.

Alexei was almost fourteen. Despite his frequent illnesses, he was as daring as Anastasia and even more inclined to play pranks. He was often seized by fits of swaggering self-importance and autocratic bullying.

The different versions of what happened at Ipatiev House, Ekaterinburg, on Tuesday, July 16, 1918, show little disagreement throughout the day and evening. The weather was fair. The daylight hours were sunny. At four in the afternoon, Nicholas took his four daughters for their customary walk in the garden. Alexei was ill. Alexandra was indisposed. The only harbinger of anything unusual involved a young servant. Yakov Yankel Yurovsky, the Bolshevik official in charge of the Imperial prisoners, ordered the fourteen-year-old kitchen boy, Leonid Sednev, out of the house for no reason that anyone could understand. Leonid had been a playmate of Alexei's.

Around 10:30 P.M., the Romanovs undressed and went to bed in their rooms upstairs. Their lights were turned out. About midnight Yurovsky climbed the stairs and entered the Czar's room. He informed Nicholas that the whole family would have to get dressed because Ekaterinburg was in danger of falling to quickly advancing Czech and White Army columns. The Ural Soviet, he said, had decided to move the Imperial Family for its own safety. Automobiles would soon arrive to pick them up. He advised them to hurry. They dressed. They found time to say prayers together.

What really happened in the next two hours is the very crux of the clash of versions. At least one theory claims the family was not at Ipatiev at all. It has all seven Romanovs removed from Ipatiev House by June 23. It is based on the subsequent finding of a day-by-day sheet calendar on the wall near Alexandra's bed.

Each day of her incarceration there, so the story goes, Alexandra had torn off yesterday's sheet to bring the calendar up to date. Then she said her morning prayers. When later visitors to the room, from July 17 on, saw the calendar, they noted that the last sheet visible was "June 23." Some reasoned that the "stand-ins" for the Romanovs had thought of keeping up all appearances except the calendar. A report quickly spread around Ekaterinburg that the Romanovs

147

had been smuggled out of town more than three weeks before their "assassination."

Most versions begin, however, with events that followed Yurovsky's midnight alert to the Czar. A widely accepted account is as follows:

All seven members of the family, with Nicholas carrying the sleepy and ailing Alexei, were led downstairs to a basement room and killed by a Cheka firing squad. Their physician and three servants were murdered with them: Dr. Eugene Botkin; Anna Demidova, Alexandra's maid; Ivan Kharitonov, the cook; and Trupp, Alexei's attendant.

By another version, not all of these eleven persons were killed; by another, Anastasia was the only one to escape; by another, none were taken to the basement, but led rather, in the gray twilight of the Siberian night, through the courtyard and as far as a small convoy of trucks, where they changed into disguises and were driven away; by another, they were ushered into the basement room, from which they were carried out to the trucks as "bodies" hidden in baskets.

By another version, Anastasia broke away from the others as they were about to leave in a car and re-entered Ipatiev House to get the dogs ("Joy," belonging to Alexei, and "Jemmy," belonging to her). This version has her barging into the basement room just as the servants were being shot, screaming and being knocked unconscious by one of the executioners swinging his pistol. The weapon discharged, so this version goes; that explains the presence of a bullet embedded in the wall outside the door, in a direction opposite to the other shots.

The ultimate key to the riddle of Ekaterinburg may be "the man" who, many versions agree, came upstairs with a lantern, after Yurovsky came down, and led the Romanovs to the ground floor. He and the "guards" who joined him below could have been agents of the liberation plot. That's the idea *Rescuing* gets across.

One of them, according to the book, dressed as "captain" of the guards, was "Fox." If so, all the others were probably agents, too; but all had probably taken the time to establish themselves in the others' eyes as reliable Bolsheviks. Goleniewski told me and several other Americans that Yurovsky shepherded all the Romanovs out of Russia and that he met the man years later in Poland. Before they left Ekaterinburg, he said, they were disguised as poor refugees, divided into a foursome, a twosome and a onesome. The foursome comprised Nicholas, Alexandra, Maria, and Alexei. Alexei was depicted as Maria's son. Olga and Tatiana made up the twosome. Anastasia traveled apart from the others but not alone.

Neither Goleniewski here, nor "Maria" in Warsaw, has described any such extensive jaunt through Tibet as that given in *Rescuing;* but whether or not Nicholas left them for Vladivostok, and whether they traversed northern India, the two, in entirely separate interviews, agree that all members of the family found their way to Warsaw after months of travel that took them through Turkey, Greece, and Austria.

Why Warsaw?

"My Father had thought it over very carefully," Goleniewski told me. "He decided on Poland for a good reason. There were in Poland at that time large numbers of Russians, not only in the cities but on the farms. He thought we could blend into that background without attracting attention. He had shaved off his beard and moustache. No one recognized him. No one recognized my mother."

He added that Nicholas also liked the idea of a locale in Poland, because it would enable him to move quickly into his old empire if a change in the political situation warranted it.

It is interesting that the same thought was echoed by "Eugene Ivanoff," according to Sheldon Whitehouse's report to the State Department in 1927, when he quoted the young man suspected of being the son of Nicholas as saying: ". . . but since 1919 I proceeded to Poland, wanting to be nearer to Russia, for I was expecting events, changes in my country . . ."

The foursome-twosome-onesome scheme of separation prevailed even while the Romanovs were in Warsaw, according to Goleniewski. He said that in 1924 his father decided their security would be better if they moved into the country. They set up humble housekeeping, first in Wolsztyn, then in Karpicko, in the Province of Poznan. This is near the German border.

"Maria's" account is in accord with all this and also with what Goleniewski said about the three other sisters: that their father sent Anastasia to the United States in 1922 with credentials to get some badly needed funds from a Detroit bank; that she never returned and thereafter was in the family doghouse; that shortly afterwards Olga and Tatiana moved to Germany to take up a new life.

But there is a conflict in what the two reported about the deaths of their parents. Colonel Goleniewski said Alexandra died in 1924, the same year the family moved into the Poznan countryside, and Nicholas in 1952, at the age of eighty-four, in the Polish village of Ciosaniec, which is about six miles from Wolsztyn. The former Emperor of Russia was buried in the Wolsztyn Cemetery, he said, under an assumed name.

"Maria" puts Alexandra's death several years later than Goleniewski does and Nicholas' several years earlier. Both, she said, were buried in Warsaw under assumed names. A Three-Gs courier reports that she is under surveillance. He has visited her several times over a period of eighteen months. He rates her as follows:

"She's a bright, hearty, and attractive woman. She has an excellent understanding of world affairs. There are pictures of members of the Imperial Family in her small living room, and two or three of them are of Colonel Goleniewski."

It was in the rustic setting of Poznan that Goleniewski outgrew the violent stomach pains of his youth, he said, and lost the "stunted figure" that promised to make him look like a child for the rest of his life. It was there also, he said, that he learned to take his father's advice about how to avoid attracting attention: "Try to look as stupid on the outside as you are bright on the inside."

It was in post-World War II Poland that powerful friends of his father's (undoubtedly Heckenschuetzes members) arranged for a waiver of his physical shortcomings and gained his admission to the Polish Army. It was the start of his career in intelligence. The secretiveness of his life in hiding had given him practice as a poker-faced anti-Communist in a Communist country.

If all the Romanovs were killed in Ipatiev House, as the world has long believed, then every living person who claims to be one of the five children is clearly an impostor. Such a thought cannot be discounted. Only a razor's edge away from it is the companion notion that some of the claimants are working together in a conspiracy. That can't be ruled out, either. But if some of these characters are, in fact, joined in an impersonation plot, they are among the most spectacularly discordant band of crooks that ever intrigued against the truth. They get all their signals confused. They can't work harmoniously. They can't agree on a story. Their motives appear to be vastly different. Indeed, if the underworld crime syndicates would only manage to get their staff work as badly scrambled as the Romanov claimants, the problems of the nation's police would be eased overnight.

Their quarrels, their divergences, their apparent insistence on steering their own courses in their own ways, have the much more familiar ring of personality clashes within a real family.

The mere chance that Goleniewski's story is true; that Nicholas' son has appealed to us after giving us his service; that his appeal was endorsed by the Heckenschuetzes, who have done more for us than any other Russian group in living history; and that we have rejected the whole business—this is a circumstance that should rest uneasily on the American conscience.

It's a prospect rendered far less incredible than it sounds by many widely separated sources mostly unknown to the public—Ackerman, Lasies, Aughinbaugh, De Shishmarev, McGarry, *Rescuing,* the "Fox" letters, the newspaper reports published from all over Europe in 1918–19, the Dowager Empress Marie's conversation in Malta; her son-in-law's complaint, in his memoirs, about his wife's and her mother's unyielding faith in the Imperial Family's survival; Sheldon Whitehouse's file on "Eugene Ivanoff"; Thomas Nelson Page's file on "highest quarters" in Rome; the "Nicholas Romanoff" Affair in San Francisco; the passport in David Prescott Barrows' papers; Hsüan T'ung's gift of fifty thousand dollars to General Semonov, in 1925, to "restore" the Romanovs; the strange reluctance of the next-in-line Romanov heirs to claim their inheritance.

These add up to something more than a "mere chance." Perhaps the most impressive manifestation of all has been the unrestrained support Goleniewski received from the Heckenschuetzes.

Importance must be given, too, to the identification of "Maria."

Hoping for a break in her case, and obviously striving not to say anything that might ruin her chances of leaving Poland, "Maria" proved to be an enigma to our courier. She was clearly so well disciplined and well bred that he said he could never be sure just how much of her emotions she was hiding.

In her interview with him, she used both Polish and English, but seemed most at ease in Polish. He gathered she was also fluent in German and French. She also bore a general resemblance to a picture of the real Maria taken in 1917 and to a picture identified by Colonel Goleniewski that was taken a few years ago. Both are reproduced in this book.

This is the woman—if our information is accurate—whom Goleniewski left in Warsaw when he defected. She underwent a long series of interrogations about him. She is the woman Goleniewski mentioned a dozen times as the one who took care of him throughout his youth and adolescence. Yet he abandoned her to face the consequences of his bolt to the West on Christmas Day 1960. She was not among those who, upon his defection to the West, he insisted be allowed to come with him.

At his court-marital, she had to testify in absentia. If she is bitter about all this, however, she didn't dwell on it to her American interviewer. She said she was eager to see "my brother and his daughter." She mentioned that she was on good terms with Goleniewski's children by a former marriage, but nothing was said about how many of them there are. Pending further notice, Maria's claims deserve serious attention.

XII

Mrs. Eugenia Smith
and the "Anastasia" Debacle

In the October 18, 1963, issue, *Life* magazine printed excerpts from Mrs. Eugenia Smith's book *Anastasia,* published by Robert Speller & Sons. As the deadline for the issue neared, *Life*'s editors became edgy. They gathered several analyses by psychiatrists and truth testers to go along with the excerpts. Polygraph expert Cleve Backster wrote the observations that included the two now-historic paragraphs converted by a staff writer as follows:

"By the time Backster had studied all the results of his renewed testing, he was virtually positive that his subject was Anastasia. His conviction was based on his interpretation of *all* Mrs. Smith's answers —not just her apparent truth responses. For example, her affirmative replies to questions about her identity, her birthday, all indicated she was telling the truth.

"But her responses were indefinite on the questions about the way her mother died and whether her sisters screamed before she did at the execution."

In other words, she didn't register much emotional response to questions about details of the "assassination." At the time, apparently, it occurred to no one that she had had no reaction because there had been no assassination. Soon afterward, however, it began

PLATE 21: William Rutledge McGarry, III, editor of *Rescuing the Czar*, 1920.

PLATE 22: The alleged Grand Duchesses Olga, Tatiana, Anastasia, and Maria, according to Colonel Goleniewski, photographed in Poland, circa 1921, approximately three years after the "assassination."

PLATE 23: The Nicholas Romanov mentioned in the San Francisco *Examiner* story, July 26, 1920, in which he urged the restoration of the Russian monarchy.

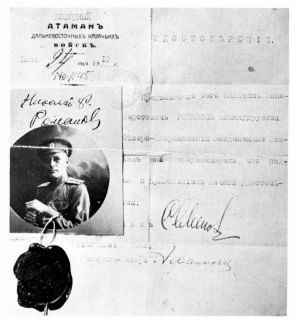

PLATE 24: The mysterious Nicholas Romanov passport found in the papers of Colonel David Prescott Barrows.

PLATE 25: A clearer photograph of the Nicholas Romanov who appears in Plate 24. Note the inscription to Barrows.

PLATE 26: An alleged Imperial trio—from left to right, the Czarevich Alexei, the Grand Duchess Maria, and the Czar Nicholas II. According to Colonel Goleniewski, this was taken in Poland in 1942.

: An enlargement of
f the alleged Czar
in the adjoining photo.

PLATE 28: The grave bearing the name of "Michał Goleniewski," in the parish cemetery, Wolsztyn, Poland. Grave of the alleged Czar Nicholas, II, deceased 1952.

PLATE 29: The mysterious Eugene Nicholaevich Ivanov, who was an "Alexei" claimant in Poland in 1927.

Plate 30: The alleged Czarevich Alexei, Colonel Michal Goleniewski, Poland, circa 1946.

Plate 31: The alleged Czarevich Alexei, Colonel Michal Goleniewski, New York, 1964.

to occur to a number of persons. And that included all members of the Speller family.

The likelihood that the mass murder was mythical was stimulated by Colonel Goleniewski's appearance in December, only weeks after the *Life* piece. It resulted in a confrontation between him and Mrs. Smith duly recorded on tape in the Speller offices, at Mrs. Smith's request. A transcript of that tape has been forwarded to the Justice Department.

It should be explained that, at the time of the confrontation, no one outside the United States intelligence services had ever heard of a "Goleniewski." The stories on him were not to be released until the following March. He didn't use the name "Goleniewski" when he first phoned the Spellers in December. He called himself "Mr. Borg." On December 28, three days before the face-to-face encounter, he asked for an appointment with Mrs. Smith, declaring he had some information for her. She consented. A date was set for December 31.

"It was quite an occasion for our firm," said Bob Speller, its president. "We had all worked with Mrs. Smith for ten months. We were thoroughly convinced of the authenticity of her manuscript, and we still are—with the exception of the part about the assassination. But then we also believed the assassination part. We had no reason to doubt it.

"We sensed this meeting might be important, somehow. Of course, we had no idea how important. I asked Cleve Backster to bring over a tape recorder and take charge of it. My wife, Maxine, came over, too. Our sons, Robert, Jr., and Jon, were there.

"When 'Mr. Borg' commenced his meeting with Mrs. Smith, it started out quite formally, but it wasn't long before it became very emotional. My sons and I were the only other persons in the room. We could follow some of what they said. Some of it was in English. Most of it was in Russian, so we had to have a Russian translator produce the transcript."

As Goleniewski explained to me, months later, he had been trying to get the CIA for two years to help him find his sister in the United States. It was not until January 1963, he said, that a "Mr. Larsen" of the CIA finally told him Mrs. Smith was in Illinois. He promised further help in bringing the two together but never lived up to it, according to Goleniewski. He said he had to find out through his own sources that the Speller firm was publishing her book. That's how it came about, he said, that he phoned the Speller offices.

The transcript of the meeting as endorsed, page by page, with Goleniewski's signature, "Alexei Nicholaevich" follows:

ANASTASIA: I am so ashamed of myself. [*She begins to cry.*] Who are you? Who sent you to see me?

BORG: I am a friend and I came to see you to speak to you. Do you remember the name Turynski?

ANASTASIA: I remember the name.

BORG: And Anastasia Turynska?

ANASTASIA: Anastasia Turynska? . . . Anastasia Turynska. I remember. I came as Anastasia Turynska but my passport is different.

BORG: Do you remember Janina Turynska? The daughter of Raymond Turynski. That was Maria Nicholaevna Romanova.

ANASTASIA: But who told you all that?

BORG: Must I tell you that you came to America as Anastasia Turynska?

ANASTASIA: Who spoke with you about Janina Turynska? How do you know? How did the Family know? I tried to see my Aunt Olga as she came to Toronto. She did not want to see me. . . . Your eyes. I remember your eyes as if I knew them. I am so afraid. Who sent you to me? . . . Maria is alive? [He shows her a snapshot.] Who is that?

BORG: Maria remained with us. I have been looking for you for two years. They didn't want me to see you. They don't want to recognize you because of the money. Because they have the money.

ANASTASIA : How can you be sure that I am Anastasia?

BORG : When I came I began at once to look for you. They did not want me to find you.

ANASTASIA : I would like the Spellers to understand . . .

BORG : I would like to speak Russian.

ANASTASIA : I am sorry, but my Russian is not very good. I see very few Russians. . . .

BORG : I came here more than two years ago.

ANASTASIA : [*To the Spellers*] He was looking for me for more than two years . . . [*To Borg*] Who didn't want you to meet me? Those who want to recognize another Anastasia? The people don't want to believe me. They printed a lot of lies. . . .

BORG : I have a photo to show you. That is your sister. . . .

ANASTASIA : There are so many complications.

BORG : But you know that all are alive.

ANASTASIA : How is that possible? Some people wrote that Tatiana is alive. But can it be that the whole Family . . .

BORG : We had to do a lot of trickery to cover the flight. . . . Your mother died from a heart attack.

ANASTASIA : I also have a bad heart.

BORG : You have the eyes of Maria, but hers are darker, like these violets I brought you and which you liked so much.

ANASTASIA : They are Anastasia blue. Who told you? Who sent you? Who told you that? I really have confidence in you. . . .

BORG : I know what you think. You see this photo. . . . Maria Nicholaevna has the other part of this photo from Warsaw. . . . She still has photos of Father and of Mother, taken in Warsaw and elsewhere in Poland.

ANASTASIA : Maria has my picture. . . . What happened to Tatiana? [*She rises*]

BORG : I didn't come to make you suffer, only to speak with

you. I wished to see you and show you a lot of things that will interest you.

ANASTASIA: The Spellers should know, because they work with me and it is really so important that they recognize me. [*Borg then shows her another photo*] Who is in this photo? That should be Olga. So old. She is older than me—six years. . . . That's the signature and writing of Maria. Why did she put Mushka? [*He had shown her another photo.*]

BORG: Mushka who was brought through the Red borders in a washbasket. Do you know who Mushka is?

ANASTASIA: It would be Maria—Mushka. It could be me. My mother said I was like a little fly.

BORG: No . . . do you know who was brought through the Red borders in a washbasket?

ANASTASIA: Yes, I know. My father wanted me to forget it. He said so. I was stolen from my family. My father, my mother, my sisters, my country, everything. . . . I have the impression you understand me. Please have patience with me.

BORG: I have to return to my family but I will always be happy to see you.

MR. SPELLER, SR.: Have you something that could help us?

BORG: Some things can be helpful. Do you have photos to give to the graphologist? [*He points to the handwriting on a photo.*] This was written in the hand of your sister, Maria Nicholaevna, and you can give it to a graphologist. Your sister is in Warsaw. . . . Your fingerprints are in London, and it is there that it should be proved that you are Anastasia Nicholaevna. . . .

ANASTASIA: In what place? If these fingerprints really exist and we can prove it, and really have it, then there would be no doubt at all. I hope you are the person I think you are.

BORG: Do you remember Father said: 'NESKIM'?

ANASTASIA: [*She cries out*] He knows. He knows. He is my

brother Alexei. [*crying*] My darling, my darling. . . . They should know. I cannot believe it. They are good people.

MR. SPELLER, SR.: Perhaps Mr. Borg . . .

ANASTASIA: No, not Mr. Borg. . . . He is my brother. It is wonderful. It is unbelievable.

BORG: Anastasia, dear, do you know when Father died? In 1952? I will show you his grave and the place where I buried him with my own hands. He was a very good Russian man.

ANASTASIA: What did you do?

BORG: The people did not let me see you. They prevented me from doing everything necessary. They say that you are not you and that I am not I. . . . But they know very well . . . Maria Feodorovna knew very well that our father was alive.

ANASTASIA: Grandmother knew that father was alive?

BORG: After Lenin's death Mother remained in Warsaw. Father, Maria, and I went to Poznan, near the German border. I was two times a child because of my sickness. . . . Do you believe you are you? So it is with me. I know and I believe that you are you. . . . They all know that I am Alexei. . . .

ANASTASIA: Mrs. Anderson is bringing a suit. The Botkins have been helping her for years.

BORG: We will arrange to bring that to order. Everybody knows who we are. . . . My dear Anastasia, the hunger that I suffered nobody could ever suffer. I could not eat at all because of my sickness. Maria also suffered terribly. She was taking care of me and Father.

ANASTASIA: Did Mama know about me? That I went?

BORG: She did. . . . I am not yet married in church. But as soon as I do so, I will let you know. . . .

ANASTASIA: How did you find where I was living?

BORG: I knew where you lived but I couldn't come and say, "My dear, how are you?" And after forty years I didn't want to give you a shock.

ANASTASIA: Do you have any things of Mother's?

BORG: Mother prayed before an icon. Maria has the icon and a little lamp. They are the only things we have from her.

ANASTASIA: But how is it possible that you have anything at all?

BORG: Some things we had with us.

ANASTASIA: I had only the diamonds. But nothing was left after the flight. Now I have only a handkerchief. . . . Are you still Orthodox?

BORG: Yes, we have never changed.

ANASTASIA: My husband was a Catholic.[1] He would have liked that I become Catholic, but I knew that my parents would have disapproved, and so I always stayed Orthodox. I was married in Bucovina. . . . My life was very difficult . . .

BORG: I also had a very difficult life. . . . Maria had a lot of trouble with me. Mother was dead. . . .

ANASTASIA: All you would like I will do for you. . . .

BORG: I came with a lot of goodwill and I was received like a dog. It was my duty to see my sister, to say hello to her, to speak about our parents. . . .

ANASTASIA: When and where can we see each other?

BORG: As soon as possible.

ANASTASIA: [*To Mr. Speller, Sr.*] Is it all right in your apartment?

MR. SPELLER, SR.: Yes, of course.

BORG: Take a good look at me. I've aged a lot. I am nearly an old man now. . . .

[*Mr. Cleve Backster enters.*]

---

[1] Although Mrs. Smith makes no mention of a husband in her autobiography, *Anastasia* (it ends with the events of 1918), she told friends here that she was once married to a Croatian, Marijan Smetisko. On her immigration papers in 1922, she listed herself as Mrs. Eugenia Smetisko. She said the marriage was dissolved a few years after her arrival in the U.S.

ANASTASIA: Hello, Mr. Backster. Can I present you to my brother, Alexei?

This highly emotional scene was followed by two or three weeks in which the reunited pair remained on the most cordial terms. They held three meetings in the Spellers' apartment in which Mrs. Smith frequently alluded to Goleniewski as "my brother, Alexei." (It should be re-emphasized, however, that the name "Goleniewski" had still to make its appearance in the life of the Spellers.) They also told the Spellers that they had held few meetings elsewhere. Then they broke up. They remain estranged to this day in December 1969. Not many miles separate them. Goleniewski lives in western Long Island, within the New York City limits. Mrs. Smith divides her time between the city and Long Beach, Long Island, which is on the South Shore, about twenty miles from Goleniewski's apartment.

One can imagine the Spellers' reactions when they were told that there had been no assassination at all at Ekaterinburg—that the Czarevich himself might be standing in front of them.

Do either or both of the two on the transcript seem to be charlatans? The reader is just as well qualified as we are to judge that to his own satisfaction. Certainly the possibility can't be overlooked that the whole confrontation scene was staged by design of the "sister" and "brother" to convince the witnesses and, through them, all others who would hear or read about it. The matter of probability is something else. Again the reader should weigh that for himself.

Assuming for a moment that it's all perfectly genuine, the transcript does provide clues to Mrs. Smith's frame of mind and why she later decided not to live up to her promise to Goleniewski, "All you would like I will do for you."

In her own words, on the same transcript, she betrays her fears and grievances: "I am so ashamed of myself. . . . Who sent you to see me? . . . There are so many complications. . . . I also have a bad heart."

The Spellers realized that her public recognition of the man as her brother would require her to admit having falsified the facts about Ekaterinburg in her book and to all in whom she had confided over the years. They heard "Mr. Borg" try to convince her that people would understand her motives and forgive her. For a while she seemed ready to go along with his pleas to support his story. The reason for her final rejection of the idea is anyone's guess. It could have been old resentments. It could have been the realization that joining forces with him would be involving herself in the dangers of his career in espionage.

Whatever her motives, she opted out. But before we turn from the transcript to other matters, we should note two facts preserved on its record. It shows what has rankled Goleniewski for years: "I came with a lot of goodwill and I was received like a dog." And it shows what has apparently long piqued Mrs. Smith: "I tried to see my aunt Olga as she came to Toronto. She did not want to see me."

With that typical Romanovian vision that sees everything only from one's own viewpoint, it doesn't occur to "Anastasia" that her aunt knew she was in extreme disfavor with the family for not returning to Poland with the money she had been sent to Detroit to collect; that her aunt knew, if she acknowledged her, she would be violating Nicholas' wishes and his "state secret."

At any rate, the next two years rained a typical assortment of Imperial Family "remembrances" on the Spellers. In March 1964, the newspaper stories on the Goleniewski case were published. Mrs. Smith's "brother" admitted he was Goleniewski and retained Robert Speller, Sr., as his agent and representative to help establish his identity as Alexei N. Romanov, son of Nicholas II. Speller embarked on a costly research program.

Then Mrs. Smith ended her relationship with the Speller firm. In a deposition, she stated that the "brother" she had acknowledged in the confrontation scene was an "invention" of Mr. Speller's. Again the reader can be his own judge of how much an "invention" of the Spellers the "brother" was.

"Looking back on it all," Mr. Speller commented, "I am sure that our interest in Goleniewski was the cause of Mrs. Smith's sudden decision to dissociate herself from us. After she decided not to support the claims of Colonel Goleniewski, she felt, I'm sure, there was conflict of interest in our representing them both."

News of all this was disseminated among all those who follow the Romanov story, and probably severed the last bond of sympathy any Americans or Russian-Americans had for the Romanov claimants. Goleniewski added a final straw.

He "dismissed" Speller as his representative and agent. After months of collaboration in which he consumed days of Speller's time at home and at his office, he neither paid Speller for his services nor returned the books, papers, and documents that Speller had obtained for him.

The whole relationship proved to be as souring and impoverishing as the treatment the Russian revolutionaries claimed they had long received from Nicholas II.

If the five children of Nicholas II were happily installed today in comfortable hotel suites, on excellent terms with each other, in common agreement on procedure, with good lawyers, and amply provided with mementos of their childhood and letters from their parents, it would still be extremely difficult for them to attain official recognition.

Only a few sentimentalists would like to see them brought out of the darkness. Almost all other influences are opposed to the idea. So, indeed, are some of the Romanov claimants themselves.

The bankers don't want the Romanovs back. Neither do the Communist rulers of the Soviet Union. Neither do the claimants' former American supporters. Neither do the White Russians who lost relatives and property in the Revolution and are not inclined to want to pay even nominal homage to a clan that managed to escape the revolutionary holocaust.

The governments of the United States, Britain, France, West Germany, Italy, and Japan don't want them back. No discernible advantage would come to any statesman or politician in these countries who invested time in unveiling aging Czarist figures.

The cruel realities are quite melancholy. The Romanovs are pariahs. Should they reappear tomorrow, far more people would feel uncomfortable or resentful about it than would welcome them. These are all factors serving as secret allies of those who want no part of any Romanov resurrection and are sure to put their weight on any coffin lid being pushed up from within.

So far we have viewed the story almost entirely through American eyes. We have given little attention to what the Heckenschuetzes may have had in mind when they sent Goleniewski over here, and how it may concern the welfare of the United States. We'll consider those subjects in the next chapter.

XIII

The Big Picture Is Different

It is not difficult to suppose that the Romanov hallmark on the Heckenschuetzes' bid for our support provided all the pretexts needed in Washington to inter the case under polite sneers and nervous bureaucratic wisecracks. The sullied charisma of the Romanov name became a handy device by which to deprecate the importance of the Goleniewski case and put the other Romanov claimants and Goleniewski in the category of eccentrics.

Right there, in that black-and-white, oversimplified form, a critic might want to rest his prosecution. He could be tempted to call it the whole answer.

He would have much to back his beliefs. He could point out that by 1963 the CIA must have noted that it had a parochial interest in hiding the story. One of its central features was the elaborate plan made to bypass the CIA in favor of the FBI because of the Heckenschuetzes' conviction that the CIA had been penetrated by the KGB. We know now that the Heckenschuetzes were right. We know it from the Philby case, the Blake case, the Wennerström case, etc. But the CIA officials didn't know it or believe it when they were first told. They felt that their agency was being wrongfully accused. Fortunately for them, and unfortunately for us, nothing can discourage the news media faster than a well-placed rumor that the source of a story was untrustworthy. Also fortunately for them, and unfortunately for us, there were days when Goleniewski behaved like an angry, Slavic Don Quixote.

A reporter who accepted these surface impressions as the whole story would have good reason to continue derogating Washington officialdom. His indictment might rise to the following climax:

The Goleniewski case was another tragic blunder in our intelligence services. We botched our chances to establish a working relationship with an organization behind the Iron Curtain that in thirty-three months had done far more for us than all other sources put together. We have only to consider what our plight would be today if Philby, Blake, Wennerström, John Vassall, Gordon Lonsdale, and twenty-five or thirty smaller fry knocked out by the Heckenschuetzes were still operating. After all, Philby himself had been one of the CIA's original 'interior decorators,' hadn't he? Didn't we ask him to help organize the CIA's Russian department in the early days of the Cold War? And didn't he accept the invitation with relish? How many of Kim's old friends are still working for the United States? And didn't Goleniewski assert at one time that there were eighteen or nineteen Americans, several in government branches, whom the KGB had found very helpful over the years? It is odd that the British, West Germans, French, Danes, Israelis, and Swedes were quick to act on Goleniewski's leads to spies in their government departments but so far there have been no reflections of American malfeasance. Did not Goleniewski tell us of one American traitor? Or is it that officialdom wasn't interested in following his leads?

All these charges and implications are fair enough. But they add up to only a fragment of the story. The chance for true discernments in the Goleniewski case didn't come within a few days or a few weeks or a few months. They were spread over

thirty-three months between April 1958 and Christmas Day 1960—
the day Goleniewski showed up in West Berlin. In most of that
time the Americans didn't have the faintest idea with whom they
were dealing. And long after the volatile Goleniewski, Irmgard,
and their entourage came out of the cold, the CIA brass had to
study Goleniewski closely to make sure they weren't being fattened
up by the Russians for some kind of kill. This is the period in
which he was being fitfully debriefed by the CIA, the American
organization he had taken such care to avoid; the period in which
he was being embarrassingly introduced as Nicholas' son to thirty
or forty American intelligence officials; the period in which he
reached the conclusion about the Americans that he expressed
to "Anastasia" in their confrontation scene: "I came with a lot of
goodwill and I was received like a dog."

He expressed the equivalent of the same thought to me and
others many times over. One doesn't have to intercept any letters
to be sure that the same word was passed back to the Heckenschuetzes. They, too, thought they had worked out a foolproof
system for outflanking the CIA.

It was the absolute nadir of Goleniewski's mission. He could see
it all clearly, though it was also the period in which he was able
to clinch the unmasking of Philby. The Americans had decided
to wash their hands of him because of his Romanov connections.
And the Romanovs had decided not to support him because
of his dangerous involvement in espionage. That much he could
glean in 1964 from Mrs. Smith's withdrawal of her recognition
of him and from similar refusals to back him up later that year
when "Olga" and "Tatiana" came over from Germany for his
Russian Orthodox marriage to Irmgard. All three women, at
various times, told others here that the perils inherent in the
Goleniewski case frightened them greatly. From their standpoint,
if ever there was going to be a right time to surface their whole
story, this wasn't it.

The grand scheme had failed. The vast store of credit built up by the Heckenschuetzes was not going to budge the Romanov story one inch toward official recognition.

The CIA hoped to convert all the data received from the Heckenschuetzes into American benefits. The rest was chaff. Especially the Romanov elements. The debriefings had run out his leads. They had milked him dry. He hadn't really made it easy for anyone. He had been trying constantly to revise United States policies, which were none of his business. It was time to put him in cold storage and hope he would quiet down.

For more than three years, the CIA saw to it that not a line about Goleniewski appeared in the nation's press. That was from January 12, 1961, the day he landed in Washington aboard a Military Air Transport plane, to March 4, 1964, the day the first story about him appeared in a newspaper, the New York *Journal-American.*

What set the background for the newspaper story was a congressional subcommittee's insistence that the CIA produce Goleniewski, for whom a private bill had been drawn that would grant him citizenship. The man who requested the private bill was Goleniewski. The CIA didn't want him to appear before the committee. It contended his security would be jeopardized. The subcommittee chairman, United States Representative Michael A. Feighan, Ohio Democrat, disagreed. The CIA stalled for several days. Finally Goleniewski was placed before the House Subcommittee on Immigration and Nationality. It was the first time he had been seen by any important persons outside the executive branch. The date was May 27, 1963.

Those three years in which Colonel Goleniewski was an invisible guest of the CIA, unsung and unnamed, constitute, I believe, Part 1 of the erroneous decisions made in his case, which have proved to be against the national interest. In all those three years, he was not introduced to Mr. Hoover, the man to whom the Heckenschuetzes' entire effort had been addressed, and the man with whom they had thought they were dealing.

This is inexcusable. We understand that Mr. Hoover doesn't see defectors, as a matter of policy. We understand that there are nice legal distinctions made between CIA and FBI responsibilities. But that is a dead letter compared with the importance of maintaining a link to an organization as helpful as the Heckenschuetzes. Mr. Hoover might be the first to state that he couldn't do anything for his visitor that the CIA couldn't. But from the viewpoint of the other side, of Goleniewski's side, it was a matter of confidence and psychology. There is no doubt that he would have imparted information to Hoover that he wouldn't tell anyone in the CIA or anyone in the FBI junior to Hoover. He would also have been able to report back to the Heckenschuetzes on a mission accomplished. Hoover, even if he refused to take a personal part in the debriefing, possibly would have named someone in the CIA he trusted completely.

Instead of meeting Mr. Hoover, Colonel Goleniewski was permitted to speak to two of Hoover's subordinates. He was taken on a tour of FBI Headquarters, in the Justice Department Building. He was shown the Dillinger, Crowley, and Bonnie and Clyde exhibits. He saw the displays on the crime laboratory, on fingerprints, on weapons. He might have seen the receptionist at the outer end of the long corridor leading to Hoover's office. He saw several pictures of the director and several American flags.

What a farce on the rituals of pecking order in the National Capital! If Gilbert and Sullivan were alive, they could do a whole musical comedy on the FBI sightseer who came out of the cold. What would have happened, it leads one to think, if a defector from the Japanese Navy, a few days before Pearl Harbor, had appeared before Mr. Hoover's receptionist with an urgent message for Hoover's ears only? Would he have been courteously bundled downstairs to see the fingerprints display?

There could have been many extenuating circumstances. Possibly no one in the CIA pressed the point with Hoover. Perhaps the CIA didn't want Goleniewski to see Hoover. Perhaps Mr. Hoover was already fed up with embarrassments resulting from the fact that the CIA rarely invited the FBI to the auspicious starts of their adventures but often asked for help at the bitter endings.

Any way you look at it, and considering what the Heckenschuetzes had already done for us, it was a mistake of historic proportions.

Another item belongs in Part I of the errors. It is the failure to find out who the Heckenschuetzes were and what could be done to resume contact with them. Clearly the CIA didn't put its heart into that inquiry. It knew the Heckenschuetzes had been anti-CIA from the start and must be getting more so as Goleniewski's wishes were ignored.

Part II in the saga of errors began on March 4, 1964, when the story of the Goleniewski case first broke into print. Both CIA and FBI spokesmen issued statements aimed at disparaging the colonel's importance. Some of the statements were deceptive. Some were outright lies. Their efforts had a certain desperation. The CIA had come through a drastic shakedown following its trials over the Bay of Pigs operation. Any more seismic upheavals threatened to sweep the agency out of existence. Goleniewski's Romanov pretensions proved invaluable to the government spokesmen in deprecating his believability and in disparaging his politics as royalist. To many Americans "royalist" and "faker" are interchangeable. In defense of these spokesmen, it must be conceded that they probably thought they were speaking the truth. It was what their seniors had told them. It is doubtful if as many as five persons in the government knew all the ramifications of the case.

Many times a thought must have come to Goleniewski. On that moment in West Berlin, on Christmas Day 1960, when he discovered he had a CIA reception committee, he should have gone back.

XIV

Who Are the Heckenschuetzes?

The Heckenschuetze organization derives from a Russian group known as the "Secret Circle." It had quite an ignominious start under Mad Czar Paul I in 1797. In a few short years, he tried to undo all the accomplishments of his mother, Catherine the Great, and he made such a mess of it that he was assassinated. The Secret Circle was started as a clandestine patriotic secret society with roots in the church, the court, the armed services, and the government departments. It waxed and waned in different periods, enlarged its base, turned into an anti-Bolshevik underground in the World War I period, and went deeply underground during Stalin's lifetime.

Colonel Goleniewski seemed always disinclined to talk about it in the ten or twelve times I interviewed him. What I was able to piece together came from snatches on different occasions.

A good deal of the formative pressure in the Secret Circle's history, he said, came in the days of the French Revolution. Royalty everywhere found their existence threatened and searched for measures to insure their survival.

The authority of the Secret Circle, as originally devised by Paul I, embodied the great influences in the motherland—God, the crown, fighting men ready to give their lives for God and country. They would be bound by secret oath. They would be permitted to enlist others in affiliated organizations, which were to include figures from a broad spectrum of Russian society, government, the professions, industry, such racial minorities as the Tartars, and such religious minorities as the Moslems and Roman Catholics.

All hereditary nobility were excluded. So were all members of the Imperial Family except the sovereign and his heir apparent. To insure the utmost secrecy, it was also stipulated, no member of the Secret Circle or one of its affiliates would know the identity of more than two other members.

The Secret Circle was decimated by the Stalinist purges of the late thirties, but it survived World War II. With Beria out of the way shortly after Stalin's death, Goleniewski claims, it enjoyed a great rebirth of power and effectiveness. It was to his position as his father's successor in the Secret Circle's top triumvirate that he owed most of his rapid strides after 1952.

The Secret Circle made no bids to the West, he said, until after it had played out its hand in the 1956 uprising in Hungary and the near revolutions in Poland and Czechoslovakia the same year. It was then that the Secret Circle decided it needed the help of the West. It was then that the code word of Heckenschuetzes was coined and the first letter to Hoover sent in care of United States Ambassador Henry J. Taylor in Berne, Switzerland, in April 1958.

But that first move was marred by an error. What made the Heckenschuetzes think, after their careful preparations in selecting Mr. Taylor as their mail drop to Hoover, that an anonymous request would cause the United States Government to rearrange its own Standard Operating Procedure? Their letter to Hoover went to the CIA. But they didn't know it. All the responses they got for nearly three years were signed "Hoover," the man Goleniewski has yet to meet.

In choosing Goleniewski for his assignments, the members of the Secret Circle entrusted him with a difficult and dangerous task. He became a quadruple agent, a man who had to juggle four balls at once.

An American intelligence official who interviewed Goleniewski on matters of their craft gave me this appraisal:

"He was an officer in Polish military intelligence. At the same time, he was employed by the Russians to keep tabs on all Polish intelligence services and personalities. He was also a member of the hierarchy of an anti-Bolshevik organization which operated at considerable peril, and under the greatest secrecy, in several Iron Curtain countries including the Soviet Union itself. Finally, while he was still 'in place' in the above roles, he maintained contact with the Americans, slipped several thousand documents and photographs to them on microfilm, and exposed dozens of KGB and GRU men of high and low rank."

A quadruple agent, of course, is another way of describing a four-role actor. This may be a practice one finds hard to shake on reaching safe ground, but it seems to me that we owe the Colonel a debt, and my impression of him—finicky as he is—is of a man who would be glad to tell the truth and the whole truth if he had absolute confidence in the one to whom he talked. We have given him every possible reason to be uncertain. Meanwhile, I hope we will lose no more time in trying to convince the Heckenschuetzes that there is really someone over here worth writing to.

It is here that the Three Gs must pass responsibility to official government authority. From here on it ought to be a federal case. Nothing less than a presidential commission should handle it.

Henceforward it's a matter for sworn testimony and cross-examination under oath. This process could have a tonic effect on some of the Romanovs, too, provided they're given fatherly advance warning on the penalties for perjury.

Common prudence should remind us that the pressures that

compelled Prime Minister Macmillan to defend Kim Philby before the House of Commons, and later John Profumo, long after they were exposed, may have been quite capable of balking Philby's chief nemesis over here.

The matter of Goleniewski and the Heckenschuetzes should be ventilated from start to finish, not to revive the old Cold War spy tensions, or to punish a few bureaucrats. It should be aired for the general enlightenment of all Russians and Americans.

Americans have lots more to value in our open society than the Kremlin does with its psychotic addiction to secrecy and its heavy reliance on KGB and GRU (military intelligence) hanky-panky.

Indeed, one of the worst features of the Goleniewski case is that America played it *à la russe*. America played it so deeply and darkly that, long after there was any need to hide it, most of our government officials who ought to have known about the case had no inkling about its important ramifications.

There are at least a dozen absorbing stories in the Goleniewski case. There are in it also at least a dozen clues to what's wrong with the Central Intelligence Agency. The CIA gets more than $500 million from us yearly, has a $47-million building, a splendid staff of scientists, scholars, readers, and electronic wizards, but somehow has failed to become an intelligence agency. For years it seemed unlikely that anything could be done with the CIA. Recently, however, a belated selection by President Nixon has aroused our hopes.

It was the appointment of Clark R. Mollenhoff to be deputy counsel to President Nixon. Mr. Mollenhoff, a Pulitzer prize-winning investigative reporter for Cowles Publications, knows better than most persons that the CIA's investigations are amateurish.

Mr. Mollenhoff's have never been. He won the Pulitzer prize for his uphill probing of labor racketeering. He was one of the few correspondents in Washington who ignored all the FBI and CIA spokesmen and kept right after the Goleniewski case until it was slated to be brought before the Senate Internal Security Subcommittee. Later on he repeatedly inquired why that subcommittee decided to duck it.

He would be ideally suited to ask the CIA why it never questioned the four men now in the United States who knew the real Alexei N. Romanov well and were in a position to determine whether Goleniewski is he. They are Kyril de Shishmarev; Count Alexis Buxhoeveden, cousin to Baroness Buxhoeveden, the Empress Alexandra's lady in waiting; and two officers on the Czar's yacht *Standart*—Baron George Taube and Paul Voronov.

He would enjoy, I am sure, trying to find out why the CIA never made the circuit followed by the volunteers of the Three Gs —never interviewed Henry Haskin in San Francisco, or dug up the Nicholas Romanov passport in Barrows' papers, or traced the McGarry papers to Saint Petersburg, or found the safe-deposit key of McGarry's marked "important." Or left a single footprint on the trails picked up by the Three Gs.

XV

Tie Score at Ekaterinburg—
What the Old Investigations Found

A primitive custom observed to this day in parts of New Guinea, Borneo, and Brazil makes a public display of the remains of a slain enemy chieftain.

The Italian partisans trussed up Mussolini's body by the ankles in a spectacle by which they sought to prove to the world that Il Duce would never again be able to smite his enemies. Pictures of the upside-down corpse were published in newspapers and magazines.

Castro, if reports are correct, staged executions of the more-despised Batista lieutenants in Cuban stadiums filled with spectators.

In the executions of such evangelical figures as John Huss and Thomas Münzer, the zealous church reformers of the religious rebellions of the Middle Ages, their detractors took delight in seeing to it that their cadavers and/or ashes, and therefore proof of their extinction, were viewed by thousands.

Only recently Iraq held public executions of the first batch of alleged Israeli spies that it had tried and convicted.

It is all the more cause for wonder, then, why the Bolsheviks treated the bodies of the hated Romanovs with all the secrecy of buccaneers burying gold in a secret cache on Treasure Island.

No photographs were taken for the world's press.

No crowds were called in to revel in the gory sight of imperial corpses and the indisputable evidence of czarism's demise.

No depositions were prepared for the benefit of historians from a committee of eyewitnesses especially chosen for the great event by the Ural District Soviet of Workers and Red Army Deputies.

The first announcement is duly recorded in the files of David R. Francis, American Ambassador to Russia in 1918, which are now in the archives of the Missouri Historical Society, in Saint Louis. It is dated Saturday, July 20, 1918, and its source is the Petrograd Telegraph Agency. It reads:

THE PRESIDENT OF THE CENTRAL EXECUTIVE COMMITTEE, SVERDLOFF, AT A MEETING OF THE PRESIDIUM OF THE COMMITTEE OF THE 18TH OF JULY, ANNOUNCED THAT HE HAD RECEIVED INFORMATION BY DIRECT WIRE FROM THE DISTRICT SOVIET OF THE URAL OF THE EXECUTION OF THE EX-CZAR, NIKOLAI ROMANOFF.

DURING THE LAST DAYS, THE CAPITAL OF THE "RED" URAL, EKATERINBURG, WAS SERIOUSLY THREATENED BY THE DANGER OF AN ADVANCE OF CZECHO-SLOVAK GANGS AT THE SAME TIME A NEW COUNTER-REVOLUTIONARY PLOT WAS DISCOVERED, WHICH HAD THE OBJECT OF SNATCHING OUT OF THE HANDS OF THE SOVIET GOVERNMENT THE CROWNED HANGMAN. IN VIEW OF ALL THESE CIRCUMSTANCES THE PRESIDIUM OF THE DISTRICT SOVIET OF THE URAL DECIDED TO EXECUTE, BY SHOOTING, NIKOLAI ROMANOFF, WHICH DECISION WAS DULY CARRIED INTO EFFECT ON THE 16TH OF JULY.

THE WIFE AND SON OF NIKOLAI ROMANOFF HAVE BEEN SENT OFF TO A SECURE PLACE. THE DOCUMENTS RESPECTING THE DISCOVERED PLOT HAVE BEEN FORWARDED TO MOSCOW. [No mention of the grand duchesses was made in the original announcement.]

IT WAS RECENTLY INTENDED TO BRING ROMANOFF TO TRIAL FOR ALL HIS CRIMES AGAINST THE PEOPLE. THE DEVELOPMENT OF EVENTS

WHICH HAVE JUST TAKEN PLACE PREVENTED THE EXECUTION OF THIS
INTENTION.

No photographs of any sort were given out.

The absence of eyewitness or photographic corroboration does
have extenuating circumstances. A hostile Czecho-Slovak force was
approaching the city. Many of Ekaterinburg's citizens were anti-
Bolshevik, and a public execution, or an ostentatious picture-taking
session around the bodies, might have led to an outbreak of riots.

But if there was time to cut up the corpses into bits and
destroy the diced fragments with acid and fire, there was time
to make a quiet photographic record of the momentous historical
event. There was time to gather a few depositions from witnesses.

But there was not so much as a picture handed out of the
lone body conjured up in the official statement. Was it because
not even that lone body existed?

This question hounded the Soviet Government for months afterward, as we shall see, and harried the various investigations launched
at the scene by the Whites—first by White Army officers, later
by Judge Nicholas A. Sokolov. As the year progressed, in fact,
the Whites seemed to develop a curious common interest with
the Reds in trying to end the spate of stories indicating that the
massacre was a myth, and it is more than likely, had there been a
photograph of any Romanov bodies to be bought, seized, or stolen,
one or the other side would have found it and used it. Let's
see what the facts are.

The theory that there *was* an assassination reposes very largely on
a base of controlled news—news handed out in 1918 by the
Communist government of Lenin and Trotsky. It has support
from other sources, chief of which are a few cursory local investigations and the monumental probe and report by Nicholas
Sokolov published in 1924. Sokolov, a White Russian, was Judge
of Instruction at the Court of Omsk.

The substance of all these diverse inquiries and findings is something like this:

Considerable evidence that an act of great violence and bloodshed took place, or was arranged to appear to have taken place, in one of the rooms in the basement of the Ipatiev House, Ekaterinburg, on the night of July 16–17, 1918. Skimpy evidence (no corpses, skulls, or identifiable large bones) that some members of the Imperial Family were shot, burned, and buried in the nearby pit of an abandoned mine, where some of the family's effects were found.

And then, completely contrary to the above:

Considerable evidence that all members of the family escaped secretly and by common agreement with the Communists that their disappearance should be enveloped in an aura of execution by a firing squad. Considerable evidence that this version is widely accepted by surviving relatives of the family.

Added to other data indicating that the story of the assassination was false, the evidence pro and con stacks up after fifty years as a kind of Mexican standoff that could give credence to either of the following two contentions:

All members of the Imperial Family were assassinated at Ekaterinburg.

Or all members of the Imperial Family made a secret, prearranged escape from a staged execution, and a pact with their captors that announcement of their deaths would not be challenged —not, at least, for a long time, and for their own safety.

Take your choice of the versions.

There is no overwhelming array of proof yet available to clinch the argument for either side. But in trying to assess the claims of Michal Goleniewski, the reader should certainly have a briefing on what evidence there is to bolster each of the versions.

Not long after the Imperial Family vanished from the Ipatiev House, a local group headed by an Ekaterinburg court investigator,

Nametkin, searched for clues in the Romanovs' second-floor living quarters. There were many signs of sudden evacuation. The occupants had left behind a wide assortment of personal knickknacks, some of which certainly must have been cherished possessions.

A few days later, another local search party concentrated on the lower floors of the Ipatiev House. This one was led by another member of the Ekaterinburg court, a man named Sergeev. In a group of rooms in the basement Sergeev noticed that the floors recently had been scrubbed, but red stains were still visible. The wallpaper showed signs of having been washed.

It was seven months before the most famous of all the investigators came on the scene. This was the moustachioed and energetic lawyer Nicholas Sokolov, the Judge of Instruction from Omsk.

His findings were later published in book form in three languages—Russian, French, and German. His work is the best known of at least five volumes written about the Ekaterinburg mystery. Four maintain an anti-Communist viewpoint. One is favorable to the Reds.

It is on Sokolov's book that there fell later most of the burden of supporting the arguments of many other authors and historians. That being the case, it is important to see exactly what his mission and methods were in the context of the time.

Sokolov was chosen for the task by the two leaders of the White Russian military forces, Admiral Alexander V. Kolchak, and that bright prodigy, General Michael C. Dieterichs, an officer who at one time had been the youngest general in the Czar's World War I army.

In the days immediately preceding July 16, the night the Romanovs disappeared, units of the Czecho-Slovak Legion and White Army had been pressing on Ekaterinburg. They took the city a day or two afterward. There had been fighting all around the area. The dead of both sides were being buried when the city capitulated. Wounded were being tended in impromptu aid stations.

The White Army command under General Dieterichs had barely set up its command post in the city when a group of officers were ordered to look into the whole question of what happened to the Romanovs. The General was fully aware of the fact that his rapid advance on the city in the hope of freeing the Imperial Family was undoubtedly one of the reasons why the Reds had been spurred into whatever hasty action they had taken.

The officers' probe didn't fare very well. Their efforts didn't suit the high command. The officers could find no hard evidence to bolster either theory—that the Romanovs had been shot, or that the Romanovs had escaped.

There were so many persons in Ekaterinburg who were sure the Imperial Family had managed to get away that their uniformed questioners, Dieterichs' officers, couldn't pin them down to sustained interrogation. Much of the citizenry, apparently, couldn't believe that the officers wanted to be taken seriously. That's when it was decided to turn to a trained evidence-finder like Judge Sokolov.

His appointment, in February 1919, came in the middle of the Siberian winter. By that time the case and its clues were cold in every sense of the word. They were as cold as the citizens were to the idea of any more inquisitions about the Romanovs.

After all, wasn't it seven months since that night of July 16–17? In all that time no imperial skulls or bodies had ever been found. What did Sokolov think he was going to dig up at this late date?

If ever an indifferent reception was waiting for a determined visitor, it was the greeting Ekaterinburg extended to Sokolov when he arrived from the city of Omsk. But Sokolov was not easily deterred.

As a staunch anti-Bolshevik in a difficult period for his country, he knew he had a twofold mission. It was (1) to prove that the Imperial Family had been massacred by the Communists, if the facts warranted, and (2) to prove that it had been done, if the facts warranted, in the most brutal possible style—a style the description of which would shock the civilized world.

An unnamed "expert artilleryman" and several junior aides helped Sokolov aim his probe at the most promising areas. One was the shot-up basement room in the Ipatiev House. The other was the reported burial site of the Romanovs—the abandoned "Four Brothers" mine, about thirteen miles from Ekaterinburg, out in the country.

Paraphrased from the Sokolov report, here are some of the findings reached after inspection of wood fragments from the room at the Ipatiev House:

Some of the bullets came from automatic pistols of the Browning type. Others came from American-made automatic pistols of the Colt .45 type. Others came from Nagant-type revolvers.

Some of the pieces of wood showed stains from what appeared to have been running or dripping blood. Other apparent bloodstains were quite dim. Five pieces of wood were submitted to scientific analysis for blood. These chemical/microscopic tests showed, " . . . it was not possible to demonstrate that the light, suspected stain [on one part of one of the wood fragments] was a stain of human blood; it is only established that this stain and similar stains [on the other part of one of the wood fragments] are bloodstains."

On the other hand, the report continues, "It was established by the present analysis that the bloodlike stains and running stains on material evidence [the four other pieces of wood] were formed by blood and that it was human blood."

The serological analysis, Sokolov stated, was made according to the Uhlenhuth method. It was used on the four pieces of wood that were adequate to its demands. On this, Sokolov wrote, "it was established that the liquid which has saturated the floorboards was undoubtedly albuminous," and "on the basis of the positive reaction obtained by the Uhlenhuth method, the specificity of which has been scientifically proved, it must be concluded that the extracts obtained by us from the suspected stains on the wood by letting them stand in a physiological solution of salt, are solutions of human blood serum, and that the stains on the floor-boards described in the record of proceedings of the Court Investigator in the matter undoubtedly came from human blood."

There was also an analysis of a part of the floor made at the request of a member of the court (Sergeev). A Van Deen test, a benzidine test, a Teichmann test, a spectroscopic examination, a microscopic examination, and an Uhlenhuth biological test were made for the presence of blood.

Results were described as follows:

1. Upon examination of the stain for the presence of blood, the Van Deen and Teichmann tests gave positive results.

2. Upon spectroscopic examination of the extracts from the given stain, two fairly clear absorption bands were produced in the yellow and green fields of the spectrum.

3. Upon microscopic examination of the scrapings from the given stains, an insignificant quantity of deformed red blood corpuscles were found, for the most part having become colorless.

4. The Uhlenhuth biological test (titer 1:1000 and 1:2000) gave a positive result.

From all this Sokolov summarized, ". . . on the basis of the microscopic and spectroscopic examinations, it must be concluded that on one of the excised pieces there are unquestionable traces of blood, which must be accepted as human since the Uhlenhuth reaction was positive."

On this hard foundation Sokolov constructs a highly imaginative and conjectural review of what had happened.

It is demonstrated that between 17 and 22 July 1918, when Ipatiev renewed the interrupted possession of his house, a murder occurred in it.

This did not occur on the upper floor, where the Imperial Family lived; there is not even a hint that violence was employed there against anyone.

The bloody carnage took place in one of the rooms of the lower, basement, floor.

The selection alone of this room speaks for itself: the murder was strictly premeditated.

From it there is no escape; behind it there is a deep storeroom without exit; its only window, with two sashes, is covered on the outside with a thick iron grating. It is deeply sunk in the ground and completely concealed from the outside by a high fence. This room is, in full degree, a torture chamber.

The murder was perpetrated with revolvers and bayonets.

More than thirty shots were fired, because it cannot be assumed that all the blows were transpiercing and that no bullets remained in the bodies of the victims.

Several people were murdered, because it cannot be supposed that one person could change his position in the room to such an extent and submit to so many blows.

Some of the victims were, before death, in positions along the east and south walls; others were nearer to the center of the room. Several were hit while they were already lying on the floor.

If the Imperial Family and those living with them were murdered here, there is no doubt that they were lured here from their living quarters by some false pretext.

Our ancient law calls such murders "foul."

By using such words and phrases as "torture chamber," "bloody carnage," and "foul," Sokolov's report shows remarkable dexterity in blending the skills of the propagandist with those of the investigator, coroner, and prosecutor. This is especially true considering that no bodies had been found and no evidence strong enough to indict anyone for anything more serious than messing up a room by firing live ammunition.

The room supplied an opportunity to seize the idea that a massacre had been committed in it. But all the evidence boiled down to three words—bullets, wreckage, and bloodstains. They are precisely what could have been put there to stage the appearance of a violent crime. Gossip to that effect was all over Ekaterinburg, but Sokolov gives it brief mention, and that later.

After focusing long and hard at the Ipatiev House, Sokolov, in the best cinematic style, pans his camera to the city and country outside.

He reports that two brothers, Peter and Alexander Leonov, whom he questioned in April 1919, "testified that late at night on July 16th a motor truck was dispatched to the building of the Cheka. They sent the chauffeur, Nikiforov, back and took the automobile [truck] to the Ipatiev House. It was returned in the morning of July 19th."

Peter Leonov described the returned vehicle as follows:

"The entire platform of the truck was stained with blood. It was apparent that the platform had been washed and swept with a broom. But the blood, nevertheless, was clearly visible on the floor of the platform."

His brother, Alexander Leonov, said: "I remember very well that the platform had a large, washed bloodstain."

Sokolov also reports that on July 17 an employee of the Commissariat of Supply, a man named Zimin, appeared in the apothecary shop "Russian Community" in Ekaterinburg, and in the name of the Oblast Commissar, Peter Voikov, presented written requisitions to the manager, Metzner, ordering more than 396 pounds of sulphuric acid. This, according to Sokolov, was brought to the Four Brothers mine by personnel of the Red Army and by one of the employees of the Commissariat of Supply.

A large quantity of gasoline was also carried to the mine, Sokolov states. After evaluating the testimony of a number of persons who claimed to have seen men moving gasoline to the site, he estimates that not less than 1440 pounds of this inflammable fluid was hauled there.

Sokolov's camera then sweeps to the mine site near Koptyaki, a small village on the shore of Lake Isetsky. In the mine, he reports, many effects of Nicholas' family were found. Among such items were miniatures, frames, a military badge, two buckles (one probably the Czar's and the other probably the Czarevich's), ladies' shoe buckles, a white vial of salts, a lens from spectacles (probably the Czarina's), two lenses from a pince-nez (probably belonging to Dr. Eugene Botkin, the Czar's physician), scorched portions of corsets (possibly the Czarina's or the Grand Duchesses' or the maid's, Anna Demidova's, or all), pieces of leather, men's buckles, military-style buttons and other buttons (several from the Czarina's lilac suit), hooks and eyes, pieces of fabric, strips of cloth, an American suitcase key, splinters of glass, a jeweled cross, a brilliant (probably the Czarina's), parts of pearls (either from the Czarina's or the Grand Duchesses' strings), splinters of emerald, splinters of sapphires, a ruby, two almandines, two adamants, two gold chains, topazes, twenty-four pieces of lead, two bullets from a revolver of the Nagan type and one steel jacket from such a bullet, a human finger and two pieces of human skin (the finger belonging to an adult woman of middle age), the corpse of a female dog (several members of the Imperial Family's suite testified that this was probably the body of Jemmy, the Grand Duchess Anastasia's pet), splinters of mammal bones (badly burned and chopped), false teeth (probably Dr. Botkin's), and other things.

Thereupon Sokolov is moved to another one of his remarkably imaginative summations. He writes:

> The mine gave up the secret of the Ipatiev House.
>
> During the evening of July 16 the Imperial Family, and those living with them, were alive.
>
> Early in the morning of July 17, under cover of the darkness of the night, an auto truck carried their corpses to the mine in the tract of the Four Brothers.
>
> On the clay area, at the open shaft, the corpses were stripped. The

clothing was crudely removed, torn away, and cut with knives. Several of the buttons were destroyed in the process, hooks and eyes stretched.

The concealed jewels were, of course, exposed. Several of them that fell with many others on the clay area remained unnoticed and were trampled in the upper layers of this area.

The main purpose was to destroy the bodies. For this it was necessary, first of all, to dissect the corpses, to cut them up. This was done on the clay area.

The blows of the sharp cutting instruments, cutting the corpses apart, cut some of the jewels that were trampled in the earth.

A commission of experts established that several of the jewels were destroyed by strong blows of some hard objects: not sharp cutting instruments. These were jewels that had been sewn into the brassieres of the Grand Duchesses and destroyed by the bullets entering their bodies at the time of the murder.

The dissected bodies were burned in the bonfires with the aid of gasoline and destroyed with sulphuric acid. The bullets which remained in the bodies fell into the fires. The lead was melted, ran onto the ground and then, cooling, acquired the shape of hardened drops. The empty bullet casing remained.

The corpses, burned on the bare ground, gave up fat. Running out, it impregnated the soil.

The torn and cut pieces of clothing were burned in the same fires. In several there were hooks, eyes, and buttons. They were preserved in burnt form. Several hooks and eyes, having been burned, remained fastened together, unseparated.

Noticing some of the objects remaining, the criminals threw them into the shaft after having first broken the ice in it. Then they covered them with earth.

Here we have the same picture as in the Ipatiev House: the concealment from the world of the evil that had been committed.

Thus it is the very best, the most valuable, witnesses which speak of the crime—mute objects.

Now let us listen to what the cunning human tongue has to say about it.

With this slightly cynical remark Sokolov introduces his gallery of "witnesses," and it is not long after starting to read their testimony that anyone can observe the difficulties under which this persevering judge had been laboring.

Almost instantly you'll agree with his earlier and unorthodox conclusion, which must come as a jolt to jurists the world over, that "mute objects" are the "best" and "most valuable" witnesses of all.

In this case he was right. The mute objects were certainly better than almost all the witnesses he was able to round up, and the reason for that was that only one person out of the dozens who gave formal testimony might reasonably be believed actually to have seen the goings on inside the room in the Ipatiev House, or looked inside the truck, or observed the activities at the mine shaft before objects were hurled into it.

All the others were hearsay witnesses, relating what someone else had told them; or perimeter witnesses who saw a portion of one event or another from afar, but nothing conclusive; or witnesses who said that they heard shots from inside the Ipatiev House; or witnesses who heard or saw a truck coming or going from the Ipatiev House or the mine site; or witnesses who saw a vehicle before or after the crucial events of the night of July 16.

The sole exception was Paul Medvediev, the guard who acted as right-hand man to Yakov Yurovsky. Yurovsky was commandant at the Ipatiev House for the last two weeks of the Romanovs' residence there. If they were executed, it is generally agreed, he planned and supervised it. If they escaped, as Goleniewski contends, he masterminded it.

Medvediev's contribution to the sum total of truth is gravely impaired by the sharp contradictions among the versions of his story that he gave other witnesses, of whom one, unfortunately, was his wife.

Like a ripple running over water in reverse, from the outer

periphery to the source, Medvediev's tales approach the Sokolov record via third-hand hearsay.

A guard, Michael Letemin, deposes that another guard, Andrew Strekotin, told him Medvediev was in the assassination room with Yurovsky. Yurovsky "shot the Czar and killed him on the spot." After that, Letemin quotes Strekotin, the Lett soldiers and Medvediev "began to shoot."

Another guard, Philip Proskuryakov, definitely fingers Medvediev as one of the assassins, saying: "Pashka himself (Medvediev) told me that he shot 2–3 bullets at the Czar and other persons when they shot. I am telling the absolute truth. Never at any time did he say to me that he, allegedly, did not himself shoot, but went out to hear the shooting from outside. In this he lies."

When Medvediev comes onto the record with his own story, however, he says Yurovsky told him, "Today, Medvediev, we are going to shoot the whole family."

Then, according to Medvediev, Yurovsky told him to "go outside and look in the street" and "listen for the shots." Just as soon as he got outside, Medvediev says, he "heard shots from the firearms" and "went back into the house to tell Yurovsky that the shots could be heard." In other words, he places himself outside the room at shooting time.

Entering the room where the Imperial Family was, he continues, he found all members had been shot and were lying on the floor in various positions.

Near them was a mass of blood, according to Medvediev's picture. The blood was thick, "like liver." With the exception of Alexei, all, apparently, were already dead. Alexei was still groaning. In Medvediev's presence Yurovsky shot Alexei two or three more times with a Nagan, and the youth stopped groaning. The members of the Imperial Family had several gunshot wounds in various parts of their bodies.

The faces of all were covered with blood, and the clothing of all was bloody.

He, Medvediev, didn't take part in any of the shooting, he said, and he didn't know where the corpses were taken and didn't ask anyone.

Medvediev also said that it was Yurovsky who woke the Imperial Family about midnight. "Whether he told them why he was disturbing them or where they were supposed to go—I do not know. I confirm that it was precisely Yurovsky who went into the rooms where the Imperial Family was. Yurovsky did not give either me or Constantine Dobrynin the duty of awakening the sleepers."

But Medvediev's wife, Maria, contradicts her husband on two vital points. She said he told her that it was he who was ordered to awaken the Imperial household about 2 A.M., and he sent Constantine Dobrynin to do it; and he was also among those, he told her, who fired at the victims.

Among those assassinated, said Medvediev, were the Romanovs' physician, Dr. Eugene Botkin; the maidservant, Anna Demidova, and the two manservants, Kharitonov and Trupp.

As varied and cryptically inconclusive as the accounts of the witnesses, were the official messages about the events at Ekaterinburg sent from there and from Moscow by the Communist officials. According to which of these you want to believe, from those sent during July 1918 Nicholas alone was killed, or his whole family was killed with him, or the Czarina and Alexei were the only ones spared, or everyone was killed including Dr. Botkin and the three servants. Sokolov finds a clear design behind this jugglery of versions, some of which were found in the files of the telegraph office at Ekaterinburg. He cites the desire of the worried Bolshevik leaders to quell the anxiety of the Germans over the fate of the German-born Czarina and her children. He contends that the Communists got wind of a plan of the Berlin government to insist that the Russians permit a battalion of the Kaiser's infantry to be stationed in the Soviet capital in order to protect the lives of Germany's nationals and diplomats there; so the Communist leaders, hoping to forestall this humiliating demand, according to Sokolov, got out new communiqués worded to set minds at rest about the safety of the Czarina, the Czarevich, and the Grand Duchesses.

A glance at the record reflects this constant change in the reports.

On July 21, for example, the official Bolshevik Press Bureau sent a telegram (No. 6153) from Moscow to the Oblast Soviet in Ekaterinburg. It was dated two days before (July 19). Its contents, reporting the execution of Nicholas and the sparing of his wife and son, appear earlier in this chapter.

That's one version—Nicholas killed, wife and son safe, no news about the Grand Duchesses.

But another version was probably given to Sverdlov, as early as a few minutes after 9 P.M., July 17 (the day after the Romanovs went to bed for the last time in the Ipatiev House), according to Sokolov. He writes: "On July 17, after 9 o'clock in the evening, he [Sverdlov] had in his possession a telegram whose contents were as follows:

TELL SVERDLOV ENTIRE FAMILY SUFFERED SAME FATE AS HEAD OFFICIALLY FAMILY PERISHED IN EVACUATION

That word "officially" could prove to be apocalyptic. It could mean, "that's the cover story."

That telegram was sent by one Beloborodov to one Gorbunov, with instructions that it be transmitted to Sverdlov. There's no proof, of course, that it was, but it represents another version—all dead.

There were other telegrams, other messages, other versions, accompanied by comments of incredulity from Sokolov that Moscow should be issuing announcements a day or two ahead of anyplace else, while Ekaterinburg, where the melodrama took place, didn't even dare to mention it until the men in the Executive Central

Committee (TsIK) took the lead. He expands on the theme that
new versions, which softened the earlier ones, were gotten out
because the Communists knew they simply couldn't face the moral
outrage of the world over the murder of innocent children and their
mother.

But when all is said and done, one must face up to the fact
that the White Army leaders under Admiral Kolchak, and even
Sokolov himself, may have been fully informed about the secret
escape of the Imperial Family. Thus there is more than a possibility
that the whole Sokolov investigation was designed, for the sake
of the Romanovs' own safety, to bolster an assassination story that
was constantly weakening under word-of-mouth tales and the continuing failure of anyone to find bodies or skeletons.

The blood that spattered the room at the Ipatiev House? The
woman's finger said to have been found in the mine? One or
two cadavers from the city morgue would have been more than
adequate.

In light of all the wavering testimony and changing dispatches
reported by Sokolov, then, one small item he unearthed appears
from the perspective of half a century to be the most portentous
of all.

He reports that Commissar Voikov, who supplied the sulphuric
acid for the operations at the mine shaft, when asked later about
the fate of the Romanovs, replied with all the tartness of the
product he procured:

"The world will never know what we did with them."

For many decades he proved to be right.

One must certainly concede, after reading his report, that the
indefatigable judge from Omsk made a valiant effort to prove
that there was a bloody assassination of the Romanovs at Ekaterinburg. What censure he deserves from members of his profession
should center around those highly imaginative scenarios he wove
from the thinnest kind of factual thread. That, apparently, was the

mission he was assigned. A fair judgment of Sokolov's ability depends on what his real motives were. If they were to shore up the crumbling legend of the assassination and thereby to improve the security of the sequestered Imperial Family, that's one thing. If they were really to "prove" there was an assassination, that's another.

It fell to two others to record far more graphically the unnerving atmosphere in which Sokolov was forced to proceed with his probe. One was General Dieterichs himself, who wrote a book also. The other was Captain Paul Bulygin, who had formerly been attached to the staff of the Dowager Czarina Marie and who was in command of her security forces. He, too, wrote a book. Both devoted more attention than Sokolov did to the trouble he experienced in persuading any of the Ekaterinburg residents to disengage their minds from the belief that all the Romanovs, as well as Dr. Botkin and the three servants, were allowed to escape.

If Sokolov's motive was merely to plug the holes in the legend, he was probably fortunate in being unable to find any better "witnesses." Their vague and conflicting statements gave him plenty of maneuvering room for his own re-enactments of what happened at the Ipatiev House, at the mine, and in the vehicles that came and went that night. If, on the other hand, his motive was a genuine search for the truth, the "witnesses" could hardly have been much worse.

Most, if not all, of the right kind of witnesses were simply unavailable. They were gone with the wind. Beyond reach and beyond the power of a Sokolov summons were the Red soldiers who followed out their superiors' orders—whatever those orders were—in the basement room of the Ipatiev House.

Similarly safe from Sokolov's beck and call were all the Communist officials in Moscow and Ekaterinburg who decreed what they decreed and did what they did in July 1918. Thus the very features of Sokolov's enterprise that militated against his being able to find "the facts" provided an ideal climate for the fabrication of fairy tales.

High in the latter category must seem, to laymen and criminologists alike, to be the contention that gasoline and sulphuric acid could obliterate all signs of the minced-up flesh, skulls, and bones of eleven persons (the Romanovs, Dr. Botkin, and the servants) in the matter of a few hours' pounding and burning near the mine shaft. Anyone who has tried to use gasoline and chemicals to destroy a small animal carcass, and knows how long it takes to do a partial job, will remain skeptical of Sokolov's story of that enigmatic July dawn. This is the same acid that moved Joseph Lasies to such heights of sarcasm in his verbal exchange with Robert Wilton.

The bodies of the Romanovs—if there was an assassination— could have been destroyed or buried elsewhere, at a site that the Communists for reasons of their own have kept secret. That is a distinct possibility.

For no one can deny that the circumstantial evidence of their disappearance, of the shot-up room at the Ipatiev House, of the coming and going of one or more trucks, etc., indicate they might have been killed and their bodies carried away, and some of their belongings thrown into the mine. But that is a very different matter from accepting Sokolov's voluminous chronicle as everlasting proof that what he claims happened actually did happen.

Yet one historian after another, impressed, in all likelihood, by the array of words, testimony, and reconstruction in Sokolov's work, or impressed, without having read it himself, by the respect others have shown it, has come to regard it as the absolute gospel of corroboration of the Romanovs' murder and extinction.

Numerous hints to the contrary, and some tangible portents much stronger than hints, now indicate that posterity—with the help of Nicholas and his family—may have been hoodwinked by one of history's major subterfuges.

But one of the greatest sources of doubt about Sokolov's findings comes from the woman *who paid for their publication—the Dowager Czarina.*

A preamble to her role and attitude appears in Sokolov's own text when he describes his final difficulties and the close call he experienced in saving the material for his book.

> On February 7, 1920, after the death of Admiral Kolchak, I was in Harbin. The situation was difficult. There was no money. In February I addressed a letter to the Ambassador of Great Britain in Pekin, Mr. Lamson, and requested that he furnish me with the means to bring the reports of the investigation and the material evidence to Europe. I stated that among the material evidence there were relics of the Imperial Family.
>
> On February 23, the Ambassador's secretary, Mr. Keith, came to me and stated that the Ambassador had submitted the request to his government, in London. Lamson, apparently, had no doubt of an affirmative reply. My car was attached to Keith's train and put under guard. On March 19 the English consul in Harbin, Mr. Sligh, gave me the English Government's reply. It was laconic. "We are unable." With General Dieterichs I turned to the French General, Janin. He told us that he would ask no one, because help in this matter was considered a duty of honor. Thanks to General Janin it was possible to save the reports of the investigation and the material evidence. I cannot pass over in silence the names of two Russians. A merchant in Harbin, I. T. Shchelokov, obtained an ingot of gold from the peasant F. M. Vlassov, from which the sum of 3000 yen was realized. With this money I was able to get to Europe and save the investigation.

Sokolov goes on to tell how money was supplied to him to get his notes, manuscript, and exhibits to Europe. Yet it is from the book by Captain Bulygin, the Dowager Czarina's former military aide, *The Murder of the Romanovs* (London: Hutchinson & Co., Ltd., 1935), that we learn precisely how the money was raised to publish Sokolov's book. It came in the form of five thousand dollars from Dowager Czarina Marie, Captain Bulygin writes. She felt, according to Bulygin, that the "evidence" or "lack of evidence" should become available to the world.

Did she also want to help her son—possibly at his own clandestine request—improve the depth of his cover? Especially when so many rumors and newspaper stories were flying around to the effect that the whole family escaped? We may never learn the whole answer to that question.

Sokolov's book, appearing first in French, was published in Paris in 1924. He died the same year. A Russian translation was published in Berlin in 1925.

But the Dowager Czarina herself supplied a clue to why she financed the publication of Sokolov's volume and how, at the same time, she disagreed with its conclusions.

To the day of her death in 1928 she kept insisting to her intimate friends that Nicholas and all the members of his family had escaped from Ekaterinburg and were alive and well.

It has been demonstrated, then, that there is far more than a good chance that the Romanovs not only escaped from the Communists but from the death knell of Sokolov.

Judge Sokolov's conclusions probably carried greater weight with scholars and historians than they did with the general public. Nevertheless, they contributed heavily to the pro side of the assassination controversy.

Thus, in the twenties and early thirties it was a matter of opinion as to which side held the edge around the world—the Sokolov and Robert Wilton side, or the contrary view espoused by Joseph Lasies and Carl W. Ackerman. The latter enjoyed the support of many stories, from several European cities, which held that the Romanovs were all alive.

But as the thirties turned into the forties, and the forties into the fifties, with still no Czar or Czarevich out of the underground, there was no question any longer about which side had the edge.

The majority of those who had any thoughts about the matter at all were fully adjusted to the notion that the Imperial Family had been wiped out. If not, any reasonable person would ask, why hadn't one or two of them showed up?

Few were interested enough, or well enough versed, to consider that the Romanovs might have been very anxious to show up but were deterred by the thought of the grim reception Stalin might have given them, by the certain opposition of some of the bankers, by the scorn of many Russians and others who detested what czarism stood for, by the long homicidal reach apparently displayed by the Kremlin when Trotsky was tracked down and murdered in Mexico in 1940, by the German invasion of Poland in World War II and Hitler's rumored plans to install another branch of the house of Romanov at the top of a constitutional monarchy in conquered Russia, by Stalin's postwar perseverance in power.

Fewer still were sophisticated enough about the case to realize that at least two members of the Imperial Family—a real or asserted Alexei (Goleniewski) and a real or asserted Anastasia (Mrs. Eugenia Smith)—might have been trying for years to "show up" despite the obstacles enumerated and despite the fact that their efforts were impaired by the congenital Romanov tendency to answer forthright questions with royal ambiguity.

Part Two

FOR THE RECORD

XVI

"The English Baby"

For two and a half centuries after the reign of Peter the Great, there had been a fabulous royal town fifteen miles south of Saint Petersburg (now Leningrad). Its grand scheme smacked of Graustark.

There were two palaces, only fifteen hundred feet apart. One, the Catherine Palace, was blue and white, with more than two hundred rooms. It was decorated with mother-of-pearl, marble, amber, lapis lazuli, silver, and gold. The other, the less ornate Alexander Palace, had one hundred rooms.

They stood on parts of 1680 acres of landscaped park and botanical gardens in which statues, pavilions, and kiosks were interspersed. There was a network of shaded walks, two bandstands, a parade ground, and an artificial lake for small sailboats and toy yachts. On one end of the lake was a pink Turkish bath and not far away a synthetic hill crowned by a red-and-gold Chinese pagoda. There was also a Chinese village, bridge, and theater as the result of an awakened interest in the land of the Manchus on the part of Catherine II.

The whole iron-fenced enclosure was protected by bearded Cossack cavalrymen of the Imperial Guard known as "The Konvoy."

They wore fur caps and red tunics and liked to swing their flashing sabers in the sunlight. They were assisted by brightly uniformed sentries from Imperial Guard regiments, and by lurking, less flashy, but more sinister, pairs of plainclothesmen of the Okhrana, the imperial secret police.

In spring and summer the colors in the gardens and shrubbery outside were matched if not surpassed by the attire of the officers and jeweled ladies of the court and by the liveries of the swarms of servants fitted into motifs to match the blue, green, purple, beige, and scarlet interiors of the different palace rooms where they were stationed. This was Tsarskoe Selo, or "The Czar's Village." For all the connection it had to the real world it might as well have consisted of sugar and spice, of chocolate soldiers and confectioners' castles. It looked like what it was—the dreams and handiwork of rich and imaginative women. Almost everything except the smaller palace had been the creation of Elizabeth, Peter the Great's daughter, or of a later and more flamboyant tenant, Catherine the Great. No one foresaw that it might prove to be a trap for the rulers who occupied it, that it might impose an optical illusion about the nature of the country they ruled.

This peril was heightened by the fact that it had always been a pampered community. It got the best of everything first. The first Russian railway, built in 1837–38, linked it with Saint Petersburg. In 1887 it became the first town on the European continent to be lighted by electricity. It got the best water supply, drainage, and sanitation systems. These combined with a dry climate to make it one of the most healthful places to live in all Russia.

It has, to this day, remained largely unchanged. The Soviets have preserved it, perhaps partly as a lesson, but mostly because they have found uses for it. Some of the villas have been converted into schools and hospitals. Parts of the palaces have become museums. Communist officials renamed it first, rather appropriately, Detskoe Selo, or "Children's Village," then changed it to what it's called today, Pushkin, in honor of the Russian poet who attended the newly formed Lyceum on the grounds from 1811 to 1817.

Gone are the saber-swinging Cossacks, the courtiers, the liveried servants, the armed sentries. But the grounds and buildings have been well preserved. Busloads of tourists can stare at the spires and castle turrets as if they were on a set for *The Prisoner of Zenda.*

One thing is not hard to understand. If you lived in Tsarskoe Selo in the days of Nicholas II, you didn't forget it. Kyril de Shishmarev hasn't forgotten it. He lived there for the best part of the first ten years of his life.

Tsarskoe Selo had a tree-lined boulevard flanked by mansions of the court's principal families. The Shishmarevs lived in one of them. It was a white, English-style country home of twenty-three rooms. It stood on four and a half acres enclosed by a brick fence. There were lawns, and two formal gardens, and stables with five English riding horses, and a carriage house with two carriages and two sleighs. One light sleigh was often used by Colonel Shishmarev in Saint Petersburg, where he also had a town house, to race his brother officers down the Nevsky Prospekt.

A staff of thirteen to fifteen servants manned the Shishmarev household at Tsarskoe. They included a butler, cook, footmen, a French maid for Kyril's American mother, housemaids, kitchen-maids, gardeners, grooms, two regimental orderlies from the Tirailleurs Regiment, and Grigori (Grisha), the peasant coachman.

Access from the boulevard was blocked by the high brick fence and an imposing iron gate. Inside the gate was a circular drive that led to the front door of the mansion. The gate was more often shut than open. Its distance from the house was not great, however, and a good loud shout from a playmate at the gate could easily be heard by Kyril or his brother, Michael, more than two years his junior.

The Shishmarevs were rich enough to build a show place of their own at Tsarskoe Selo. But one simply didn't dream of trying to upstage the Imperial Family on their own home grounds— not if one was connected with the court, not even if one was a grand duke.

On the paternal side, the Shishmarevs were related to many of the nation's influential families, among them the Vassilchikovs. They were rooted to ancient, land-owning, untitled boyar nobility, and their ancestors were among the members of the council of boyars that elected Michael Romanov, another untitled boyar, as Czar of Russia in 1613. The boyar, or untitled line, contrasts with the *tchin,* or "service-to-the-state" nobility, which Peter the Great originated partly to offset the power of the land-owning boyars.

For generations, however, the Shishmarevs had served the state. They were diplomats, explorers, and officers of the Army, Navy, and Guards Corps. To this day there is a village in Alaska, Shish-maref, near Bering Strait, named in honor of a family forebear, Gleb Semënovich Shishmarev. He was a navigator of the Kotzebue Scientific Expedition of 1815–18. The Shishmarevs owned agricultural tracts in the cold northlands and the warmer southlands near the Black Sea.

On the maternal side, Kyril's generation of Shishmarevs was linked to the Frys of Kentucky, the Gurneys and Cadburys of England, the Rohans of Austria, and the Chandors of Hungary and the United States. The mistress of the Tsarskoe Selo household, Kyril's mother, Louise Alfredovna, was a wholly American product who had been born and schooled in France. Her father was John Alfred Chandor, a Harvard-educated diplomat who was second secretary of the American Embassy in Paris when Louise was born there in 1882.

On a visit to Saint Petersburg, Louise met her handsome Russian suitor when he was a captain in the Imperial Army. They were married in 1906 in the private chapel of the Grand Duchess Xenia, the Czar's sister. Xenia and her husband, the Grand Duke Alexander, served as the pair's Christian sponsors in the wedding ceremony.

Kyril, the Shishmarevs' first child, was born the following year. One of his two godmothers was the Grand Duchess Serge, the Empress Alexandra's older sister. Michael, the Shishmarevs' second child, was born about two and a half years later. In the years of her sons' development at Tsarskoe, Louise Shishmarev was a dynamic and diminutive, blue-eyed brunette who packed a wallop out of proportion to her small frame. She busied herself on literary and cultural matters, but she held a tight rein over the servants and nurses. They called her "Barina" (the Russian equivalent of Lady). They executed her orders as if she, too, were a colonel, if not a general. Her friends called her "Louise."

Compared with the two palaces at Tsarskoe, the Shishmarev residence was modest. It was also rather small compared with the size of the family's properties in the Crimea and at Kuerovo, eighteen miles west of Tsarskoe. It was Kuerovo where regiments of the Guards Corps almost invariably ended their summer maneuvers while their officers stayed in the two great houses as guests of the Shishmarevs. The estate measured in square miles. There was no servant problem. Approximately five thousand families, including tenant farmers, abided on the Shishmarev estates in northern and southern Russia.

Though Kyril was almost three years younger than Czarevich Alexei, he was in the circle of children approved as playmates for the emperor's son. His part in this role began with a pair of nicknames—"The English Baby" and "The Russian-English Baby." He won these sobriquets, he said, even before he graduated from a baby carriage powered by a Russian nurse to a state of romping self-propulsion under the watchful eye of a real English governess, Miss Mathews.

In the course of a recent interview in his New York apartment,

Mr. de Shishmarev told me, "My mother was enamored of English nannies, English clothes, and English baby carriages. When my brother and I were in baby carriages, at different times we had Russian nurses. But they dressed as English as mother could make them. When we went outside at Tsarskoe Selo we cut a figure as totally British as a fleet review of Spithead.

"The baby carriages were large, complicated things with big wheels and brakes and movable covers. I think they came from Harrods, London. They were definitely not Russian. The nurses. The nurses' uniforms had big white cuffs and collars—all linen. Our clothes and sailor suits came from London, too. We must have looked like a British fifth column in the nest of the czars.

"When I matriculated from nurse to governess, my doom was sealed. Miss Mathews not only looked English. She *was* English. She was erect and slim. She was a pretty brunette, and her diction was perfect Oxonian. Mother had chosen her with care. Having started out at Tsarskoe on wheels, so to speak, as 'The English Baby,' I remained 'The English Baby' no matter how much I grew, as long as Miss Mathews in her prim English dress was hovering around. That was just about all the time. It got to be a joke. I got damn' tired of it. Even Alexei and the Emperor were in on it a few times.

"Someone would say—'Oh, there's the English baby!' Then up would come the answer, 'Oh no—he's not English. He's Russian-English. Only his nurse and clothes are English!' But the nickname stuck."

His sometimes rambunctious reaction to the "English Baby" albatross often fitted the mood of the high-spirited heir to the throne. Their inclination for each other's company was strengthened by a friendly relationship that sprang up between the immaculate Miss Mathews and the more scholarly, but equally well-groomed, Miss Schneider, Alexei's German tutor. Especially in the last two years before the Revolution, said Mr. de Shishmarev, Alexei frequently came over in the afternoon to play or attend a party. He would be accompanied by Miss Schneider and one of his two body-guards, the two sailors from the Imperial Navy "Dena" Derevenko and Nagorny.

Often a call would be a surprise. The Alexander Palace was only fifteen minutes by carriage from the Shishmarevs'. Any time of day Alexei would step out of his carriage, run to the gate, and shout for Kyril. Kyril, on his part, was invited to the palace to play with Alexei while Miss Mathews chitchatted happily with Miss Schneider. In the summer Kyril never missed the military reviews on the palace parade ground, where his father, at the head of his regiment, could be seen marching past the Czar with the Czarevich at his side. Once, before the Revolution, Mr. de Shishmarev remembers, both Nicholas and Alexei came to Kuerovo for the ceremonies marking the end of the Guards Corps summer maneuvers. All the Shishmarevs were there, and the imperial visitation brought great excitement to the tenants of the estate, though Mr. de Shishmarev recalls that some of the older residents couldn't understand what all the fuss was about, reminding the younger sons, "In the old days the Czar came here every year."

Russia's great upheaval in 1917 ended everything Tsarskoe Selo stood for. It turned the fairyland into an imperial jail when the Provisional Government ordered the Romanovs confined there minus most of their armed and liveried retinue. It put Kyril, his mother, and his brother into flight to the United States. It took the life of Colonel Shishmarev. But it left Alexei, then twelve and thirteen, and Kyril, then nine and ten, with a store of common memories. As the months passed, Mr. de Shishmarev said, and he was speaking fifty-two years later, those memories came to mean more and more to him after he heard the grim news of the assassination.

The Shishmarevs reached California after an exciting trip on the Trans-Siberian Railway. Their train started a few hours behind

one that left Moscow with an American flag flying on its locomotive. It was the official train of a U.S. munitions and supply
mission headed by former Secretary of State Elihu Root. Imperial
Army officers on the second train persuaded Mrs. Shishmarev to
use her American charm on Mr. Root to borrow an American flag
for their locomotive, too. They thought it would provide better
insurance against marauding revolutionaries. Her chance came
when a blown bridge stalled the first train and the second overtook
it. Mrs. Shishmarev trudged up to Mr. Root's car. He graciously
handed her a spare Old Glory nailed to a stick.

"It went right on our locomotive," said Mr. de Shishmarev. "We
had no more trouble all the way to Vladivostok."

In California young Kyril and his brother began a new life as
cadets in the Mount Tamalpais Military Academy in San Rafael.
The uniforms and martial music, the shakos and swords, were
helpful in the change-over. They seemed like bits of Tsarskoe
Selo. But the boys knew they were in exile. The formal change in
the family name reminded them of it—from "Shishmarev" to "de
Shishmarev." The prefix "de" meant they were out of their native
land.

Bits of Tsarskoe Selo kept haunting the boys more forcefully
all the time. As he grew older, said Mr. de Shishmarev, his boyhood
memories of that incomparably colorful compound continually became more poignant and bittersweet, like the living picture of his
father, whom he knew he would never see again. And the memories,
strangely enough, he added, instead of becoming hazier, seem to
grow clearer and clearer with the years: years as a student at
London University, in the Foreign Legion, in Paris and Hollywood
as a writer and movie scenarist, in Alaska and Europe, with the
United States Army of World War II, in a Spanish hospital re-
covering from a roadside accident that hurled him off a bridge
and impaired his health for several years.

It was particularly in those interminable months in a hospital bed, he observed, that the flashbacks of Tsarskoe Selo sharpened into a set of recurring patterns: the number of times he would respond to the shouts of Alexei and other kids from the iron gate; the afternoon at the Alexander Palace parade ground when Alexei stood next to his father on the reviewing line, dressed in a Cossack uniform—red tunic, white hood, black boots, and striped papakha. Something happened then that was unforgettable. Miss Mathews and those damned mocking voices: "Oh, there's the English baby!" "No, he's Russian—only his nurse and clothes are English!" the Christmas party in 1916, when the long-legged Kyril kicked over a lamp, the window drapes caught fire, and there was a mad scramble of servants; the big to-do when Alexei fell on the Shishmarev lawn and everyone thought he was going to bleed; Alexei's flare-ups with his sisters over making room for Kyril in their carriage.

Mr. de Shishmarev said these memories all figured in his confrontation with Michal Goleniewski, so I asked him to elaborate on them. Here's what he said:

"The incident at the parade ground, when Alexei was uniformed as a member of the Cossack Konvoy—that started when he and I were far removed from each other. He was next to the Emperor on the reviewing line with all the rest of the brass. Miss Mathews and I were some distance away.

"I was surprised when a Cossack aide came up and told me that His Imperial Highness, the Grand Duke Alexei Nicholaevich Romanov, wished me to join him on the reviewing line. Well, that suited me fine. I hadn't any idea what I was getting into, and I stepped right along with the aide. Miss Mathews stayed behind. I guess she was taken aback.

"Alexei nodded to me, but stood stiffly until the last line of troops swung by. My father and his regiment were among those being reviewed. Alexei then turned to me and declared in a loud voice: 'Now I'm going to drill you!'

"His voice was loud enough to attract the attention of his father and other officers. They watched as Alexei put me through the paces—right face, left face, about face, and so forth. I gave him his money's worth. I never had such an audience.

" 'Get your shoulders back!' he yelled. 'I'll make a Guardsman out of you yet! How do you think you'll get into the Imperial Guard if you stand there like a—like a—' I don't remember what it was he compared me to. Something terrible, I'm sure.

"It was the Emperor who rescued me. There wasn't a general or colonel who'd have dared interfere with the Czarevich. The Emperor told him he'd drilled me enough. The officers laughed. So did I. We all knew the Emperor was proud of Alexei's interest in military affairs. He must have been happy, too, that his son was feeling so full of life that day. There were times when Alexei missed parades because of hemophilia attacks."

Then Mr. de Shishmarev discussed the Christmas party "that could have burned down the house."

"Alexei was there," he said, "with his bodyguard the sailor 'Dena' Derevenko. It was at our house. I guess there were ten or twelve kids and a phalanx of nurses and governesses.

"We'd had our supper and ice cream and cake, and I was in the mood for a little hell-raising. I formed the kids into a line and led the line into a rotating ring in the big playroom. It was filled with toys and tin soldiers and model sailboats and stuff. There was a kerosene lamp held to the wall on a metal fixture. I was proud of my long legs, and you know how kids are—they always like to start a game they think they can win.

"I decided to offer a prize to the first kid who could kick high enough to hit the lamp.

"We went around and around a few times, but no one could kick high enough, including me. Then, on about the fifth or sixth round, I got limbered up. I made it. My foot crashed into the lamp and broke it up and sent it thundering to the floor. The kerosene spilled all over the place. The flames spread and caught on to the drapes around the windows. All hell broke loose. Nurses and servants screamed. My father's orderlies came running. So did 'Dena.' They put out the fire, and pretty soon my father came in and gave me the devil. He was chewing me out loud and hard when Alexei stepped up. He told father a damn' lie. He said he'd done it, that I shouldn't be blamed. My father's rank of colonel, of course, didn't impress him. Before anyone short of the Czar, I guess, Alexei felt he was the senior presence, and he might just as well make use of the fact to protect a friend and playmate, namely, me. It was very sporting of him. It worked for a while, but as soon as Alexei left, it didn't work any more. Then I really got it in the neck. I deserved it, too. I was reminded over and over that I had to be especially careful not to endanger Alexei in any way, because a mere scratch could set him bleeding for hours and upset the whole Imperial Family. My father was especially angry because he had warned me before about this and felt that my deliberately egging the kids on showed I shirked my responsibility."

Alexei's tumble on the Shishmarev ground and his trouble with his sisters about the carriage were telescoped into the same memory pattern:

"Quite often I would hear a call from Alexei at the gate," Mr. de Shishmarev said. "I'd go out and find him standing there near a carriageful of sisters—two, three, or even four of the grand duchesses. He'd invite me to drive with them, and I'd accept. Then the trouble would start. There'd be no room in the carriage. He'd ask them to make room for both of us, and they wouldn't do it. He'd scold them. He'd put on a scene. It never had much effect. If any of them moved, she didn't move far. It would be a tight squeeze. Sometimes I'd go, sometimes not. Once this situation developed, and when Alexei saw his sisters wouldn't budge, he ran through the gate and onto our lawn and shouted back that they could go without him. He ran very hard and took an awful belly-whopper when he tripped. Immediately everyone rushed to him.

There was a great fuss. It looked as if he'd cut himself. The women all fluttered around, looking for the telltale sign of blood. There wasn't any, but once more I caught hell for not preventing the accident."

THE CONFRONTATION IN NEW YORK

Fifty-two years and forty-five hundred miles from Tsarskoe Selo, Kyril Feodorovich de Shishmarev lives in an eighth-floor apartment bordering New York's Central Park. The half century of time between him and Tsarskoe has brought him more than an average share of traumatic change and varied experiences.

At sixty-two, Mr. de Shishmarev is tall, slim, and handsome in the rakish style of a Russian general making the best of his loose civvies. He walks erectly. He's a little too lanky: six foot three, 174 pounds. He has a thin moustache, a ready smile. His voice is usually soft, until he gets excited. He uses a form of English that would do credit to the Old Vic. There's no trace of a Russian accent. His sense of humor seems always impatient for a workout. On the other hand, there are times when he's anything but a quietly amiable drawing-room presence. On the infrequent but memorable occasions when he's knocking back a few (whisky is his preference, though he wouldn't exactly refuse a beer), his voice and manner may more closely approximate that of a Cossack commander rallying his troops in the teeth of a blizzard. Then he seems very, very Russian.

He lives in obviously comfortable circumstances with his attractive, sable-haired wife, Emilie, the former Countess Bruzzo, and her teenage daughter, Alice. They have a summer home on Long Island. Mr. de Shishmarev has been an American citizen since 1942. Emilie was born here. Thus the Americanization process would appear to have played its own part in increasing the distance from, and weakening the old ties to, Tsarskoe Selo, but that is not exactly true.

One thing he liked about his World War II service, Mr. de Shishmarev said, was that it put him back in Europe. After a few other tours of duty he wound up as a junior officer (lieutenant) in the special intelligence missions section of SHAEF, under British Brigadier Kenneth Strong. Brigadier Strong has since become Sir Kenneth Strong and the author of a book, *Intelligence at the Top.* It was published in 1968 by Cassell & Co., Ltd., London. It spells out many of the reasons and political undercurrents that made the assignment seem so interesting to Mr. de Shishmarev.

In Europe, he said, he was able to renew his acquaintances from the old days, many dating back to Tsarskoe and Saint Petersburg. The continent was full of Romanov stories. Some annoyed him for their flagrant fantasy. Others amused him. It was not until the postwar claims, however, that he became conscious of being riled. He was quite sure, in those days, that the whole Imperial Family had been wiped out.

"The years went by," said Mr. de Shishmarev, "and then came another 'Anastasia'—Mrs. Eugenia Smith. She was really the third I had heard about. That was three too many for me.

"Then I heard about Goleniewski and his claims to be Alexei, the Czarevich. That was too damn' much altogether. That was a desecration of my old friend!"

About the same time, he said, he heard that publisher Robert Speller was in touch with Goleniewski. He had never met Mr. Speller, but he sat down in considerable pique and wrote him a letter. The gist of it was that if Mr. Speller was wondering whether Goleniewski was telling the truth, then all he had to do was ask him one little question: "Just ask him who 'The English Baby' was at Tsarskoe Selo," Mr. de Shishmarev wrote.

He put his name, address, and phone number on the letter to

Mr. Speller. In a day or two Speller phoned and invited De Shishmarev over to his office.

"Well, who *was* 'The English Baby'?" asked Mr. Speller.

"Never mind," said Mr. de Shishmarev. "I'll tell you that later. First ask him, and let me know what he says."

A few more days went by. Then Speller called de Shishmarev.

"He remembers 'The English Baby,' all right," said Speller. "He thought 'The English Baby' was dead. He wants to talk to you."

"How can I talk to him?"

"I can't give you his phone number. It's a secret. But if we can make a date and you come to my home, I'll get him on the line for you."

Several more days went by. Mr. de Shishmarev was in no rush. At first, he said, he didn't have much stomach for the idea of the phone hookup or much faith that it would lead him to anyone but an impostor who had been well coached. Finally his curiosity got the best of him. He made a date and appeared at Mr. Speller's midtown office.

Maxine Speller, Mr. Speller's wife, presided over the telephone rendezvous.

"It was annoying as well as exciting," she said. "After a very few words in English, it was all in Russian. I couldn't understand a word. I could tell that Mr. de Shishmarev at first was very skeptical. I'm sure he thought Goleniewski was a faker. I'm sure he thought the man had read about 'The English Baby' some-where or heard about it somewhere. I think Goleniewski had simi-lar doubts about Mr. de Shishmarev. But after a while I could tell that Mr. de Shishmarev was becoming greatly affected. Tears began to come down the sides of his face. It was a long talk. For quite a while Mr. de Shishmarev didn't say much after he hung up. After that, of course, they got together. After that we were out of it."

Now for Mr. de Shishmarev's version:

"Mrs. Speller is dead right about my being affected," he said.

"I certainly was. I was shaken up. I think we both started that conversation believing the other was a phony. When that wore off, there came a sensation that doesn't come to many in a whole lifetime—the shock of talking to someone you imagined in his grave. The tone—the voice inflections—they gave me goose-pimples. They were so damn' familiar. Right there in Speller's office I was convinced. Yet after a night's sleep I began to be a little uncertain again. It took the face-to-face session to convince me once and for all."

Thereafter, said Mr. de Shishmarev, he and Colonel Goleniewski met many times in their respective apartments. Their relationship grew increasingly close and cordial. For more than a year they conferred once or twice a week.

"Looking back," said Mr. de Shishmarev, "I believe that even in the first few minutes of our facing each other in his apartment we both harbored reservations. We had an eye out to see what was behind the trick. We were ready to determine where the right answers of whoever had coached the other were going to run out. You can imagine why he had every reason at that point in his life for being damned suspicious.

"But after a while there was simply no more question. Each of us in a rather politely indirect way had been feeding the other the first half of an old situation at Tsarskoe Selo, and, as it were, challenging the other to finish it. Both of us missed a couple. After all, fifty years is fifty years. But there were too many others that we didn't miss. There was just no doubting any more. No one could have readied up or filled in the other on all the old times we hashed over. As for me, I found that all his familiar mannerisms, his explosive way of speaking, his sudden bursts of emotion and rising inflection—they were the same as ever. Even the features behind the moustache weren't a bit different from the Alexei of my youth. He had always been very attractive to me—so alive, so full of fun and impetuous actions. I found him so all over again.

It was really a great feeling. I'd thought he was dead. I guess he'd heard about my father's death and decided I was gone, too.

"My wife, Emilie, found him as attractive as I did. He came here, and she talked to him often on the phone.

"My first reaction to his situation was a strong impulse to try to help him. He seemed to be having a hard time coping with the Americans. I could see he·made a good deal of this problem for himself in his impatience and overbearing manner. After all, my father was Russian, my mother was American. I thought I could bridge the gap. I gave him a pretty stern lecture, and he took it very well. I gave him hell on the subject of his arrogance. I pointed out that all the Americans I knew who had any interest in him were getting fed up, one by one. He seemed to be saving his sharpest invective for those who had given him the greatest support. I found that he had been switching from one lawyer to another and from one person to another, and I advised him to come to his senses—settle on a program and stick to it. The funny part of it was, he agreed, sweet as a lamb."

"Did you ever get the impression that his faculties were cracking up?" I asked.

"Absolutely not," Mr. de Shishmarev answered. "That's a myth put out by someone in Washington. I'll admit that his ways and moods and temperament play right into the hands of his detractors. The fact is, he has a fine mind. On some things it's positively brilliant. But there's no question about his moods and peccadilloes. He had them at Tsarskoe. They're not much different. In a boy, though, they're not so grating on his peers. Of course, I forget—we weren't his peers then. I guess that's part of his trouble. We're all his peers now, but he doesn't know it."

Mr. de Shishmarev's Russian heritage sometimes impels the same kind of volcanic soliloquies for which Colonel Goleniewski is renowned in the offices of the CIA at Langley, Virginia. My next question inspired just such a reaction.

"Is it true you and he have busted up?" I asked.

He shot to his feet. He began pacing fretfully around the book-lined room of his apartment as if it were one of those old Okhrana detention chambers at Saint Petersburg.

"We haven't busted up," he said, in a booming tone. "I don't abandon my friends. I simply decided that his case was too damn' important to be left to him. It's one of the most important matters of this century. I decided to disassociate myself from all his mixed-up plans and strategies so I could proceed in my own way— and that's just what I'm doing. I well understand why he doesn't like it.

"Just consider how important it is," he continued. "The American people probably don't think they owe anything to the son of the Czar. But there is no end to what they owe to Lieutenant Colonel Michal Goleniewski. . . . By our bungling of the Goleniewski case we cut ourselves off from the Heckenschuetzes network. I don't say they didn't make mistakes, too. Maybe one of them was using Alexei. But I don't think the damage is beyond repair. That's one thing I'm working on . . ."

"Did he ever talk to you about the subject of the family inheritance?" I asked.

"My word, yes—many times. He has a very exact list of banks and cash figures. The banks are all over the world, from Switzerland to California. I don't think the list is all fanciful, either. On a visit to Paris not long ago, I sounded out the official of one large French bank and an executive of the French Finance Ministry. They seemed quite familiar with the matter. The banker indicated he would honor any claimant from Nicholas' family who could show the proper credentials and proof of identity. He displayed no surprise at all."

"Were the sums on his list large?"

"The largest, I think, was about $80 million in a French bank. There were pretty sizable sums in London and New York."

"Does he have a plan for suing and collecting?"

"Yes, but the plan was always changing or stalling or passing from the hands of one lawyer to another. He's certain, you see, that the British and American governments between them have all the documents and positive evidence he needs to prove his identity in court. He says he's determined to get it before starting the litigation."

"Do you believe it?"

"I believe there's lots about his identity in the government files —yes. But now I'm not so sure he wants to force his case into the open. There's some factor holding him back. It's really quite mysterious. It makes him back away at the last moment—makes him shrink from the brink—as someone said. He may be afraid of something quite beyond my calculation. In his own mind, I think, it may have to do with preserving his life against something threatening him, but he'll always tell you it's really something else.

"Another project I'm working on he doesn't like, either. It's a little less mortal than the whims of a Czarevich. I'm talking about a proper revision of history. I'm working on his case with that in mind. I happen to be a member of the Sovereign Order of Saint John of Jerusalem. It's an old Christian order of chivalry and knighthood, which is better known as the Knights of Malta. It has many ties to Russia. Czar Paul I offered sanctuary to its members when they were forced off the the island of Malta in the Napoleonic Wars. Later he served as the order's Grand Master.

"Other Russians, from time to time, have been Grand Masters. It has members in many countries. As a matter of fact, the present chairman of the order's military committee is a former Commandant of the Marine Corps, General Lemuel C. Shepherd, of La Jolla, California. I'm the Associate Security General of the order. My wife, Emilie, is head of the hospital committee. The order's headquarters are in Shickshinny, Pennsylvania. I'm happy to say

PLATE 32: The alleged Grand Duchess Anastasia, Eugenia Smith, Illinois, 1963.

PLATE 33: The alleged Grand Duchess Maria, 1968.

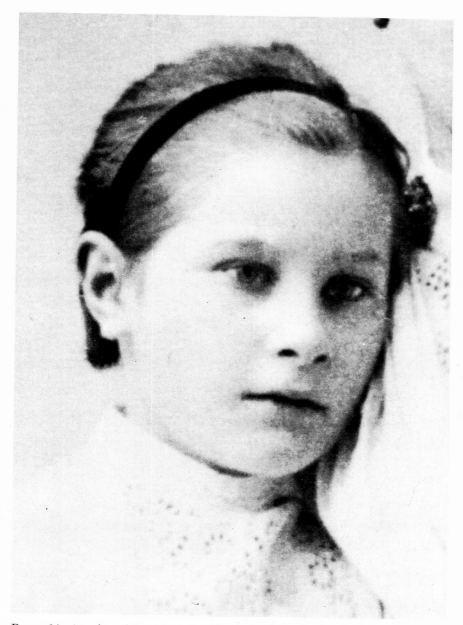

Plate 34: Another claimant to the Romanov fortune, Anna Anderson, circa 1902.

PLATE 35: Group photographed at the time of the Russian Orthodox marriage ceremony uniting the alleged Czarevich Alexei and the former Irmgard Kampf, New York, 1964. The couple is seated in the center, with the officiating priest, Count Georgi Grabbe, the Protopresbyter, on the left, and the alleged Grand Duchess Olga on the right. Standing in the back is the alleged Grand Duchess Tatiana.

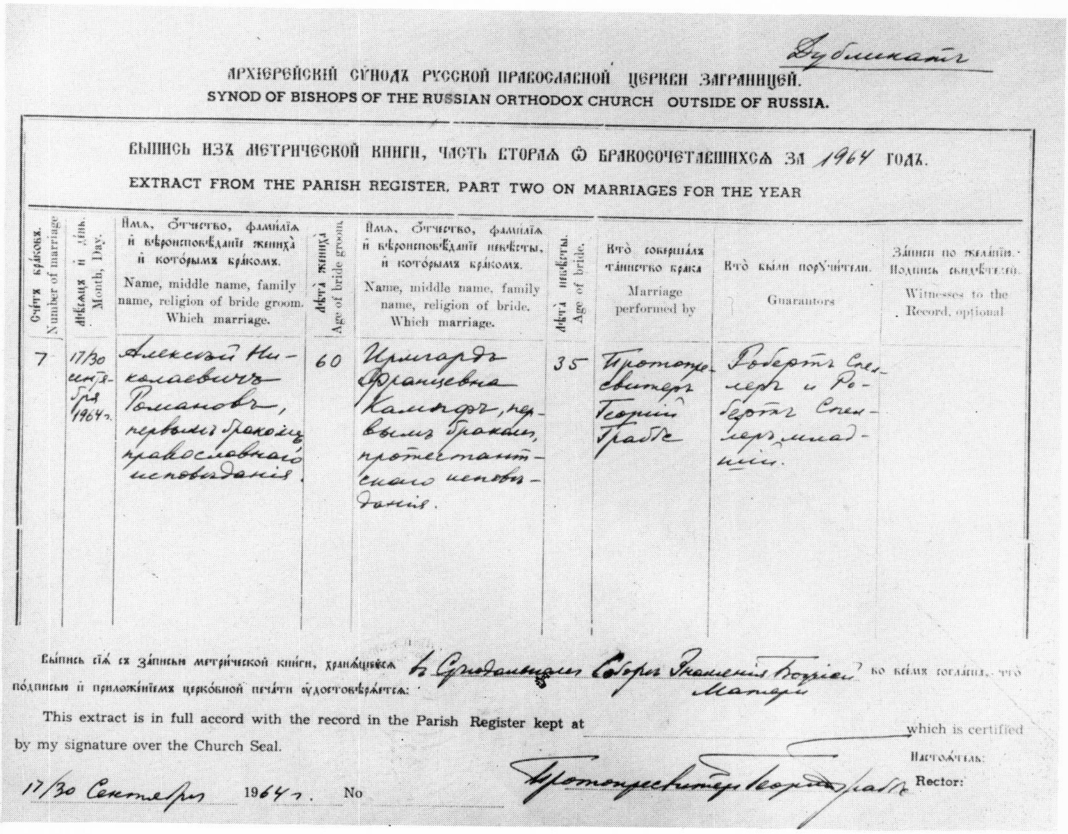

Дубликатъ

АРХІЕРЕЙСКІЙ СЇНОДЪ РУССКОЙ ПРАВОСЛАВНОЙ ЦЕРКВИ ЗАГРАНИЦЕЙ.
SYNOD OF BISHOPS OF THE RUSSIAN ORTHODOX CHURCH OUTSIDE OF RUSSIA.

ВЫПИСЬ ИЗЪ МЕТРИЧЕСКОЙ КНИГИ, ЧАСТЬ ВТОРАЯ О БРАКОСОЧЕТАВШИХСЯ ЗА 1964 ГОДЪ.
EXTRACT FROM THE PARISH REGISTER, PART TWO ON MARRIAGES FOR THE YEAR

Счетъ браковъ. Number of marriage	Мѣсяцъ и день. Month, Day.	Имя, отчество, фамилія и вѣроисповѣданіе жениха и которымъ бракомъ. Name, middle name, family name, religion of bride groom. Which marriage.	Лѣта жениха. Age of bride groom.	Имя, отчество, фамилія и вѣроисповѣданіе невѣсты, и которымъ бракомъ. Name, middle name, family name, religion of bride. Which marriage.	Лѣта невѣсты. Age of bride.	Кто совершалъ таинство брака. Marriage performed by	Кто были поручители. Guarantors	Записи по желанію. Подпись свидѣтелей. Witnesses to the Record, optional
7	17/30 сентября 1964 г.	Алексей Николаевичъ Романовъ, первымъ бракомъ, православнаго исповѣданія.	60	Ирмгардъ Францевна Кампфъ, первымъ бракомъ, протестантскаго исповѣданія.	35	Протопресвитеръ Георгий Граббе	Робертъ Спеллеръ и Робертъ Спеллеръ младшій.	

Выпись сія съ записью метрической книги, хранящейся въ Синодальном Соборе Знамения Божией Матери во всемъ согласна, что подписью и приложеніемъ церковной печати удостовѣряется:

This extract is in full accord with the record in the Parish Register kept at ________ which is certified by my signature over the Church Seal.

Настоятель:
Rector: Протопресвитер Георгий Граббе

17/30 Сентября 1964 г. No

PLATE 36: The Russian Orthodox marriage certificate of the alleged Czarevich, Alexei Nicholaevich Romanov, and Irmgard Frantsevna Kampf, 1964. It is noteworthy that the officiating priest, Count Grabbe, the Protopresbyter, is the nephew of Count Arkhip Grabbe, the Chief of the Czar's personal Guard, the Konvoy. It seems unlikely that he would have married Goleniewski in the name of the Czarevich unless he were convinced of his identity.

PLATE 37: Lieutenant Lawrence Butler, circa 1924, courier who allegedly brought *Rescuing the Czar* to the United States.

PLATE 38: Kyril de Shishmarev, who was the childhood friend of the Czarevich at Tsarskoe Selo.

PLATE 39: The Czarevich Alexei being held in the arms of Paul Voronov, an officer on the yacht *Standart*, circa 1911.

that the Grand Chancellor of the order has appointed me to a sizable committee which has been investigating the Goleniewski case for some time. We're well along in the task of establishing the truth or falsity of Goleniewski's claims. I have already sworn out a long affidavit in accord with the laws of Pennsylvania, and this is now an acceptable legal document in any court or for any revision of history in respect to what happened at Ekaterinburg.

"We have reason to believe that all Alexei's sisters are alive under cover names in different parts of the world. We're well along in the process of establishing contact with them. I don't want to say any more about that right now—only this: I think we'll do better in dealing with them than he has. They've never liked the bossy side of his temperament. I remember how they would never move over when he yelled at them in the carriage at Tsarskoe Selo. They still don't want him to boss them, as he always tries to do. And they don't want to get mixed up in international politics. Well, it looks as if they were going to respond to a different approach."

"You feel no bitterness, then, about his attitude?"

"None at all," he said. "Better than that, I understand it perfectly. He's playing a game for his life. He's under tremendous pressures, and he has been for years. He knows that the Poles have sentenced him to death. He knows there are others who would love to help the Poles carry out the sentence. He's got one hell of a security problem. He's got to make decisions on a very different frame of reference. That's why I decided to operate independently. His problems are not mine. My obligations are different from his. I think the obligations of the American people are the same as mine. And they can't expect him to see everything their way, either."

Mr. de Shishmarev paused in his pacing to look out the window. More as an afterthought to the window and himself, he added:

"Anyone who decides to help Alexei in a way he doesn't like

must be ready for double jeopardy. Not only will Alexei's enemies be arrayed against him; Alexei will be, too. You know the names he called you after your book came out [*Imperial Agent*]. Just think of the names he's going to start calling me. We must take comfort from the fact that it isn't the voice entirely of the real Alexei. Either he's saying something to suit the CIA, which has been paying him a stipend, or he's speaking to the ears of the Heckenschuetzes ring, or he's speaking to disarm those on whom he must depend for protection until he can speak for himself."

XVII

Hunting Notes—Other Game Sighted, Etc.

There are some side lights on certain facts and personages discovered in the day-by-day detective work on the Romanov mystery that ought to go into the record.

SIR THOMAS PRESTON—As senior British Government representative at Ekaterinburg at the time of the alleged assassination of the Romanovs, Sir Thomas, now 83 and a distinguished retired civil servant, was one of many persons who responded several times to Robert Samborski's letters. Sir Thomas made it clear that he didn't want to get involved in the Romanov imbroglio. He wrote that he didn't know anything about the Goleniewski case. He expressed the opinion that Goleniewski was an impostor if he said he was Nicholas' son. Then Preston made what seemed to be a slip. In one of his letters to Mr. Samborski, Sir Thomas discussed at some length the writings of the late Pierre Gilliard, Swiss tutor of the Romanov children. He added this cryptic sentence: "The Heir knew Gilliard well and must remember him."

What was in his mind when he wrote that?

If Sir Thomas didn't believe that Colonel Goleniewski was the "Heir," why would he have written such a sentence? Was it intended that the reader tack on the thought, "But, of course, Goleniewski *doesn't* remember him"?

The fact is, on many occasions Goleniewski made it clear that he recalled all the principal figures in Nicholas' household, Gilliard included.

I called Mr. Samborski's attention to this sentence. He didn't agree with me that it had significance. He contended that Sir Thomas, at his advanced age, was entitled to coin a few inscrutable phrases. I have read over that sentence many times since, however, and it still strikes me as a signal—though perhaps an unconscious one—from some unofficial area of Sir Thomas' brain. Sir Thomas, it must be remembered, is not only a retired civil servant. He was knighted for his service to the crown. It is still the official British line that the Romanovs were assassinated.

THE BREST-LITOVSK THEORY—Germany and the Central Powers signed a separate peace treaty with Bolshevik Russia on March 3, 1918, in the Russian city of Brest-Litovsk. In a memo found in his files, McGarry makes this point: "Germany was in a position to dictate terms and did dictate the terms of the Brest-Litovsk Treaty with the Bolsheviki and would have annihilated the Bolsheviki had not their first terms for the safety of the *Kaiser's Relatives,* namely the Imperial Family of Russia, been granted and actually PROVED by satisfactory evidence before the treaty was signed."

This is in accord with evidence now occupying a team of investigators in Switzerland that the liberation of the Romanovs was arranged and paid for in Zurich, possibly before Lenin left Switzerland in the Spring of 1917, to arrive in Petrograd on April 3, via Germany and a sealed train.

THE HELPFUL PRINCESS—So far in this book there has been no mention of Princess Marina D. Kropotkin, the hearty and outgoing mother of four children who is among the few persons responsible for bringing the Goleniewski case out of hiding. She is a Russian émigrée related to the nobility of old Saint Petersburg. Her mother, born Princess Marina A. Obolensky, had become famed as "Pani (Lady) Marina" for the help she rendered Ukrainian Freedom Fighters in the 1920s.

It was Marina Kropotkin who first interested the Russian Orthodox Church in the Goleniewski case. She helped to arrange his marriage to Irmgard in a Russian Orthodox ceremony in New York on September 30, 1964. (This was the "nick-of-time" wedding that took place only a few hours before the birth of Colonel Goleniewski's daughter, Tatiana.) She introduced Goleniewski to the Russian Orthodox priest who performed the ceremony—the Very Reverend Archpriest and Protopresbyter of the Synod of Bishops of the Russian Orthodox Church Outside Russia, Count George P. Grabbe, better known as Father Georgi. Goleniewski was married with a license that named him as Alexei Nicholaevich Romanov, son of Nicholas Alexandrovich Romanov and of Alexandra Feodorovna Romanov, née von Hesse. It listed his birth as August 12, 1904, at Peterhof, Russia.

There was not much mistaking who the groom was—or said he was.

These were no small achievements. Marina had no ax to grind in the matter. She had never seen or heard of Goleniewski up to a few weeks before. She had no inkling of the ruckus Father Georgi's role in the marriage would cause in Russian-American circles.

Letters attacking the priest promptly appeared in the Russian-American press. His seniors in the church punished him. He was forbidden to christen little Tatiana, though he had married her parents. He was obliged to make the rounds of a number of writers, myself included, to inform them that "Goleniewski couldn't possibly be Alexei N. Romanov"; that as a priest, he was obliged to marry any pair who asked him and who were otherwise qualified; that the name "Romanov" was as common in Russia as

"Smith" was in the United States; that his performance of the wedding was no indication that the church recognized Goleniewski's claims.

It was all very humiliating for Father Georgi, a scholarly prelate with a beard and drooping moustache. It was also very unconvincing. As the nephew of Major General Count Arkhip N. Grabbe, an aide-de-camp of Czar Nicholas II, Father Georgi was well versed in the lore of the Imperial Family. Before he agreed to perform the wedding ceremony, he had visited Goleniewski in his Long Island apartment six times. He had received from him two multi-page memorandums describing Goleniewski's life in exile. When he agreed to conduct the ceremony, he must have known that he wasn't dealing with any old "Smith."

Goleniewski, for his part, undoubtedly magnified Father Georgi's acquiescence in the matter of the wedding to the much larger proportions of an official Russian Orthodox acceptance of his claims.

The backlash stirred up, and the rapid reversal of the church's position, are two more mysteries still to be plumbed. Marina Kropotkin is among many observers who believe the church's actions are examples of its subordination to State Department pressure.

After Father Georgi refused to christen Tatiana, Marina Kropotkin said: "I was shocked and surprised by Father Georgi's actions. I expected much more integrity from a man of the church."

According to Marina, it had been Father Georgi, after he had once made up his mind about it, who insisted on the importance of the full-ritual wedding and the christening ceremony to follow. His sudden switch prompted some Romanov buffs to theorize that the priest unknowingly had collided with plans of higher-ups in the church. By this theory, the church, of which the Czar was titular head, planned to work with a group of next-in-line Romanovs who were not in the immediate Imperial Family for a share of the inheritance. Recognizing the survival of any of Nicholas' children would put a crimp in such a strategy.

Marina is a buxom, energetic brunette with a keen mind and a contagious laugh. Her father, Prince Dimitri D. Kropotkin, was an officer in the Czar's Army. Once reported killed in the Bolshevik Revolution, he later turned up in the Polish anti-Communist underground. This fact, and Marina's contagious laugh, became the keys to her interest in Michal Goleniewski. How the two came together is quite an eerie story.

The deep bursts of Marina's laughter are accompanied by a certain tilt of her head and sweeping arm gestures. On her first meeting with Goleniewski, in 1964, he stopped talking to study her features pensively.

"Your laugh reminds me of someone," he said. "I'm trying to think who."

He didn't manage to recall, immediately, she said, but before long, he exclaimed: "Now I know who your laugh reminds me of."

He named a man in Poland, she said. It happened to be her father's cover name in the underground. She added that only a few persons in the world knew the secret. She had never mentioned it to anyone in the United States.

MCGARRY'S EMPLOYMENT RECORD—In checking with the Foreign Service and elsewhere in the State Department, we found there was no record of William Rutledge McGarry's employment. This jarred us for a few days. We asked more questions at the federal departments. We read more of McGarry's papers. Soon we learned that in the old days U.S. embassies granted many Americans temporary status as "attachés" for business or other reasons without putting them on the payroll. Ambassadors often did it on a personal basis. If the attachés were hired for intelligence purposes, sometimes by the ambassador himself, they were paid out of a separate fund, of which there was no public record. McGarry's own files bolster his claims of far-flung peregrinations

in Europe, conferences with foreign dignitaries, responsive telegrams and mail from them, etc. Considering his financial resources, his way of operating, his obvious disinclination to be
pinned to a desk job from 9 to 5, his ready access to the ambassadors themselves, it is understandable that his name is not on
the personnel records. He was an undercover man. Even less-
glamorous agents of the State Department's Intelligence Branch
were not always named on the rosters.

THE DESCENDANTS' DILEMMA—The McGarry and Fox
clans have a common problem. They have been made aware, in
belated small fragments, of the full extent of their forebears' achievements. The experiences of the children and grandchildren of William Rutledge McGarry, in this regard, have already been described.
Not so, however, on the Fox side. There the initial incredulity
was even slower to disperse. James M. Fox of Alexandria, Louisiana,
son of Charles James Fox, was far more confounded than the
McGarrys when we first broached the subjects of the Romanov
liberation and the "Fox" diary in *Rescuing the Czar*. James Fox
is a tall, rangy, handsome former investment counsel who served
as an MP officer in the World War II Army. He retired from
business to live in San Diego, where his father spent the last years
of his life with him. More recently he moved to Alexandria, where,
in World War II days, he had met his wife, the former Mary Jane
Chesley. They were married in 1953.

James Fox was still in San Diego when he told us over the
phone that he had never heard of *Rescuing,* from his father or
anyone else. After we outlined the contents of the book, he expressed the opinion that its "Fox" couldn't be his father. Shortly
thereafter, he and his wife moved to Alexandria. We brought him
a copy of *Rescuing* to read. He spent a day on it and maintained
the same skepticism. No, he said, the diary didn't sound like his
father. No, he said, his father had never mentioned any experience
with the Russian Imperial Family or any other imperial family

that resembled the events of the book. He spent several weeks amassing what he called "negative evidence" to prove that it couldn't be his father. Then, little by little, his doubts began to recede. He recalled that he and his mother had been separated from his father in the summer of 1918. They had gone to Japan to escape the heat in Tientsin. His father, he thought, remained in Tientsin all the time they were away, but he wasn't sure. He had to admit that his father could have been anywhere, Siberia included. Then, reflecting on the escape route described in *Rescuing,* James Fox began to consider a few other points. Yes, it was true that his father had been a great hiker. Yes, it was true that he spoke several languages. Yes, it was true that he had a great interest in military affairs and had served as a major in the National Guard of the District of Columbia. Yes, it was true that he had a good friend in the U. S. Secret Service. Yes, it was true, come to think of it, that his father had a windfall of money at the end of the summer of 1918—enough to buy the newspaper *North China Star*—but James always had the idea, he said, that the money had come from the sale of 120 acres of Maryland farm property.

Yes, it was true that his father had friends among influential Germans, Britishers, Japanese, French, and Chinese. Yes, it was only too true that his father was the kind of man who would keep a secret in the marrow of his bones, whether a friend's secret or a state secret, if he had promised.

As more weeks passed, and more letters were exchanged, it was noticeable that there were coming to be too many coincidences on the affirmative side for James Fox to cope with in comfort. He was beginning to believe that his father *could* have done it and *would* have done it, if asked. But he was still not quite convinced that his father *had* done it.

It was Henry Pu-yi who proved the one coincidence too many for James Fox. When we discovered that Pu-yi (destined to be the puppet emperor of Manchukuo, with Japanese backing) stated in his autobiography that he had contributed $50,000 to help restore the Imperial Family of Russia, James Fox instantly remembered that his father had known Pu-yi well. They had both been in Tientsin at the time of the contribution (1925). James remembered very clearly hearing his father speak of Pu-yi to his mother at the dining-room table. James had never met Pu-yi, he said. He had left his parents in China in 1921 to attend the University of California at Berkeley; but if his father was the "Fox" in *Rescuing,* and Pu-yi wanted any firsthand corroboration that the Romanovs had escaped, Charles James Fox, the distinguished publisher and editor of the *North China Star,* would have been just the man to give it. There was no doubt about that. Not even for James Fox.

ANOTHER OLD PLAYMATE ?—According to Colonel Goleniewski, "Howard E. Roman" was the cover name of an expert linguist whom the CIA sent to meet Goleniewski in Frankfurt, Germany, on January 5, 1961. "Roman" proved to be familiar with the most minute details of the Imperial Family. Later, Goleniewski told some of his confidants in the United States that "Roman's" real name was Romanov; that he was a distant cousin; that the two had known one another as youngsters at Tsarskoe Selo. "Howard Roman," by whatever name, may be another person in the United States who is qualified to identify Goleniewski.

THE SECOND ASSIGNEE—"Peter Skov" was the cover name of the second man assiged by the CIA to Colonel Goleniewski after he was put in a "safe-house" at McLean, Virginia, in January 1961. Thanks to the East Germans, "Skov" has lost the anonymity that still shrouds "Roman."

"Skov" is listed in a handbook published in East Berlin in 1968. Few Americans have ever seen it; it is titled *Who's Who in the CIA* and is edited by Dr. Julius Mader. It proclaims itself

"A biographical work of 3000 officers of the civil and military branches of the secret services of the United States in 120 countries."

This 605-page volume reveals "Peter Skov" as a CIA operative with impressive credentials; his real name, it claims, is Dr. Herbert Scoville, Jr. Some of his past tours of duty are given as "1946–48: Nuclear Weapons Researcher in Los Alamos; 1956–63: Assistant to Director of CIA for Science and Technology; Adviser U. S. President's Scientific Council; Scientific Consultant to Air Force; Specialist in Photochemistry; 1964–present: Assistant for Science and Technology in Arms Control and Disarmament Agency."

"Howard Roman" does not appear in this manual, only a "Paul Roman." Perhaps this indicates that "Howard Roman" was a contract employee, hired for the mission because of his knowledge of the Romanovs. But the choice of "Roman" and "Skov" to work with Goleniewski does tend to bear out Goleniewski's story that the CIA had advance notice of his identity claims, and that they had made appropriate preparations; and that in the person of Dr. Scoville the CIA assigned an important and knowledgeable operative to the case. "Roman" and "Skov" remained with Goleniewski for months.

XVIII

Fox's Diary—
A Man for All Seasons, Climates,
Countries, and Crowns

No one will ever accuse "Fox" of excessive modesty. His self-portrait reveals a man who flashes more colors than a Venetian glass vase. Nothing daunts him. He's as fast with a bon mot as he is with his fists. He's also keen in the art of soldiering. One minute he's parleying with the Czar on matters of high statecraft. The next minute he's bloodying a burly Bolshevik guard. The next he's conducting a fey and rather wordy flirtation with the young Grand Duchess Maria; the next, in sight of freedom and foreign gunboats in China, he's striking "herculean blows" in a free-for-all with a "tatterdemalion mob" of coolies.

How Fox left London and filtered in and out of the German lines, going from Berlin to the Balkans, is described in this book's first chapter. Those portions of his diary are omitted here, to avoid repetition. We pick him up at Ekaterinburg at what appears to be his first moment alone with "my Imperial prisoner" (Nicholas II).

There are several interesting references in these opening passages at Ekaterinburg, which the Soviets now call Sverdlovsk. One is to "Syvorotka." He's the "Alexei" of the second diary, which makes up Part II of *Rescuing the Czar*. Another is to the "NUN" who might very well be the same one mentioned in New York *Times* correspondent Carl W. Ackerman's dispatches from Ekaterinburg in 1918. She is later quoted again in Mr. Ackerman's book *Trailing the Bolsheviki* as assuring the world that all seven Romanovs escaped.

Another early reference is to the "old valet, Parafine Domino," who, outside of *Rescuing,* gains a living entity in no other place but Mr. Ackerman's writings. Another is to "Ekhart's tunnel." This, no doubt, is the cistern tunnel through which Fox later leads the Romanovs away. Ekhart, furthermore, must be the same man to whom Mr. Ackerman refers as "Colonel of the General Staff Ekhart," among those accused by the Ural District Soviet of having plotted Nicholas' escape. Another notable item here is one of several clues to Fox's nationality. He tells the Czar, in French, that although he was born in Paris he is in fact an American.

As the diary continues, one gets a glimpse of Fox's tactical plan. He manages to become "captain of the guard" around the Imperial Family. He and several other members of that guard who are working with him loudly abuse the Romanovs, while Bolsheviks are around, but, when opportunity offers, actually conspire with Nicholas on the projected getaway.

Fox's entries are numbered, unlike Alexei's. Fox also uses liberally the device of upper-case lettering in words, phrases, and sentences he wants to emphasize. Alexei doesn't.

But the two diaries have a number of things in common that are not necessarily explained by the fact that they were prepared by the same "arranger and translator." All the way along in both of them the reader is fed infuriatingly censored tidbits about the identities of certain persons. His first reaction may be outright resentment. It seems that the writer is playing a game. It becomes a mental tussle like a crossword puzzle, where the given information is always exceeded by that withheld.

As one continues, however, and possibly because there's nothing else to do but read on, the game becomes quite engrossing. Once resigned to the fact that it is less of a book than it is a mental bout, the reader is apt to be drawn into it on its own terms. Sooner or later he is bound to realize that the clues are interesting, adroit, and generously provided.

22. Then the following odds and ends appear:

". . . . . The Metropole performer is a Baroness sure enough. . . . . She knows a Syvorotka but declines to give his rank or whereabouts. . . . . She tells me that this place was founded by Count Tatishchëv in 1721. . . . . when Catherine was a baby. . . . . The Monastery of 'Our Lady of Tikhvin' looming up before me is a very graceful compliment to the Mosque of St. Sophia it resembles in so many ways. . . . . fine place to radio from to friends at Odessa. . . . . especially if the NUN has been obeying orders. . . . . Lvov is out of the way, over in the city prison, cooking, where he can't betray the prisoners at Ipatiev's. . . . . When I was alone with my Imperial prisoner I tore the patch off from my shirt sleeve and handed it to him. . . . . 'Sa lettre!' he exclaimed in an undertone. . . . . His manner was exceedingly polite. . . . . 'Ouvrez, lisez,' I advised. . . . . 'Oui, oui, je sais! je sais!' he said softly, 'mais malheureusement cela est impossible!' . . . . 'Soak it in water,' I replied. . . . . 'Et vous, monsieur, êtes-vous américain ou francais?' he came back. . . . . 'Je suis né à Paris, mais je suis américain, and if the prisoner has no objection I'd rather speak in English.' . . . . 'That will be delightful,' he said; 'I shall do as you say.' . . . . He ran back to the bathroom. In a moment he returned holding the patch up before him. . . . . 'Ah!' he continued aloud, 'this merely says that the Heir Apparent will make a cruise of the world in a man-of-war; what does that signify?'. . . . 'If you recognize the writing,' I replied, 'you will, doubtless, remember the methods of its author when extending an invitation.' . . . . 'Yes, yes, I see; how clever of you!

Had you been a subject of mine I should have made you an ambassador!' . . . . . "That would imply infinite wisdom on my part, Sire!' I bowed very humbly. . . . . It made a hit with my prisoner."

This entry follows:

"Alice will give up her wheel chair when the NUN gives the word. . . . she is worrying about my prisoner's sister, Olga, and her two companions, who insist on offering their services to the poor in the Crimea. . . . . and well she may! . . . . 'Facing the East,' they are likely to travel south! . . . . I must get rid of this old valet, Parafine Domino, who makes a nuisance of himself hovering around my prisoner like a hawk. . . . . Gallipoli says he'll get rid of Alice's physician before the TENTS arrive,—substituting a fake doctor from the Red Guard, who'll tell me when the prisoners are fit to travel. . . . . As 'Captain' of this Soviet Guard I am as cold-blooded as Gallipoli before the spies and hangers-on. . . . . 'Captain?' . . . . that title seems to stump the old Russian soldiers,—they claim that there is no such animal. . . . . The Sergeant has suggested that I put the prisoners under a SMALL GUARD when we take them to the Ural District Soviet Court of Workmen. . . . . Nice trap to catch me. . . . . If I agreed to this I'd be in the same category as Denikin or Dutov or Ekhart and be shot by the gang outside by mistake, so as to fulfill the prophecy of my lady of Buckingham. . . . . My Answer was to order the guard on the balcony to keep their guns pointed at the prisoners whenever they appear in the garden. . . . . this will satisfy that suspicious Sergeant that there is no Japanese money secreted by the prisoners. I have ordered my men to use their bayonets against the walls and ceilings. . . . . even the frame of the bathroom is not to escape! . . . . Gallipoli is growling around that I'm doing my work too damned well to seem reasonable! . . . . The poor boob! His idea of being reasonable seems to consist in spreading rumors that the prisoners have been disposed of in a dozen different ways. . . . . When Maria and Tatiana mounted the truck in the yard this confiding swaggerer started the gossip that they were being loaded up to be taken out of town and shot. . . . . Now I am told by some of the excited guard that that report is TRUE because they heard someone in the attic of the red brick building yelling: 'The baggage is at the station!' . . . .

"When I asked them what we wanted with 'BAGGAGE' they went away growling that I wasn't playing fair! . . . . To my somber-robed lady of Buckingham, who seems to have deserted me, as well as the slender guard at the Huis ten Bosch, as well as those at the Wilhelmstrasse and Odessa, who are part of this 'BAGGAGE,' my guard's agitation will assume the humorous character of unconscious prophecy. . . . . Suspicion is in the air! . . . . This undisciplined gang of cutthroats under that half-baked Sergeant are demanding HOSTAGES from me for my conduct of this business . . . . they want 'the Grand Duchess Olga,' her two companions, and FIFTY other women! . . . . AT LAST! . . . . the planes are buzzing in the sky. . . . . The Ikon of Holy Nicholas is being wrapped up. . . . . The NUN has copies of the letters to Oldenburg and Gendrikov. . . . . It's time to say to my prisoner: 'Come with ME to the U. D. S. of W. A. R. A. D.' . . . . If he has the code from Odessa he will ask: 'Are you taking me to be shot?' . . . . 'RUNMOBS' . . . . I'll have the guard go through his pockets to find the letters that'll turn him over to my 'vengeance' . . . . then for Ekhart's tunnel and OBLIVION!"

23. Then this entry follows. It seems to be sufficiently circumstantial to justify its reproduction here:

"Murder, like jealousy, in this country is a disease," begins the narrative. "My part in this international murder will paralyze the politician and mystify the sober mind of intelligent belief. . . . . History will not be satisfied, however, without a VICTIM, and I must furnish a victim that will satisfy the mob outside! . . . . The Order has been given. . . . . There are celebrations among the banditti. . . . there are moistened eyes among many peasants; there are strong men and gallant men among the gang out yonder whose very looks betray the HATRED they entertain for the suspected executioner of their former ruler and his excited family. . . . . They fear, they try to avoid me; and I can see in their looks that, given a favorable opportunity, they will hang me to the highest electric-wire pole in the city! . . . .

"I am not so certain, though, that EVERYONE outside will accept my theatric 'slaughter' as the Gospel truth.

"Diagonally across the way there has been a Red Cross nurse eternally peeking through her window in this direction. . . . . If we go into the courtyard she can see us plainly behind the other buildings, for there is nothing to obstruct her vision. . . . and she seems mighty anxious to keep tab on all proceedings in the yard. . . . . I have tried to figure out a resemblance between this nurse and the capricious Metropole Baroness, but the nurse seems much older. . . . . Perhaps she is disguised. . . . ."

24. This entry follows:

"To satisfy the mob I had to perform a very unpleasant duty. . . . . I use the word duty advisedly, remembering the instructions I committed to memory in the underground office of the Wilhelm-strasse. . . . . Knowing that I am continually WATCHED and spied upon, not only by that nurse in the window over there, but by a number of crazed lunatics in uniform, I was compelled to treat a very pretty Princess shamefully. . . . . News was spread yesterday that Japan had loaned Siberia $250,000,000, and the mob was clamoring for the jewels of the prisoners. This unoffending Princess—this girl, hardly more than seventeen—was holding a conversation in French with her brother, Alexis, a little lad of fourteen, in the courtyard. The boy was pale and emaciated from abuse, solitude, and confinement. The Princess, a radiant beauty under this hot July sun, was trying to cheer Alexis up. Her gown was badly soiled and of a simple, soft material that seemed to accentuate her modest resignation and glorify her courageous cheerfulness in gloom. Her three older sisters, in gowns that spoke of yesterdays, were walking moodily down the path, when a crowd of ruffians burst by the sentries, tore through the doors, and dashed into the yard in the direction of the startled girls. . . . . Taking in the situation quickly, I raised my voice and began swearing like a demon, and prancing around like a skberny madman. . . . . Then rushing up to Tatiana I TORE FROM HER EARS the jewels that had descended from her early ancestors and howled: 'Aha! you'll wear those cursed things, will you, when your betters are starving in the gutters! Get back, all of you, into your Ipatiev SEPULCHRE and get me ALL the jewelry in the place or I'll turn these men loose upon you in three quarters of an hour! . . . . Soldiers,—attention!!' . . . The mob crawled into line. . . . . 'The next time any of you men come into this yard without any orders,' I said, 'I'll have you SHOT WITH THESE PEOPLE IN THE MANSION! . . . . Column right! . . . . March! . . . . I heard them mumbling as they passed the first sentry that the cursed interloping tovarishch intended to keep all the loot!' . . . . Following Alexis and his sisters into the ex-Emperor's study I laid down the earrings upon the flat-topped desk and apologized for my apparent act of cowardice and cruelty. . . . .

"There was pathos in that father's soft and courteous voice as he looked at me and said: 'I understand,—yes, yes, I know. You are quite right—quite right. My darlings, you must not blame this man.'"

WHEN ROYALTY FACES DEATH

25. This entry follows:
"I must jot this down now—who knows what may happen? . . . Reminding the family that I had promised results in three

quarters of an hour, I instructed them in the part each one must take. . . . . Alexis appeared to be listlessly unconcerned and sat upon one corner of the large flat-topped desk, swinging his feet indifferently; but when I started for the door he sprang to attention like a well-trained soldier and awaited the results. . . . . Going to the door fronting in the main street, I called the sentry and ordered him to CALL OUT THE GUARD. . . . Shortly my selected guard appeared. . . . .

I conducted them through the dining room and told them to help themselves. . . . . Then we roamed through the living rooms, the boudoirs, straight through to the washing room and bath; then back through the oblong archway into the little square room beyond the study, where I halted them and said: 'Men, these women will die before they'll tell us where the treasure is at present. The OLD MAN and WOMAN seem utterly indifferent to their fate; we can get nothing out of them. Now, what do you say to giving them a night to think the matter over before we line them up? We may get more by waiting than by closing their mouths FOREVER. . . . .'

'Not another day!' said one of the men whom I had all along suspected of being suspicious of MY conduct. . . . . 'What say the rest of you?' I asked. . . . . 'Well,' droned the most courageous of them, with a hangdog expression, 'we might give them until midnight.' . . . . 'Very well,' I snapped viciously, 'I'LL PUT OFF THE EXECUTION till that hour; then if they don't disgorge I'll kill every one of them myself!' . . . . 'Not so fast, comrade!' returned the rebellious one; 'as a member of the guard, I believe I'll keep you company.'

". . . . I knew better than to object. . . . . That man is a cutthroat beyond redemption and will hesitate at nothing to satisfy his lust. . . . . 'That'll be fine,' I rejoined; 'YOU STAY WITH ME; the rest of the men are dismissed!' . . . . when the men disappeared I made a run and jump at my diabolical 'comrade' and struck him squarely on the nose. Then I smashed him on the mouth, and, with a down drive of my left, I bored into the pit of his stomach and sent him sprawling on the carpet, where he BLED as profusely as a corn fed bull. . . . . This blood was exactly what I wanted, and in my anxiety to make a good job of it I kicked him several times in the face until he lay there, motionless and senseless, bleeding from every gash. . . . . In the joy of giving this remorseless bully what he needed to overcome his pride I OVERLOOKED ENTIRELY THE PROPRIETY OF MAKING HIM BLEED IN ALL THE OTHER ROOMS. . . . . This little oversight may cost me a well-earned reputation for efficient management I have hitherto enjoyed among many great men of our times, if the omission be detected by some enterprising commission, some journalist or SERVICE man who will certainly check up my report if I leave this place alive. . . . ."

26. This entry follows:

"It was a long wait till midnight when the mob outside expected to be invited to a division of the spoils. . . . but my plans were taking shape gradually as the moments slipped away. . . . . In the few hours left to us before the time set for their 'execution'—in these evening shadows of July 1918—we have been discussing the effect of THEIR SACRIFICE upon the history of the world. . . . . I put this down from memory:

" 'It is understood already in certain chancellories,' my prisoner significantly replied, 'how my execution will be publicly accounted for. . . . . Each Ministry will appoint a Commission, suggested by the Crown, to investigate and publish its own report. . . . The report published will be given out under the name of a Naval or Military Commission to impart an official sanction to the supposed inquiry and support the authenticity of the document agreed upon. . . . Naturally these prearranged reports will vary so as to satisfy the state of mind in each particular country.' . . . . 'If regicides are so easily arranged,' I observed cautiously, 'perhaps

the duration of this "Revolution" is also definitely determined?'
. . . . 'There'll be a period of revolution and distress,' my prisoner
remarked, 'before our country settles down to industry and con-
tentment. But the desire of "self-determination" will mislead the
unfortunate and cause them to embrace a tyranny of the most
cruel and selfish type. This will last for a time until gluttony
destroys itself, as all excesses do. When the country is dismembered
by the activities of rival greeds, my poor and honest peasants
will turn upon their masters and restore this nation's power. They
need but education to accomplish glorious results. They will obtain
this education while they suffer and evolve a science of self-
government while learning to govern themselves. The boy or girl
that is doomed to Royal birth steps into a prison with the first
breath he breathes. . . . . Take my own case; I longed to get out
and play rough-and-tumble with the boys I saw staring at me in
the streets. But I was taught by my English tutor, Heath, that it
would be lowering my dignity to associate with those fine young
boys. My "dignity" was placed in a straitjacket and, in a namby-
pamby way, I was taught to play ALONE. I had cousins scattered
over Europe who took their lot more happily than I; but even
they regretted the mocking barriers that laid down a barrage
between us and the more fortunate chaps outside,—outside, they
enjoyed FREEDOM,—within, we were ALL prisoners in our little cells
of etiquette and traditionary bondage. At fifteen I was dragged
away to the Military Academy at Petrograd[1] and made to listen
to old Danilovich until I actually hated the very name of war.
I could not map out my own general education, even; forced
by the traditions of my family I was placed in charge of the
Holy Synod and taught by Pobedonostzev to regard myself as the
source of SPIRITUAL POWER and instructed to regard an unorthodox
opinion as a transportation offense. Now, while I reverence pro-

---

[1] Nicholas used "Petrograd," not the German nomenclature.

foundly the sacred tenets of my holy religion, I regard religious freedom as indispensable to the dignity of spiritual belief. For that reason I made that reformation in 1905. As I grew up I rebelled against my intolerable confinement—I went out among the PEOPLE and TALKED WITH THEM. They were friendly in most instances and gave me good advice. I did not need a bodyguard to go about. I was as safe among the people as I would be in the Winter Palace. Often have I walked to the hotels alone to call on some particular friend without any thought of fear. Nor was it necessary—I liked the people as genuinely as I believe they respected me. I learned their hunger for land by going around; and it was on that account that I projected and completed our Siberian railways so as to give our people the coveted opportunity and an outlet to the markets of the world. Given an opportunity to accumulate and prosper, men will hesitate about going to war unless THEY ARE MISLED. I saw such an opportunity in international trade. . . . .' My prisoner spoke regretfully. His voice was soft and courteous, breaking at times into the altisonance of the tragic muse. He does not think that any act of his can be wrong; the mere fact that HE ran counter to accepted standards divests, in his mind, the act itself of turpitude. That seems to be the way he looked upon his former Eastern encroachments. That's the way he justified his subterranean deals with the KAISER; and he even goes so far as to assert that 'if the Vyborg-Bjorkesund treaty had not been denounced the present war would not have happened.' He speaks of this a little passionately, scorning the very memory of Count Witte for 'questioning the morality of that arrangement.' That great Minister my prisoner refers to as 'an uncouth bully who bellowed like a mad bull.' In this respect it is my impression that the ex-Empress indorses his state of mind. What he likes, she will place in the superlative; what he merely hates, she elevates to positive abhorrence. In this way she seems to flatter his decisions, which makes him smile quite indulgently at her, and hold her ascendancy over his apparently veering mind. I can notice this in so many little things: She oozes delicate flattery and he likes it; she plays upon his prejudices, and he seems to have a lot of them submerged beneath his inalienable urbanity and instinctive grace of manner that even this misery and abysmal gloom have not relieved of polish. Beneath it all I get the impression that he is very much in love with every member of his family. . . . that he would like to be alone with 'Alice,' whom he addresses as 'my darling' and experiences a shell-shock if she stubs her toe. His final words are: 'Now it is ALL OVER and I WILL WELCOME THE OBLIVION that will release us all from the memory of our devoted bondage!' . . . . . While my prisoner conversed, Alexis assisted his stately mother and his four beautiful sisters while putting on their superannuated wraps. . . . . One by one they filed out the door leading into the open yard. . . . . My prisoner stood up and stretched himself. . . . . He was about to resume his seat when the report of a revolver resounded in our ears. . . . . The brute on the floor, wallowing in his blood, was raised upon his elbows and firing recklessly. . . . After he had fired six rounds without apparent injury, I drew my own revolver and fired deliberately INTO THE WALL. . . . . The fellow slunk back to silence. . . . . My prisoner and I followed the ladies out into the night, forgetting a jewel or two in our leisurely departure. . . . . Out in the open WE DESCENDED into the old abandoned tunnel that formerly led from Ipatiev to the medical office of a foreign consulate a thousand feet away. . . . ."

WHAT IS LEARNED IN A SECRET TUNNEL

27. The next entry is mystifying.

"We are between the devil and the deep sea! . . . . which gives me time to write. . . . . The beastly tunnel has caved in mid-

way in our passage. . . . . It seems, from the roar overhead, that
we are somewhere, as there seems to be a draft of air through
this passage . . . The family are congregated off to the right, in a
kind of stoping where the dirt has been removed, leaving a small
room like one meets with in the Gogebic iron mines in Wisconsin
and Michigan, back in the United States. . . . . Our little electric
bull's-eyes come in handy just now. . . . . With my bull's-eye
propped up on a sand-encrusted box I am noting down some
things that must not be forgotten. . . . . While trying to find a
passageway out of this hole in the ground, we gyrated back and
forth for the last two or three hours until the women became
exhausted. . . . . Then my 'prisoner' and I returned to the mouth
of the entrance. There we heard a horrible row between the unruly
brute we left on the floor and his wild-eyed fellow conspirators.
. . . . They accused him of DOUBLE-CROSSING THEM and making
away with the treasure that they insisted should be theirs! . . . .
He insisted that there was NO treasure EXCEPT the JEWEL he
apparently was exhibiting. . . . . We could hear, quite distinctly,
a sullen voice saying: 'I do not believe you; you are trying to
steal the whole of it! . . . . . We'll give you ten minutes to
produce ALL you have hid away, and if you don't do it, we'll
fill your body so full of lead that your rotten carcass won't float
in the Kolunda.' . . . The culprit replied: 'Let me explain. You
remember that I was suspecting that interloper when I insisted on
watching him; well, my suspicions were correct,—he was a TRAI-
TOR to our cause. He was planning to steal away with his precious
gang when I covered them with my pistol. Then when I had the
drop on them I made them open all of their trunks and boxes.
Nothing was found. I felt sure they were holding out on me,
so I took a shot at the kid. The interloper made a dive at me.
I knocked him down with that chair there. . . . then in my rage
I emptied my pistol into the hearts of the whole gang. . . . .
That's all there's to it.' . . . . 'He's lying!' 'Traitor!' 'Betrayer!'

'Down with the thief!' flew back and forth from one to another above our heads. . . . . Then in a more subdued voice we heard 'Hist! Silence! Some one is coming!' A moment later I heard distinctly the unmistakable growl of my hero of Gallipoli overhead demanding, 'WHAT HAVE YOU CUTTHROATS DONE WITH OUR PRISONERS?' . . . . There was a silence that could be felt. None offered an explanation that I could hear. . . . ."

ROMANCE IN SIGHT OF DEATH

28. This page of the diary is badly blurred and torn, but the following can be made out:

"We are all about played out. . . . . The boy is exhausted and lying over in a little excavation upon his sisters' wraps, his fingers bleeding and one eye blinded with the sand. . . . . The passageway behind us is almost closed up. . . . . In front of us we have hit a solid wall. . . . . The exhausted mother is binding her boy's hands with a portion of her petticoat. . . . . As she kneels there, with the faint flicker of light falling on her finely chiseled profile, she resembles Botticelli's magnificent Madonna in the Uffizi Gallery at Florence. . . He is using his hackknife against the concrete wall with great patience and whistling softly and slowly an air from 'The Blessing of the Waters.' . . . . WATER! . . . . I know those girls are CHOKING for a drink as I have been for the last ten hours myself. . . . . Still, not one of them has murmured at our grief and Anastasia has become quite chummy in pretending to cheer ME up. . . . ."

29. Then there follows the entry:

"Water has burst through the hole my prisoner has been making in that wall! . . . ."

30. The next entry has been evidently water-soaked and is entirely blotted out.

31. This entry seems sufficiently distinct to make out what the writer has been through:

"I tried in the foregoing to jot down enough of what was happening to enable anyone who would find our bodies to make out how we had died. . . . . What I forgot to record in the excitement I'll put down now. . . . . When the wall caved in and the water burst down upon us it seemed that we would soon be drowned alive. . . . . The small hole in the wall had allowed enough water to filter through at first to slake our thirst and make us all quite happy. . . . . But gradually the ground beneath us became damp and sticky and the blue mud clung to our shoes like glue until we could hardly move. . . . . The little air that crept in with the water, though, was a positive blessing to us all. . . . . We should have stifled. . . . . Finally the water ceased and our hearts began to sink. . . . ."

36. In this entry the Emperor spoke of Rasputin:

" 'May I ask your actual estimate of creatures like Rasputin?' I ventured. . . . . 'Our Rasputin was a hardened criminal beyond a doubt until his conversion by Father Zaborovsky, the good Rector at the Theological Academy at Tomsk,' the ex-Czar replied. . . . 'He would have made an excellent subject for investigation by Lombroso, by Havelock Ellis or other eminent criminologists. . . . . but I believed the man was sincere in his repentance and accepted him as a sort of text for other sinners to point a way toward regeneration. . . The higher Rasputin rose, the greater his fame became, the more impressive would be his textual example to other aspiring souls—even a criminal should not be denied the consolation of hope where crime is the result of ignorance or misdirected patriotism. . . . . If I sinned in pardoning a sinner then sin must be an unpardonable crime! . . . . Nathan treated David as I treated Rasputin, although both were guilty of the same offense. . . . . He was grossly illiterate—the only schooling he ever got was in the Monastery Abalaksky and what he acquired from the lips of monks while making his rounds as a barefoot pilgrim from place to place. . . . . His claims of having visions I ascribed to his empty stomach, although others gave credence to the nonsense. . . . . Alice at first abhorred him; finally she began to regard him as a rare specimen in self-hypnosis who was worth studying to learn how far the fascinations of self-delusion were capable of deluding and swaying stronger wills and more cultivated minds. . . . . We both learned, by observing him, that an ignorant mujik, like an egotistical Minister, if granted the semblance of authority for any length of time, will demoralize the finest organization in the world. . . . . That was the lesson both Alice and I acquired from Rasputin. . . . . And I am accepting Rasputin as a standard to estimate what will happen when men of his type and origin attempt the government of the world. . . . Without education, with no experience in governing even the smallest unit of society, unfamiliar with the trend of history, ignorant of military and commercial strategy, building their philosophy of life and their science of administration upon some isolated text, they will overturn the whole structure of civilization by arrogating to themselves the supernatural privileges and persuasiveness of the Voice of God! . . . The prospects are not inviting. . . . . There are Rasputins in all the chancellories of Europe. . . . You have them in North and South America,— some educated, others like Marat and Danton, while some are simple Cagliostros who deceive the people and themselves. . . . . If they were only Gideons instead of Joshuas their strategy might be reassuring—but they are merely Rasputins and Papuses, after all! . . Against all laws of nature they will try to triumph by commanding the heavenly and mundane bodies to stand still until they readjust the motions of civilized society to some dissolving and ruinous invention of emotional insanity where everything runs wild!' "

(Editor's note—Rasputin's daughter, Mrs. Maria Rasputin Soloviev, now lives in Los Angeles. She said she is in the process of preparing a manuscript that, among other things, will deny a published contention by her father's alleged assassin, the late Prince Felix Yusupov. In his book *Lost Splendor* (London: Jonathan Cape, 1953), Prince Yusupov charged that Mrs. Soloviev's husband, Boris Soloviev, deceived several persons seeking to free the Romanovs by offering his help—and then exposed them to the Bolsheviks. Quite the contrary, according to Mrs. Soloviev, her husband aided members of the Imperial Family in their confinement by giving them food and clothing. The Bolsheviks imprisoned him for his actions in Tobolsk, she said, and she had to go there and help to get him out. She said he died later of "malnutrition.")

THE INVISIBLE DIPLOMAT APPEARS

37. This entry is mystifying:

"Last night I waited until there was not a sound overhead. . . . . I knew it would be taking chances—but I HAD TO GET WATER. . . . . We could no longer survive on MUD! . . . . I began pushing against the planking overhead to see if there was anywhere an opening, but every plank I pressed against seemed as solid as a stone sidewalk. . . . . Finally I began thumping with my clenched fist. . . . . and this brought on the fracas. . . . I heard a heavy pair of feet bounding on the floor directly above my head. . . . Then there was a scraping and a sound like the tearing up of carpets. . . . . Presently I heard an iron bolt crack back and the floor above my head began rising slowly until I found myself looking into the muzzle of a Mauser held in the clenched hands of a tall, square-faced man with a jaw like a prize fighter. . . . .

". . . . . Another pair of hands reached down and caught me by the collar and I was yanked like a squirming spaniel out of my hole into a large, oblong room that was only slightly lighted by a blue student lamp upon a small roll-top desk. . . . . Against the wall was a large steel engraving of King George of England, and I could see the Union Jack displayed upon another wall. . . . . There were papers and documents and army tents in piles here and there round the room. . . . . BUT THE IMPRESSION THAT FLASHED UPON ME was not at all reassuring for a man who had made his way into SUCH SURROUNDINGS directly from the other underground corridor in Berlin! . . . ."

38. Then this entry follows:

"From that very hour I AM STRONGLY FOR THE BRITISH . . . I will not attempt to describe that MEAL. . . . . It was all a King in Exile or any of his suite could ask for; and the silent men who prepared it will always be remembered for their discretion and manly hospitality. . . . . Neither of them appeared to KNOW me NOR ANY OF OUR PARTY. . . . . But those gallant fellows are adept at dissimulation. . . . . I'm certain that the tall, slender, and soldierly bearing officer will remember the day we had our STRAW-BERRIES at Carlton Terrace, and the slender, willowy Duchess who forgot her fan until he picked it up and brought it to her AT MY TABLE, where she paused for a moment to say to me, 'MY FATHER IS IN LONDON AND WISHES TO SEE YOU BADLY.' . . . . I am certain he remembers what I told her about the Gordons and the Devons in that slaughter at the Somme—when so few of those brave lads returned! . . . . If we ever meet again I shall thank him for the robes and provisions and motor trucks he furnished to transport us safely rolled up in army tents for many rough miles across the country in the direction of CHANYI LAKE. . . . ."

39. We find this entry of the diarist next:

"I have never beheld a more beautiful landscape than the scene before me. . . . . I am writing this on the banks of Altai Lake. . . . . The balsam from the conelike firs along the gorges sur-charges the air with an intoxicating flavor and reflects their in-verted gracefulness in the calm waters of the lake. . . . . The

mountains sloping up from either side are delineated in the
mirroring surface and form an archway for the snow-capped and
broken pinnacle that towers above the others like a sentinel brooding in his frosty and eternal isolation. . . . . Far off in the distance
I can see the black and white walls of the KATUN GLACIER and
know that, throughout this region, gold and silver, as well as lead
and copper, most certainly abound. . . . . In our unending tramp
today I have discovered many evidences of the presence of zinc
and nickel and other minerals lying around. . . . . My 'prisoner'
tells me that there are mines already working in the upper part
of the Talovsky River and that the copper runs very high in the
vicinity of Chudak. . . . . Alice wrote to Princess G——— today
at T———. . . . . I am NOT much impressed nor FAVORABLY by the
attitude of these natives in the hills. . . . . They seem to be a
mongrel mixture of Tartar and Mongolian, who are always ready,
like the huge ungainly bears we have encountered in our pilgrimage, to grapple and devour one for the mere pleasure of
seeing blood! . . . ."

40. There seems to have been quite a skip in the notations
of the diary. Evidently the diarist has become MORE INTERESTED
in something else:

"The fact that we have been on FOREIGN SOIL during the last
fifteen days has considerably relaxed our nerves. . . . . Aside from
the rumor constantly reaching us that the Mongolian mercenaries
are in the employ of the Bolsheviki and offered BIG REWARDS
for our capture, we have not been disturbed in mind or bodies.
. . . . Maria asked me today if I were any relation to CHARLES
JAMES FOX, whose oratory she claims to greatly admire. . . . .
When I informed her that I had never met this gentleman, her eyes
grew very big. . . . .

'What ARE you?' she inquired. 'Are you an Englishman, or a
Russian—you CANNOT BE A GERMAN—or ARE YOU AN AMERICAN? Oh,
I just hope you ARE an AMERICAN! . . . .' When I informed her

that my ancestors fought beside Kosciusko and Pulaski and that
their names might be found on the muster rolls of the First Line
Regiment of New York Colony and State, along with the names
of Goose Van Schaick and Jeremiah Van Rensselaer, she burst her
sides with laughter. . . . . 'What a happy family you must have
been!' she rippled. 'When a Fox and a Goose may dwell in peace
and amity together, there is nothing that is not possible for their
race!'

" . . . . . This quick-witted girl, certainly, BELONGS in the UNITED
STATES—the plains of Eastern Turkestan are NO place for
her. . . . ."

41. There seems to be another skip in the neglected diary.
Evidently the scenery has lost all its charms. . . . . He merely
notes:

"My 'prisoner' seems VERY MUCH interested in my family connections. . . . . He seems jolly enough about it. . . . . BUT I can
see that something is DISTURBING him. . . . . He is very obstinate in
little things, lately. . . . . When we get into Cashmere perhaps
his mind will be diverted. . . . . He loves the languid charm of
scenic beauty nearly as much as the flattery of his wife. . . . .
Anyway, WHAT can I do? . . . . There is a naturalness about this
whole affair that one simply CAN'T get away from. . . . . Danger
has a generous way of bestowing blessings on the BOLD. . . . ."

42. Then we find the following critical entry:

"I shall NEVER read 'Lalla Rookh' again! . . . . . The Vale of
Cashmere may sound fine in poetry but it FEELS TOUGH beneath
one's feet whenever one dismounts. . . . . I might overlook the
rough spots easily enough had not OLGA suddenly interested herself in my ANCESTRY while she found employment for Maria with
her brother, who seems sadly out of breath. . . . . My 'prisoner' has
forgotten all about me in the absorbing interest he displays in
what he declares to be EARLY MISSIONARY WORK OF JESUS in these
very interesting stretches. It has been no easy matter for me to

pilot this party outside the range of camel caravans and soldiers on their way from the Punjab Valley toward RAWAL PIND! . . . . . The rattle of our tongas might be heard at any moment, and then our little caravan, disguised as Buddhists, might spend some time in the GUARD HOUSE at Murree. . . . . We will not regret the shade and comparative coolness of that pleasant Summer Resort—but none of us are longing for any more confinement. . . . . The road from Murree down the valley was gullied by the terrific rain we have been wading through. . . . ."

WHERE THE PRISONERS DISAPPEARED

49. Then this entry reveals the sequence:

"We had been a number of days on the road—our lives imperceptibly growing into a closer and more intimate companionship as the days ambled slowly away with the bleak snow-clad mountains that we left behind. . . . . Descending down the slopes into a fertile valley, the hillsides terraced with a series of rice yards, and our paths softly shaded with the mulberry tree. . . . . Behind us was the white-fringed mountain of the Lama, before us loomed the SACRED PINNACLE OF OMAY and off to the south spread an ancient walled city with steeples pointing heavenward surmounted by the CROSS. . . . . Where the pagoda stood a thousand years ago now rise the hospital and the Christian missionary school. . . . . Here the people walk on well-paved and broad, sweeping streets, and the tourists spend their afternoons promenading along the smooth and high and broad city wall. . . . . As we approached this city, a stream of rickshas came dashing in our direction, commanded by the TALL, slim 'lama' I had supposed we left behind! . . . . The coolies appeared to understand their parts. . . . . Quickly making a circle around us they pulled the women from their camels and tried to rope and bind my 'prisoner' and myself.

"Of course we were in full view of the consular flags of a dozen different nations; but that did not seem to bother the ringleader of this tatterdemalion mob. . . . . My 'prisoner' fought like a demon. . . . . He well remembered the lessons he received from Heath in the manly art of self-defense. . . . . Right and left he boxed like a well-trained athlete delivering his dynamic punches well. . . . . But finally the gang overpowered him and turned their undivided attention to me. . . . . I was vainly attempting to reach the side of Maria and her sisters, whom the tall bully was forcing into a waiting 'ricksha manned by two barelegged men—a dozen coolies pounded upon me, tore my clothing into fragments, furrowed my face with their infernal nails and actually attempted to bite me on the ears! . . . . .

"I have no notion how well or hard I fought, but as I knocked one down another took his place as I fought my way to the side of the now bound and helpless girls. . . . . Their hair was streaming down their backs, their faces flushed, their eyes filled with tears. . . . . that sight maddened me! . . . . I have been in many fights before, I have lain beside the dead in Flanders and among the Balkan highlands, I have seen blood flowing by me like a river—and the thought of all these seemed to electrify my soul and fill my veins with steel. . . . . I tore madly right and left. . . . . I never struck such herculean blows before or since.

"I literally grabbed the tall man by the heels and whirled him round like a flail and tore into that gang of snarling hellhounds with cyclonic fury. . . . . I literally mowed them down. . . . . But finally a dull thud sounded in my ears. . . . . A wave of light blinded both my eyes. . . . . I knew nothing more until this morning when I awoke in a tent. Beside me was a loaf of bread and a canteen of cool water. . . . . NOT ANOTHER SIGN OF A LIVING CREATURE IS IN SIGHT. . . I am in a deep mountain gorge, leading to the south along a narrow roadway that has apparently witnessed the procession of unnumbered ages."

50. Then this entry:

"After tramping all day I finally emerged in the sight of a swift-flowing river on either bank of which, in the distance, appeared two walled-off cities of considerable size. . . . . Foreign GUNBOATS were lying in the harbor in holiday attire. . . . . As I approached the city a courier came running to meet me. . . . . When he approached I drew back prepared to fight. . . . .

"But his friendliness disarmed me and I allowed him to draw near. . . . . 'Li'l' ladee wantee see you quick; you cum foller me,' he said, and turned back from where he came. . . . . I followed him with beating heart. . . . . On the dock at the landing where the gunboat was steaming up MARIA met me with moistened eyes. . . . .

"She informed me in a low voice that the officer was ready to receive me and accept my orders. . . . . And then she said:

"'Before you go I wish to thank you for all you have done for us. . . . . If our paths should ever meet again I want you to know my heart will beat more quickly when I shall see you coming up the path.' . . . . That said, she flung her slender arms around my neck, impulsively, and looked calmly in my eyes. . . . . When, involuntarily, my arms showed signs of being prehensile, she sprang away quickly and flashed along the gangway to disappear, like a holy vision, behind that gray storm door! . . . . ."

51. The last entry reads:

"It has been a habit with me for many years to never be surprised. . . . . When I appeared on deck to give the code to the commander of that vessel this habit was unmoored. . . . . A tall, square-jawed man approached me with a twinkle in his clear, blue eyes. . . . . I looked at him inquiringly and a little reminiscently until I heard him speak. . . . . 'I see the loaf of bread came in handy,' he said, extending me this bony hand. . . . . 'I thought

I left you at Ekaterinburg,' I exclaimed, recalling the moments we spent after our escape from the abandoned tunnel. . . . . 'Oh,' he laughed, 'YOURS was not a one-man job; there are others in the world besides yourself intrusted with state secrets. . . . .' 'But what do you know about the bread, you just spoke of it?'

" 'My company was following on behind,' he answered. 'When we came round the bend we saw you scrappling with that outlaw from Trebizond. You did quite well; you had all but three of them laid out in manly fashion when you got that clip on the back of the head. Then we stepped in and conducted your party to their present quarters. . . . thought it better for you to remain in the tent while the authorities here locked up those cut-throats for your disappearance.'

" 'Have you the CODE WORD?' I asked. . . . . He whispered it in my ear. . . . . Then I lettered the order. . . . . Finally he asked, 'Would you not like to meet my SISTER who has been so much interested in you?'

"His sister! I had never heard of her! . . . . 'Of course!' I answered amiably enough for one completely stumped. . . .

"He called a petty officer and said a few words in an undertone. . . . . In a minute a radiant young woman with springing steps glided gracefully down the deck. . . . . She was not, in her present attire, much different from Maria. . . . . but as she drew near I noted the difference at a glance. . . . . She came forward quickly and held out her hand. 'Congratulations, Mr. Fox!' she said smiling. . . . . 'The Metropole!' I gasped—'what brings YOU here?' 'Still asking questions!' she coquetted prettily. 'I merely called, of course, to inform you that the sapphire is in America!' . . . . I thought hard for more than a minute. . . . . Then it occurred to me that I had seen her in a dozen disguises shadowing me from Buckingham to the room upstairs on Downing Street—to charm me later at the Hague—to disappear like a will-o'-the-wisp—then to fascinate me at the Metropole.' . . . .

"Well, the commander of the vessel tells me that it is fourteen hundred miles downstream to Woosung and that the voyage will take seven days from there. . . . . With this code word still ringing in my ears to be repeated to one man at Berlin, to another man in England, another in Japan, and to a dignitary in Italy, the mission I have undertaken shall have been successfully discharged, so far as history and public policy is concerned. . . . . But there is another mission that I shall, some day, undertake that will be enshrined in lovely memories and lively fancies until that day shall come."

Bibliography

Accoce, Pierre, and Pierre Quet, *The Lucy Ring* (London: W. H. Allen), 1967.

Ackerman, Carl W., *Trailing the Bolsheviki* (New York: Charles Scribner & Sons), 1919.

Alexander, Grand Duke of Russia, *Twilight of Royalty* (New York: Ray Long and Richard R. Smith), 1932.
——*Once a Grand Duke* (London: Cassell), 1932.
——*Always a Grand Duke* (London: Cassell), 1934.

Alexandrov, Victor, *The End of the Romanovs* (London: Hutchinson), 1966.

Almedingen, E. M., *An Unbroken Unity. A Memoir of Grand Duchess Serge of Russia* (London: The Bodley Head), 1964.

Anastasia, Grand Duchess of Russia [Anna Anderson], *I am Anastasia: The Autobiography of the Grand Duchess of Russia* (London: Michael Joseph, 1958; Penguin 1961).

Anastasia, Grand Duchess of Russia [Eugenia Smith], *Anastasia; the Autobiography of H.I.H. the Grand Duchess Anastasia Nicholaevna of Russia* (New York: Robert Speller and Sons), 1963.

Anonymous, *The Russian Diary of an Englishman, Petrograd, 1915–1917* (London: Heinemann), 1919.

Asprey, Robert, *The Panther's Feast* (London: Cape), 1959.

Auclères, Dominique, *Anastasie, qui êtes vous?* (Paris: Hachette), 1962.

Aughinbaugh, William E., *I Swear by Apollo* (London: Gollancz), 1939.

Benckendorff, Count Paul, *Last Days at Tsarskoe Selo* (London: W. Heinemann), 1927.

Botkin, Gleb E., *The Real Romanovs* (New York: Fleming H. Revell Co.), 1931.
——*The Woman Who Rose Again* (New York and London: Fleming H. Revell Co.), 1937.

BIBLIOGRAPHY

Bulygin, Captain Paul P., and Alexander F. Kerensky, "The Sorrowful Quest," in *The Murder of the Romanovs* (London: Hutchinson), 1935.

Buxhoeveden, Baroness Sophia, *Left Behind: Fourteen Months in Siberia During the Revolution* (New York and London: Longmans, Green), 1929. *The Life and Tragedy of Alexandra Feodorovna, Empress of Russia* (New York and London: Longmans, Green), 1928.

Bykov, Paul M., *Posledniye dni Romanovykh* [The Last Days of the Romanovs] (Sverdlovsk, U.S.S.R.: Uralkniga), 1926.
——*Les Derniers jours des Romanovs* (Paris: Payot), 1931.
——*The Last Days of Tsardom* (London: Lawrence and Wishart), 1934.
——*The Last Days of Tsar Nicholas* (New York: International Publishers), 1934.

Cowles, Virginia, *1913: An End and a Beginning* (London: Weidenfeld & Nicolson), 1967.

Dehn, Lili, *The Real Tsaritsa* (London: Thornton Butterworth), 1922.

Dieterichs, General Michael C., *Ubiistvo tsarskoi sem'i i chlenov doma Romanovykh na Urae* [The Murder of the Imperial Family and Members of the House of Romanov in the Urals] (Vladivostok: Vladivostok Military Academy), 1922, 2 volumes.

Dulles, Allen, *The Craft of Intelligence* (London: Weidenfeld & Nicolson), 1964.

Francis, David R., *Russia from the American Embassy, April 1916–November 1918* (New York: Charles Scribner's Sons), 1931.
——Reports and personal papers in Missouri Historical Society, St. Louis, Missouri.

Frankland, Noble, *Imperial Tragedy: Nicholas II, Last of the Tsars* (London: Kimber), 1960.

Fülöp-Miller, René, *Rasputin, the Holy Devil* (London: Putnam), 1928.

Gilliard, Pierre, *Le tragique destin de Nicolas II et de sa famille* (Paris: Payot), 1921.
——*Tragicheskaya sud'ba Russkoi imperatorskoi familii* (New York and London: Revel), 1921.
——*Tragiona sudba Nikole II i njegov porodice* (trans. Nikola Andric) (Zagreb: Kr. Zemaljska Tiskara), 1921.
——*Thirteen Years at the Russian Court* (trans. Appleby Holt) (London: Hutchinson and Co.), 1921.
——*Thirteen Years at the Russian Court* (New York: Doran), 1921.
——*La fausse Anastasie: histoire d'une prétendue grande-duchesse de russie* with Constantin I. Savitch (Paris: Payot), 1929.

Graves, Major General William S., *America's Siberian Adventure 1918–1920* (New York: Jonathan Cape and Harrison Smith), 1931.

Janin, Général Maurice, *Ma mission en Sibérie* (Paris: Payot), 1933.

Katkov, George M., *The February Revolution* (London: Longmans), 1967.

BIBLIOGRAPHY

Kerensky, Alexander, *The Catastrophe* (London: Appleton), 1927.
——*The Crucifixion of Liberty* (London: Arthur Barker), 1935.
——*Russia and History's Turning Point* (London: Cassell), 1966.
——*The Murder of the Romanovs* (see Bulygin, Paul).

Kschessinska, Mathilde, *Dancing in St. Petersburg* (trans. Arnold Haskell) (London: Gollancz), 1960.
——*Souvenirs de la Kschessinska* (Paris: Librairie Plon), 1960.

Lasies, Joseph, *La tragédie sibérienne: le drame d'Ekaterinbourg, La fin de l'amiral Koltchak,* preface by Marcel Gounouilhou, letter preface by Général de Maud-huy (Paris: L'Edition Francaise Illustrée), 1920.

Lockhart, R. H. Bruce, *British Agent* (New York and London: Putnam), 1933.

Majolier, Nathalie, *Step-daughter of Imperial Russia* (London: Stanley Paul and Co.), 1940.

Marie, Grand Duchess of Russia, *A Princess in Exile* (London: Cassell), 1932.
——*Things I Remember* (London: Cassell), 1931.

Markov, Serge V., *How We Tried to Save the Tsaritsa* (New York and London: Putnam), 1929.

Massie, Robert K., *Nicholas and Alexandra* (London: Gollancz), 1968.

McGarry, William R., *From Berlin to Bagdad* (Portland, Oregon: International Publishers), 1912.

Mal'gunov, Serge P., *Sud'ba Imperatora Nikolaya II poslye otracheniya* [The Fate of the Emperor Nicholas II after Abdication] (Paris: La Renaissance), 1951.

Melnik, Tatiana, *Vospominaniya o Tsarskoi Semye i eya zhizni do i posle revolyutsii* [Memories of the Tsarist Family and Their Life Before and After the Revolution] (Belgrade: M. U. Stefanovich and Co.), 1921.

Moorehead, Alan, *The Russian Revolution* (London: Hamish Hamilton, 1958; Panther, 1960).

Narishkin-Kurakin, Elizabeth, *Under Three Tsars* (New York: Dutton), 1931.

Obolensky, Serge, *One Man in His Time* (London: Hutchinson), 1960.

O'Conor, John F., *Nicholas A. Sokolov's Investigation of the Alleged Murder of the Russian Imperial Family,* including sections, translated by Mr. O'Conor, of *The Murder of the Imperial Family* by Judge Sokolov (New York: Robert Speller and Sons), 1970.

Page, Bruce, David Leitch, and Phillip Knightley, *Philby: The Spy Who Betrayed a Generation* (London: André Deutsch), 1968.

Parkes, Dr. Oscar, *British Battleships* (London: Seeley, Service and Co.), 1958.

Preston, Sir Thomas H., *Before the Curtain* (London: Murray), 1950.
——"Last Days of the Tsar," *Sunday Telegraph,* London, July 14, 1968.

Pridham, Vice-Admiral Sir Francis, *Close of a Dynasty*, with a foreword by Her Imperial Highness the Grand Duchess Xenia Alexandrovna of Russia (London: Allan Wingate), 1958.

Pu-yi, Emperor of Manchukuo, *From Emperor to Citizen, the Autobiography of Aisin-Groro Pu Yi* (trans. W. J. F. Jenner) (London: Collets), 1964-65, two volumes.

Rathlef-Keilmann, Harriet von, *Anastasia, the Survivor of Ekaterinburg* (trans. Stewart Flint) (London and New York: G. P. Putnam's Sons), 1928.

Reilly, Sidney George, *Adventures of Sidney Reilly* (London: Matthews), 1931.

Richards, Guy, *Imperial Agent—The Goleniewski-Romanov Case* (New York: Devin-Adair), 1966.

Rodzianko, Michael V., *The Reign of Rasputin* (London: Philpot), 1927.

Sayers, Michael, and Albert F. Kahn, *The Great Conspiracy; The Secret War Against Soviet Russia* (London: Collets), 1947.

Smythe, James P., *Rescuing the Czar, Two Authentic Diaries Arranged and Translated by James P. Smythe, A.M., Ph.D.* (San Francisco: California Printing Co.), 1920.

Sokolov, Nicholas A., *Enquête judiciaire sur l'assassinat de la famille impériale russe* (Paris: Payot), 1924.
——*Ubiistvo tsarskoi sem'i* (Berlin: Slovo), 1925.
——*Der Todesweg des Zaren—Dargestellt von den Untersuchungsrichter* (Berlin: Stollberg), 1925.
——*So Begann der Bolschewismus, Leidensweg und Ermordung der Zaren-familie* (Berlin: Deutsche Verlagegesellschaft), 1936.

Spiridovitch, Général Alexandre, *Les dernières années de la cour de Tsarskoie-Selo* (Paris: Payot), 1928, 2 volumes.

Tarsaidze, Alexander G., *Czars and Presidents—The Story of a Forgotten Friendship* (New York: McDowell, Obolensky), 1958.

Tisdall, Evelyn Ernest F., *The Dowager Empress* (London: S. Paul), 1957.

Tokoi, Oskari, *Sisu: Even Through a Stone Wall* (intro. by John I. Kolehmainen) (New York: Robert Speller and Sons), 1957.

United States Senate, Internal Security Subcommittee, Part VIII, Hearings on State Department Security, containing testimony by two State Department officials on Michael Goleniewski's intelligence information (Washington, D.C.: United States Government Printing Office), 1966.

Viroubova, Anna, *Memories of the Russian Court* (New York and London: Macmillan and Co.), 1923.

Vorres, Ian, *The Last Grand Duchess: Her Imperial Highness Grand Duchess Olga Alexandrovna* (foreword by Her Imperial Highness Grand Duchess Olga Alexandrovna) (London: Hutchinson), 1964.

Wilson, Colin, *Rasputin and the Fall of the Romanovs* (London: Arthur Barker), 1964.

BIBLIOGRAPHY

Wilton, Robert, *The Last Days of the Romanovs* (New York: George H. Doran Co.), 1920.

——*Les derniers jours des Romanofs* (Paris: G. Cres et Compagnie), 1920.

——*Posledniye dni Romanovykh* (Berlin), 1923.

——*Russia's Agony* (London: Edward Arnold), 1918.

Wise, David, and Thomas B. Ross, *The Invisible Government* (London: Cape, 1965; Mayflower, 1968).

Wrangel, General Baron Peter N., *Always with Honor* (foreword by Herbert Hoover) (New York: Robert Speller and Sons), 1957.

Yusupov, Prince Felix, *Rasputin* (London: Cape), 1927.

——*La fin de Raspoutine* (Paris: Librairie Plon), 1927.

——*Avant l'exil,* 1887–1919 (Paris: Librairie Plon), 1952.

——*Lost Splendor* (trans. by Ann Green and Nicholas Katkoff) (London: Cape), 1953.

——*En exil* (Paris: Librairie Plon), 1954.

Index

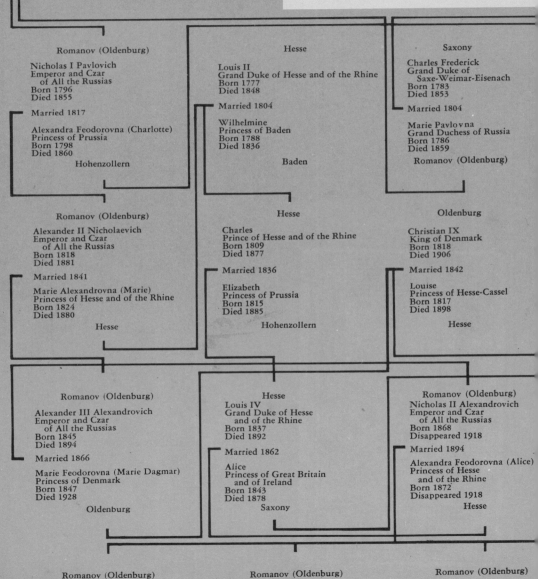

Genealogical Chart Showing
Closest Relationship Among
Nicholas II,
Alexandra Feodorovna,
George V,
and
William II.

Explanation of Their Relationship:

1. Nicholas and Alexandra are second
   cousins (Nicholas' paternal grandmother
   and Alexandra's paternal grandfather
   are sister and brother).

Romanov (Oldenburg)

Paul I Petrovich
Emperor and Czar of All the Russias
Born 1754
Died 1801

Married 1776

Marie Feodorovna (Sophia Dorothea)
Princess of Wurttemberg
Born 1759
Died 1828

Wurttemberg

Romanov (Oldenburg)

Nicholas I Pavlovich
Emperor and Czar
   of All the Russias
Born 1796
Died 1855

Married 1817

Alexandra Feodorovna (Charlotte)
Princess of Prussia
Born 1798
Died 1860

Hohenzollern

Hesse

Louis II
Grand Duke of Hesse and of the Rhine
Born 1777
Died 1848

Married 1804

Wilhelmine
Princess of Baden
Born 1788
Died 1836

Baden

Saxony

Charles Frederick
Grand Duke of
   Saxe-Weimar-Eisenach
Born 1783
Died 1853

Married 1804

Marie Pavlovna
Grand Duchess of Russia
Born 1786
Died 1859

Romanov (Oldenburg)

Romanov (Oldenburg)

Alexander II Nicholaevich
Emperor and Czar
   of All the Russias
Born 1818
Died 1881

Married 1841

Marie Alexandrovna (Marie)
Princess of Hesse and of the Rhine
Born 1824
Died 1880

Hesse

Hesse

Charles
Prince of Hesse and of the Rhine
Born 1809
Died 1877

Married 1836

Elizabeth
Princess of Prussia
Born 1815
Died 1885

Hohenzollern

Oldenburg

Christian IX
King of Denmark
Born 1818
Died 1906

Married 1842

Louise
Princess of Hesse-Cassel
Born 1817
Died 1898

Hesse

Romanov (Oldenburg)

Alexander III Alexandrovich
Emperor and Czar
   of All the Russias
Born 1845
Died 1894

Married 1866

Marie Feodorovna (Marie Dagmar)
Princess of Denmark
Born 1847
Died 1928

Oldenburg

Hesse
Louis IV
Grand Duke of Hesse
   and of the Rhine
Born 1837
Died 1892

Married 1862

Alice
Princess of Great Britain
   and of Ireland
Born 1843
Died 1878

Saxony

Romanov (Oldenburg)

Nicholas II Alexandrovich
Emperor and Czar
   of All the Russias
Born 1868
Disappeared 1918

Married 1894

Alexandra Feodorovna (Alice)
Princess of Hesse
   and of the Rhine
Born 1872
Disappeared 1918

Hesse

Romanov (Oldenburg)

Olga Nicholaevna
Grand Duchess of Russia
Born 1895
Disappeared 1918

Romanov (Oldenburg)

Tatiana Nicholaevna
Grand Duchess of Russia
Born 1897
Disappeared 1918

Romanov (Oldenburg)

Marie Nicholaevna
Grand Duchess of Russia
Born 1899
Disappeared 1918